RVing in Alaska
CAMPGROUNDS & SERVICES

RICHARD D. ANDERSON

Billiken Press

RVing in Alaska: Campgrounds and Services

by Richard D. Anderson

Cover Design by Bob Parsons, Anchorage, Alaska
Map Designs by Erin Quinn, Friday Harbor, Washington
Black and white photographs by Richard D. Anderson

ISBN 0-9629325-3-1

Billiken Press
Post Office Box 240866
Anchorage, Alaska 99524-0866

TABLE OF CONTENTS

SECTION I

Introduces the user to the layout and features of the overall book;
planning an itinerary; available highway options and how to use
them; preparation for the trip and other information.

Describes parks and campgrounds including a typical Alaska
campground and other pertinent details; it also describes animals
in the wild, fish, birds, and wetland habitats.

Describes campgrounds and services in Skagway, Juneau and
Haines. Options include the Klondike Highway, the Haines Cutoff
Highway, and the Alaska Marine Highway System.

SECTION II

Describes campgrounds and services on the Alaska Highway
between the Canadian border and its termination in Delta
Junction at the Richardson Highway. Options include the Glenn
Highway and the Richardson Highway.

Describes campgrounds and services in Fairbanks; the Chena Hot
Springs Road; the Steese Highway; the Elliott Highway; and the
Dalton Highway. Options include the Richardson Highway and the
George Parks Highway.

SECTION III

We are everything that you are
But with a difference you will find
It's Alaska's guiding Northern Star
It's a certain state of mind

It's a different kind of living
It's a variance of pace
It's a loving, caring, giving
It's a special kind of place

So leave the world behind you
Let us host you in our way
Let the nearest future find you
Where the midnight sunrays play

We welcome and invite you
You are friends we haven't met
Let us meet you and excite you
On your best vacation yet

Come Northward to Alaska
Where the world is great and grand
Come join us in Alaska
Meet our people, see our land

Larry Beck
Alaska's Ambassador of Good Will

Permission to use excerpts from "An Invitation to Alaska" by Larry Beck granted by the Alaska Heritage Review Board and the estate of Larry Beck. © 1984

Dedicated to the memory of Larry Beck

who recognized Alaska as a state of

mind as well as a state of being

Introduction

Alaska – Your road to adventure.

A driving vacation through Alaska is something you'll never forget. It's an opportunity to travel at your own pace and see parts of Alaska that few others see. As you travel along the road, let the beauty of our state dictate your itinerary. You'll find white mountain peaks shimmering on the horizon, spectacular roadside glaciers, and countless wildflowers. Stop often to take in the view, meet the friendly people, and experience the grandeur of the Great Land.

Alaska is big, so be sure to allow plenty of time to enjoy that "perfect" spot when you come to it. With over 3,000 rivers and 3 million lakes, the temptation to stop and drop a fishing line will be hard to resist. Or you may just want to relax and enjoy the view, take a walk, or explore a glacier. Whatever activities you enjoy along the way, be sure to keep your camera handy – wildlife can appear at any time.

All along Alaska's roadways you'll find a wide array of restaurants, grocery stores, souvenir shops, and laundry facilities to make your trip more comfortable. And when it's time to stop for the evening, you'll find our campgrounds have that touch of Alaska you came north for.

Information on the many state, federal, and private campgrounds throughout Alaska will be invaluable as you travel. *RVing in Alaska: Campgrounds and Services* includes maps and drawings, making our campgrounds easy to find. You'll also find useful information on service stations, waste dump sites, where to buy propane, emergency phone numbers, RV rentals, and campground amenities such as showers, laundry and activity booking services.

An excellent option for those areas not accessible via roads is the Alaska Marine Highway System, which provides year-round ferry service. The Marine Highway allows you to combine the luxury of a cruise with the independence of a driving trip.

Start planning your trip today and discover the true Alaska. With the open road in front of you and the wind at your back, you'll experience untold adventure along Alaska's roadways. For a vacation you'll always remember, come to a place you'll never forget.

Tina Lindgren

Executive Director
Alaska Tourism Marketing Council

Author's Note

Studies show that independent travelers are the fastest growing segment of visitors to Alaska. This book is intended to be a guide for RVers or car-top tent campers who want to make their own decisions on the highways they travel as they explore Alaska, the "Great Land."

"I don't know what I expected," one visitor commented, "but the quality of camp sites changed markedly as we drove across Western Canada and into Alaska." Comparing Alaska's campgrounds to their sophisticated cousins in the "lower forty-eight" is difficult since both private and public campgrounds in Alaska tend to be more primitive and rustic in structure.

Campgrounds frequently appear to have been arbitrarily punched out by someone with a D-8 cat and not planned by an engineer. The Department of Environmental Conservation is working to bring older, established campgrounds into conformance with current state codes regarding sewage disposal and septic areas, especially along creeks and rivers.

The Bureau of Land Management has long-range plans which include upgrading BLM campgrounds as well as bringing them into compliance with "The Americans With Disabilities Act". Furthermore, the Department of Natural Resources and the Department of Fish and Game have completed cooperative projects which have enhanced camping opportunities for all.

Special thanks are extended to Tina Lindgren, Executive Director, and Kathy Dunn from the Alaska Tourism Marketing Council; to BLM staff members, Jan H. Burris, Outdoor Recreation Planner, and Gene Keith, Glennallen District Manager; and, of course, to my wife Joanne who can not only spot a fire ring from forty yards but can spot an awkward sentence nearly as far.

RVing in Alaska: Campgrounds and Services describes Alaskan campgrounds as accurately as possible, but the author recognizes that things are not always as they appear to be. If descriptions are inaccurate or need revision, please send your welcome comments to me at the following address:

Billiken Press
Post Office Box 240866
Anchorage, Alaska 99524-0866.

Dick Anderson

RVing in Alaska:

Campgrounds and Services

Section I

Prudhoe

Coldfoot

DALTON HIGHWAY

Livengood

ELLIOTT HWY

Manley

STEESE HWY

Circle

Circle Hot Springs

Chena Hot Springs

North Pole

Eagle

Fairbanks

RICHARDSON

TAYLOR

Kantishna

Delta Junction

Cantwell

DENALI HWY.

Tok

GEORGE PARKS HWY.

Paxson

GLENN HIGHWAY

Talkeetna

Nabesna

Glennallen

Wasilla

Palmer

EDGERTON HWY

Anchorage

Portage

Valdez

Chitina

RICHARDSON

McCarthy

Kenai

SEWARD HWY

STERLING HIGHWAY

Seward

Homer

Cordova

GULF OF ALASKA

Alaska's
highway system

Dawson

KLONDIKE HIGHWAY

Beaver
Creek

ALASKA HIGHWAY

Haines Jct.

HAINES HWY

Whitehorse

KLONDIKE HWY

Carcross

Teslin

ALASKA HIGHWAY

Watson
Lake

Skagway

Haines

Juneau

Chapter 1

THE ALASKAN EXPERIENCE

This chapter is divided into four sections: How To Use This Book; Planning an Itinerary; Preparing for Adventure; and Driving the Highway. It introduces the reader to the layout and features of the overall book; to available options and how to use them; to preparation for the trip; and to information relevant to highway conditions and border crossings.

HOW TO USE THIS BOOK

FEATURES: Each chapter begins with an indented chapter summary. The summary is followed by introductory comments relevant to the geographic area; maps showing the highway, major intersections and towns; locations of visitor centers and points of interest; and a listing of health and emergency services within the region. Sections on RV campgrounds and RV related services follow. Finally, travel options at major highways are described; options are identified by the billiken logo as shown on page four. Highway options allow RVers to deviate from the route as presented at any intersection or junction along the way.

LAYOUT: There are four divisions to this guidebook. The first two chapters of Section I present the structure of the book, pertinent information for RVers who are unfamiliar with Alaska, and a chapter on campgrounds in Skagway, Haines and Juneau.

Chapters in Section II describe highways and campgrounds in the interior and southcentral regions. This portion, which presents four highways as conceptually forming a loop, begins at the Canadian border and leads to Fairbanks, Denali, Wasilla/Palmer and Anchorage, then returns to the Canadian border through Glennallen and Tok.

Chapters in Section III describe the Kenai Peninsula including Seward, Soldotna, Kenai and Homer. The Appendices represent the remaining portion and includes information on national airlines serving Alaska; RV rental agencies; golf courses; and other items of interest.

MILEPOSTS: Major highways in Alaska are marked by small, numerically sequenced signs known as mileposts (MP). MP 1221.8 marks the border entering Alaska from Canada on the Alaska Highway. The first campground is Deadman Lake Campground at MP 1249.2 or 27.4 miles from the border. Milepost markers are always whole numbers. Tenths of a mile are used in the text to more precisely mark campground entrances or roads and give drivers approximate distances to their destination.

RVing in Alaska: Campgrounds and Services

NORTH, SOUTH, EAST, WEST: Compass headings are *generically used* throughout this guidebook. In a few cases more specific directions are used such as with the option from Tok to Glennallen "southwest" on the Glenn Highway.

Most Alaskan drivers think of the George Parks Highway as running north and south, but in fact the first fifty miles from Fairbanks are westerly. The option from Fairbanks describing the Parks Highway refers to it as "south to Denali National Park." Maps describe each geographic region and should help the RVer to overcome confusion on directional points.

RV CAMPGROUNDS: The name, milepost number or address, and times of operation follow the same pattern for all campgrounds. Privately operated campgrounds include mailing addresses and phone numbers including Alaska 800 numbers. This information is followed by driving directions to the campground and a detailed listing of its amenities: number of spaces, **sewage dump station** or **propane** if offered (always in bold print), tables, grills, and so on. A separate paragraph includes a brief, four-to-five sentence general impression of the campground. Campgrounds are not rated on an arbitrary scale or ranked in any order. Prices, which are subject to change, are not included.

RV SERVICES: The name, phone number and type of RV service, followed by driving directions to the service, are presented separately. An effort was made to include representative facilities which offer towing, emergency road service, propane and sewage dump stations. Not all such facilities could be included.

THE BILLIKEN: The billiken, as defined by Webster, is ". . . a squat smiling comic figure used as a mascot." Billikens have been popular as good luck charms in Alaska for decades and are seen in practically every gift shop. Alaskan mythology documents the power which billikens have to bring good luck as expressed in the following rhyme:

Rub his belly,
Rub his toes,
Good luck follows,
Wherever you goes.

It is certainly the author's wish that good luck will follow you as you make decisions in planning your trip whether it is for a weekend or a summer. Half the fun of taking any trip is planning for it ahead of time.

PLANNING AN ITINERARY

OPTIONS: Each chapter offers options or alternatives to the traveler at major points along the highway. Each option has a brief description and is marked with the billiken logo. Alaska's highways offer many options.

Here is an example of how the book can be used to plan your trip. Three separate highways lead from Tok: 1. the Alaska Highway east to the

Canadian border; 2. the Alaska Highway west to Fairbanks; 3. the Glenn Highway southwest to Glennallen.

The description to Fairbanks reads "west leads to Delta Junction and the terminus of the Alaska Highway at the Richardson Highway. Further west is Fairbanks and the George Parks Highway to Denali Park and Anchorage." A decision might be made to follow the Alaska Highway west to Fairbanks, south to Denali National Park, east to Paxson, then either north to Delta Junction or south to Glennallen and Valdez.

Options on the Kenai Peninsula and the Sterling Highway could lead the angler to fishing opportunities on the Kenai River in Soldotna or to charter boats in Homer.

One exciting option to consider is traveling by ferry on the Alaska Marine Highway System either to or from Bellingham, Washington, using Haines or Skagway as points of arrival or departure.

Here is an *extreme example* of how options might be used from the Alaska Highway approaching Whitehorse. Although this scenario would allow the RVer to drive the most scenic highways in Alaska and retrace fewer than fourteen driving miles (Tok to Tetlin Junction), it is unlikely that many Rvers would choose to do so.

Option 1: The Klondike Highway from the Alaska Highway to Skagway.

Option 2: The Alaska Marine Highway System from Skagway to Haines.

Option 3: The Haines Highway from Haines to Haines Junction, Yukon Territory, and re-entry to the Alaska Highway.

Option 4: The Alaska Highway from Haines Junction to Tok, Alaska.

Option 5: The Glenn Highway cutoff southwest from Tok to Glennallen.

Option 6: The Richardson Highway south from Glennallen to Valdez.

Option 7: The Alaska Marine Highway System from Valdez to Seward.

Option 8: The Seward Highway north from Seward to Anchorage.

Option 9: The Glenn Highway east from Anchorage to the George Parks Highway junction.

Option 10: The George Parks Highway north to Denali National Park and then to Fairbanks.

Option 11: The Richardson Highway east from Fairbanks to Delta Junction.

Option 12: The Alaska Highway east from Delta Junction to Tetlin Junction.

Option 13: The Taylor Highway north from Tetlin Junction to the Canadian border and Dawson City, Yukon Territory.

TOP TOURIST ATTRACTIONS:

Attraction	Location	Annual Visitors
Portage Glacier	Seward Highway	238,800
Marine Highway	Ketchikan to Skagway	227,700
Mendenhall Glacier	Juneau	200,000
Glacier Bay	Southeast Alaska	181,500
Ketchikan Totems	Ketchikan	178,500
Mount McKinley	Denali National Park	175,200
Historic Skagway	Skagway	175,000
Museum of History & Art	Anchorage	149,700
University Museum	U of A Fairbanks	124,500
Kenai River	Kenai Peninsula	121,200

THE ALASKA MARINE HIGHWAY SYSTEM

The Alaska Marine Highway System is supported in part with federal highway funds because it connects both interstate and international highways. Ferries depart Bellingham, Washington, and travel the "inside passage," the world's longest sheltered waterway. Juneau, Haines and Skagway (see chapter three on Southeast Alaska) are served as are many smaller Alaskan towns and villages. Haines and Skagway, which are points of both arrival and departure, connect with the Alaska Highway. An estimated one of every twelve visitors to Alaska will use the marine highway system at some point.

RVers who would like a taste of the Alaska Marine Highway System but who still want the pleasure of driving can also board or depart ferries at Prince Rupert, British Columbia. This allows them to see the Tongass National Forest as well as Petersburg, Wrangell and Ketchikan. Prince Rupert accesses the Alaska Highway via the Yellowhead Highway at Prince George.

RV campgrounds are also located in many of the communities on the marine highway system. They are not described in this guidebook since they are not directly accessible from the road system. A resource for people considering stopping along the way is *Alaska's INSIDE PASSAGE Traveler: See More, Spend Less!* by Ellen Searby, Windham Bay Press. Information can also be obtained through the U.S. Forest Service.

Fares on the inside passage are based on a port-to-port structure. However, stopovers are permissible without additional cost if they are reserved at the time that the itinerary is booked. Vehicle rates are based on vehicle length.

Winter tariffs (October 1 through April 30) are reduced. There is no charge for the driver which represents a substantial reduction to RVers who can arrange their travel to correspond with those dates. Summer travel reservations, which are accepted after the first week in December, should be made as far in advance as possible because vehicle deck space is limited. Advance ticketing is less critical on ferries in southcentral Alaska (Valdez, Seward and Homer) but still should be arranged when travel dates can be confirmed.

Any person who is 65 years of age (not just Alaskans) can obtain a senior citizen pass for the marine highway which allows walk-on boarding for a small fee. These passes are issued at the point of embarkation only. Passes are good on all vessels during the winter (October through April) but certain restrictions apply during the summer season. Vehicles, cabins, food and other charges are priced at the normal rate.

Disabled persons (70 percent disabled) can apply for a marine highway pass which is good for two years. Application requests must be made through the Alaska Marine Highway System in Juneau, Alaska. Certain restrictions also apply to these passes.

Animals are required to have current health certificates and must be kept in appropriate containers. Animals are restricted to the car deck and are allowed out only at times specified by the purser.

Marine highway vessels are "working ships" and not cruise ships. They provide comfortable but not luxurious quarters, meals and facilities. Cabins are available but are limited in number. Meals are served cafeteria style. First aid is available only; there are no ship doctors.

The Alaska Marine Highway System offers free summer and winter schedules which detail restrictions, fares, check-in times and other information. Write to Alaska Marine Highway, P.O. Box 25535, Juneau, Alaska 99802-5535 or call toll free 1-800-642-0066 for reservations (FAX 907/277-4829).

PREPARING FOR ADVENTURE

OUTFITTING THE RV: The secret to trouble-free driving on the Alaska Highway and the highways in Alaska is to take a few preventative steps in preparation. The first step is to have *in your possession* the warranty packet and card information that came with the motorhome, fifth wheel or travel trailer at the time of purchase. Know the name of the dealer and location of the original purchase, factory telephone numbers, warranty numbers, as well as year, make and model in order to expedite delivery of replacement parts if that should become necessary.

Mount Spurr which is located west of Anchorage erupted on August 18, 1992. Prevailing winds carried volcanic ash over Anchorage which was soon covered with ash. Air quality standards are exceeded when dirt particulates in the air measure above 150 during any eight hour period. The day following the eruption, the air quality reading in Anchorage was 989. The silicon-based ash is highly abrasive and can be very destructive to automobile engines. Automobile filters were sold out in a matter of a few hours and became impossible to obtain. The likelihood of a visitor experiencing a volcanic eruption in southcentral Alaska is slight, but it is nevertheless wise to carry extra oil filters and air filters for the engine as well as for the generator.

Factory made wheel cylinders, radiator hoses, dimmer switches, electrical and hydraulic parts are not always available even at the appropriate dealer's service department much less fifty miles away from anywhere. Therefore, it is imperative to have a thorough tuneup which includes checking belts, filters, hoses, batteries, fuses, cooling systems, brakes, propane fittings, wheel alignment and tires. Also check for loose screws and rivets and loose skin panels, wires and hoses underneath the RV. Perform the normal maintenance tasks *but be certain to do them all* before heading north on the Alaska Highway.

Is it necessary to install screens for headlights and windshields or special materials to cover holding tanks? Probably not on today's highways. However, it is a good idea to carry extra belts for various engine components, extra radiator hoses, and an extra section of heater hose in addition to replacement ignition parts such as fuses, plugs, points and condensers. In all likelihood small garages will have neither the equipment nor parts to do more than temporary repairs on your RV.

Low air pressure is the primary cause of radial tire failure. Tires should be checked each morning for proper air pressure and outer edge wear. Air pressure for maximum weight should be maintained during extended periods of highway driving although some RVers believe that slightly reducing the air pressure on rear duals on motorhomes provides better stability and handling. An inexpensive precaution for tire maintenance before, during and after the trip is a computerized alignment check; one replacement tire can cost twice what a front end repair and alignment would cost.

Note: many truckers driving gravel roads in Alaska such as the Dalton Highway and the Denali Highway reduce air pressure slightly on all tires in order to cut down on rock cuts and sidewall punctures. This procedure is for gravel roads exclusively and proper air pressure is restored as soon as their rigs return to blacktopped highways.

PREPARATION FOR WINTER DRIVING: Preventative action for cold winter driving is not significantly different than it is for summer driving. Winter driving requires studded tires or tire chains, and the installation of a tank-type heater for the cooling system and/or an oil pan heater plug. Windshield scrapers for ice and a broom for snow removal are also necessary. A small shovel and battery booster cables should be carried as well.

All water lines, including the hot water tank, should be drained. Once drained, the lines should be blown out under pressure and anti-freeze added to the water lines. Anti-freeze good to at least thirty degrees below zero should be added to the cooling system, and windshield washer fluid should be replaced with washer fluid designed for cold weather use. A portable chemical toilet can substitute for the conventional flush toilet during winter months.

OUTFITTING YOURSELF: Alaska has a seat-belt law in effect although state troopers in the past have not stopped drivers for noncompliance to the law. Troopers check seat-belts if some other violation has caused a motorist to be stopped. Drivers are liable for a $50 fine if any nonbelted occupants are under sixteen years of age. Car seats for infants are also required.

Alaska is such a large state that it encompasses six unique climates and the RVer who drives the Alaska Highway could experience three of those. Southeast Alaska is cool and wet while the interior is hot and dry; southcentral is a combination of the two.

Average monthly precipitation for Anchorage (southcentral) nearly doubles each month from May through September. May gets a mere .57 inches of precipitation (the driest month). June at 1.08 inches nearly doubles May's output. July offers another near doubling at 1.97 inches while August comes in with 2 inches. Finally, September, the wettest month, produces 2.45 inches of measurable precipitation.

Most of the summer rain comes in the form of long, light rainfalls rather than intense showers. Average high temperatures in Anchorage on the Fahrenheit scale during those same months are 54°F for May; 62°F for June; 65°F for July; 63°F for August; 55°F for September.

Therefore, clothing should include raingear, rainboots, wool sweaters and a stocking cap or some form of warm headgear for cool evenings. Denim jeans, a pair of good walking or jogging shoes, and a windbreaker will get a lot of wear during summer months as will lighter clothing such as denims and short sleeved shirts. Winter clothing would include down-filled jackets, polypropylene underwear, heavy gloves, insulated boots, and some form of moisture-proof outer shell as well.

Layering clothing provides better protection against the elements and greater warmth especially in the southcentral and Prince William Sound regions of the state. Dress casually and wear clothing that does not require much in the way of ironing; anticipate warm days and cool evenings between May and September. Your best guess will probably be pretty close in terms of actual temperatures and conditions. What to wear in Alaska is always a judgment call, but it is better to bring too much than too little.

MEDICAL: Followers of the television series, "Northern Exposure," may be lulled into thinking that each Alaskan town has its own doctor as does Cicely, Alaska; nothing could be less true. Most towns and villages have a health center at best, and maybe not even that. In all likelihood, the center, if there is one, will be staffed by volunteers.

Therefore, it is important to know that in the event of an emergency, you could very well be medivaced by air to a larger community for medical attention. Be certain to carry enough medication (in appropriate containers) to provide for your needs while you are on the highway. If your condition is such that it is out-of-the-ordinary, it would be wise to carry a doctor's statement describing the condition and any special instructions that might be deemed important for another medical provider to know. Living wills, expectation for hospitalization and care, and other important documents should be readily available.

MOSQUITOES: The question always arises, "What about mosquitoes"? The secret is out: there *are* mosquitoes in Alaska. Big ones! How big are they? Maybe not quite big enough to mount on a wall plaque.

Mosquitoes are especially populous in the spring following a warm, wet fall. They usually reach their peak around mid-June. It may be of some comfort to know that Alaska's mosquitoes are not disease-bearing. Certain foods affect mosquitoe behavior more than others; for example, bananas seem to attract them whereas garlic repels them, especially if worn in a garland around the neck.

DEET (diethyl-meta-toluamide), a chemical commonly used in mosquito repellents, has become suspect in terms of its safe use by humans; several of the better known repellents containing DEET are not available across the counter in Alaska. New York state health officials recommend that repellents contain no more than a thirty percent DEET concentration.

An interesting substitute for DEET-based repellents is Skin-So-Soft, an Avon bath oil product. The jury is out in terms of Skin-So-Soft's effectiveness, but it is the author's belief that it keeps mosquitoes at bay under ordinary mosquitoe conditions; furthermore, it moisturizes the skin in the process. A quick disclaimer: the author has no association with Avon Products, Inc. but does use Skin-So-Soft in lieu of other repellents.

White-sox, also known as black flies, are blood-sucking insects which have a particularly nasty bite; a small dab of ammonia applied with a cotton swab provides an element of relief from their bites.

WATER PURIFICATION: Most Alaskan campgrounds have potable water. Posted signs identify those campgrounds where water is unsafe. Water should never be used directly from streams or lakes for drinking or cooking purposes no mater how clear and pure it appears to be.

A campground set in a pristine area against a stand of trees and a clear-water stream can be deceptively inviting. Although it is against the law to drain RV holding tanks and human waste directly onto the ground, the practice does occur especially in isolated public campgrounds. Therefore, harmful bacteria can be present in water where least expected.

State epidemiologists issued the following bulletin in 1991: "There is a constant risk of ingesting giardia cysts from consumption of water obtained from any untreated surface source in the state." Symptoms of giardiasis, commonly known as "beaver fever" include gas, abdominal pain, bloating, fatigue, nausea, vomiting and loss of appetite. These flu-like symptoms can occur within hours of the time of infection or not appear for days or even weeks and vary from person to person.

Alaska's Division of Public Health suggests that the best method for water purification is to bring the water to a long, rolling boil for at least three minutes and longer at higher altitudes. A second recommended method is to add one drop of Clorox or Purex bleach (5.25% chlorine) to each quart of water. Two or three additional drops can be added to cloudy water. Allow the water to stand for thirty minutes before using.

DRIVING THE HIGHWAY

ALASKA'S HIGHEST HIGHWAY PASSES: These are the seven highest mountain passes on Alaska's highways: Atigun Pass (4,800 feet), Dalton Highway; Maclaren Summit (4,086 feet), Denali Highway; Eagle Summit (3,624 feet), Steese Highway; Eureka Summit (3,222 feet), Glenn Highway; White Pass (3,290 feet), Klondike Highway; Isabel Pass (3,000 feet), Richardson Highway; Twelvemile Summit (2,982), Steese Highway. The Denali Highway is closed during the winter. Permits are required to travel beyond Disaster Creek (MP 210) on the Dalton Highway. Drivers without permits are subject to citation.

THE TRANS-ALASKA PIPELINE: The 48-inch oil pipeline begins at Prudhoe Bay on the North Slope of Alaska and ends eight hundred miles later at the Valdez Marine Terminal. It took thirty-eight months, sixty million manhours, and three million tons of material to construct. The pipeline crosses permafrost, tundra, three mountain ranges, and fifty-seven bridges. The pipeline is the largest privately financed construction project ever undertaken. The first oil began flowing on June 20, 1977.

THE OIL SPILL: The events following the night of March 24, 1989, when the 987 foot tanker, Exxon Valdez, went aground on Bligh Reef have been well documented. Nearly 11 million gallons of North Slope crude oil spilled into Prince William Sound. Questions related to oil company beach cleanup efforts and the quality of the cleanup will undoubtedly be in the courts for years.

RVers are unlikely to see any shoreline from the highway that has been impacted by oil. This is not to say that the natural resources of Prince William Sound have been fully restored. The impact of the oil spill on fish, marine and animal life has not been fully determined. Oil is still present in places such as the Kenai Fjords National Park, Kodiak and elsewhere, but for the RVer, it is almost impossible to discern the damage at a distance.

CB OR NOT CB? Is it necessary to equip your RV with a CB radio? The answer is no; most RVers who want CB's already have them. Granted, long stretches of highway are without services, but to install a CB radio as a precautionary measure is questionable unless you expect to be on roads far from the main highway system.

Channels 9 and 11 are monitored as emergency channels, but there is frequently no response when they are used. Truckers prefer to use channel 19 on the Richardson Highway and channel 14 on the George Parks Highway.

HIGHWAY CONDITIONS: The Alaska Highway is entirely paved and and generally has good driving conditions throughout its length. However, driving conditions in Canada do become more difficult north of Kluane Lake. The driver seems always to be in the process of turning or going up or down hill. From Beaver Creek to the United States border, the road becomes worse and narrows with more pavement breaks. In mid-summer dust can also be a factor. These minor conditions, however, should not dissuade the hardy RVer from driving the Alaska Highway.

Highways in Alaska would be designated as roads at best almost anywhere else in the country. They are very similar in design and construction to highways in the contiguous states in the 1950s. Most of the highways are two lanes with narrow shoulders and unbanked curves. Only near cities such as Fairbanks and Anchorage do highways expand to four or six lanes.

Therefore, RVers cannot crank up the old motorhome to 65 or 70 MPH and let cruise control take over. In fact, 55 MPH is the legal speed limit throughout the entire state with the exception of the George Parks Highway between Nenana and the Susitna River which is legally posted at 65 MPH.

Bumps or dips are commonly the result of frost heaves beneath the road surface and seem to appear almost overnight. Expansion and contraction of freezing water destroys Alaskan roads through a cycle of freezing, thawing, and refreezing many times over. Permafrost, which is permanently frozen subsoil, is not normally a contributing factor to bumpy stretches of highway.

Driving Alaska's highways and roads should not be a problem if attention is given to road conditions. Department of Transportation highway signs that offer warnings such as "rough road" or "pavement break" should be heeded. Less obvious but equally important warnings of hazardous driving conditions come in the form of small wooden stakes set on road shoulders with attached fluorescent orange or pink flags.

Another clue to bad road conditions is a rash of short skid marks caused by vehicles that "bottomed out" as they hit an unmarked bump too fast. As soon as highway signs, markers or skid marks are seen, the driver should begin slowing the vehicle. Brakes released just before the moment of impact help to reduce damage whereas locked brakes can cause serious damage to the vehicle's suspension or front end alignment.

EMERGENCY ROAD SERVICE: Emergency road insurance is one of the options an RVer purchases and hopes never to use; however, when a medium-sized wrecker in Fairbanks costs $80 for the service call and $4 per mile, emergency road service is an option which can pay for itself in one phone call. The Good Sam Club has a reputation in Alaska for quick response to RV emergency service calls because of its service provider network. Other agencies may be equally responsible but, in any event, some form of emergency coverage is desirable.

BORDER CROSSINGS: Customs agents may claim that RVs are not singled out from other vehicles, but the fact remains that RVs are frequently searched at the time of border crossing between the United States and Canada. It is in the RVer's interest to have the following documents in possession and in order:

U.S. citizens should have evidence of nationality in the form of birth certificates, naturalization certificates, or voter registration; driver's licenses are not recognized as such evidence. Non-citizens should have an Alien Registration Receipt Card. It is not necessary to have passports or visas.

Parents traveling with young children absolutely must have certified copies of their birth certificates in their possession. Otherwise, long delays may be experienced and entry into Canada is not assured.

Evidence of vehicle insurance, motor vehicle registration forms, current license registration and plates or tags, and related documents should be in the vehicle glove compartment or easily accessed. A *Canadian Nonresident Interprovince Motor Vehicle Liability Insurance Card* can be obtained through your insurance company which will expedite the crossing process. Vehicles not registered to the driver will not be allowed to cross the border unless the driver has a letter of authorization from the owner (preferably notarized).

Small animals such as cats and dogs must have current rabies vaccination cards signed by a licensed veterinarian.

Elephant ivory and products made with bone, skin, or feathers from animals on the endangered species list will be confiscated. Alaskan ivory products should be accompanied with evidence or certificates obtained at the time of purchase verifying that the product is not made from elephant ivory. A tag on the product that reads "made in Alaska" may not suffice and could lead to confiscation of ivory products.

Firearms can be transported across the Canadian border but certain restrictions do apply. The three categories which are recognized are *prohibited*, *restricted*, and *long guns*. Handguns are not allowed into Canada.

Prohibited rifles and shotguns have barrels that have been adapted to less than 18 inches (457 mm) or which are less than 26 inches (660 mm) in overall length.

Restricted firearms, including handguns, are those designed to be fired by the action of one hand as well as those which are "capable of discharging centre fire ammunition in a semi-automatic manner."

Long guns are ordinary hunting rifles and shotguns, as described by the manufacturer, which do not fall into the prohibited or restricted categories.

A person who has been convicted of driving while under the influence of alcohol (DWI) can be prevented from entering Canada even as a passenger in a vehicle. In Canada a DWI is a felony and a lifelong offense. Proof of rehabilitation or affidavits confirming good behavior can be demanded by customs personnel. Although this is not normally a problem, it can become an issue especially if alcohol has been consumed by the driver or others just prior to the time of crossing. More information on this point can be found in the publication, *Employment and Immigration Canada, Immigration Manual, Part III, Exclusion and Removal, 19 (2) a, b, c..*

An excellent brochure, "Canada: Travel Information (for visitors from the U.S.A.)," gives more complete details. Write to the following agencies for current border crossing and customs information:

United States Customs
P.O. Box 7407
Washington, D.C. 20044
(202) 566-8195

Canadian Customs
Connaught Building
Sussex Drive
Ottawa, Ontario K1A OL5

M/V Tustumena car-deck: Alaska Marine Highway System

Chapter 2

PARKS AND WILDLIFE

This chapter describes state parks and campgrounds including a description of a typical Alaska campground, fees, periods of operation and the campground host program. An overview of animals in the wild, fish and birds and wetland habitats is also included.

NATIONAL PARKS: AN OVERVIEW

The nation's first national park was created as a "public park or pleasuring-ground for the benefit and enjoyment of the people." Congress established the National Park Service in 1916 in order to "conserve the scenery and the natural and historic objects and the wild life therein and to provide for the enjoyment of the same in such manner and by such means as will leave them unimpaired for the enjoyment of future generations."

Mount McKinley National Park was created in the territory of Alaska in 1917 and was soon followed by several other parks and monuments. *The Alaska Native Claims Settlement Act* (ANSCA) was passed by Congress in 1971. The settlement established large blocks of land for Native Alaskan use and included a controversial section (17, d-2) which allowed the Secretary of the Interior to define other tracts of Alaskan land which could be considered for new national parks, preserves, refuges, and monuments.

The Alaska National Interest Land's Conservation Act (ANILCA) was signed by President Jimmy Carter on Sunday, December 2, 1980. The act added forty-seven million acres of national park land in Alaska and doubled the acreage in the national park system. Also created were seven new Alaskan national parks, including the Wrangell-St. Elias National Park and Preserve, while existing parks were enlarged, not the least of them Denali National Park and Preserve (formerly Mount McKinley National Park). Additional wildlife refuges (10), monuments (4), and wild and scenic rivers (25) were set aside by that signature. Considered by many people to be the greatest act of conservation in the nation's history, President Carter has written that it gave him "particular satisfaction" to sign the act into law.

Three basic groups comprise the fifteen administrative units in Alaska's National Park System: Pacific Rim Parklands; Interior Parklands; Far North Parklands. Of these fifteen national parks, the RVer can visit four directly from the highway system: Klondike Gold Rush National Historic Park; Kenai Fjords National Park; Wrangell-Saint Elias National Park and Preserve; and Denali National Park and Preserve. Three others—Glacier Bay National Park and Preserve, Sitka National Historic Park, and Yukon-Charley Rivers National Preserve – although not directly accessible, can be viewed by making special charter arrangements for flightseeing or watercraft.

FEDERAL RECREATION PASSPORT PROGRAMS: Many national parks and refuges can be entered and used with no charge while others do require entrance fees or user fees.

The Golden Eagle Passport, for persons under age sixty-two, permits the holder and passengers in a noncommercial vehicle access to national parks, wildlife refuges, monuments, historic sites and recreation areas which charge entrance fees. An annual fee is charged for the passport.

The Golden Age Passport, for persons age sixty-two or older, is a free life-time entrance pass which also provides the holder, passengers and vehicle admittance to the above mentioned areas. In addition, this passport allows a fifty percent discount for camping, boat launching, parking and use of other facilities and services.

The Golden Access Passport, for blind and disabled persons, provides essentially the same privileges as does the Golden Age Passport. None of these passports provides fees for private concessionaires or other contractors operating within federal recreation areas.

For further information regarding these passports, write to the U. S. Department of the Interior, National Park Service, Post Office Box 37127, Washington, DC 20013-7127. The regional office for the National Park Service in Alaska is located at 2525 Gamble Street, Room 107, Anchorage, Alaska, 99503.

ALASKA'S PARKS AND CAMPGROUNDS

Alaska's park system, with more than three million acres under the direction of the Alaska State Division of Parks and Outdoor Recreation, is the largest in the nation; it provides 2,500 campsites in 120 state parks. The parks host six million visitors each year, about twenty percent of whom come from out-of-state. The state uses a number of designations to define its offerings; the most common designations are State Parks (SP), State Recreation Areas (SRA), and State Recreation Sites (SRS).

State Parks are the largest entities. Denali State Park, for example, contains 324,240 acres and borders on Denali National Park and Preserve which contains six million acres. State Recreation Areas usually encompass several smaller campgrounds: Rosehip Campground and Tors Trailhead Campground are part of the larger Chena River State Recreation Area.

A State Recreation Site is an individual campground and may, or may not, be part of a larger SRA. Other state designations are used, but they are of less importance to the RVing public. RVers most commonly stay in an SRS if they use a state campground.

A TYPICAL STATE CAMPGROUND: A typical state campsite has tables, fire rings, litter barrels or dumpsters, potable water and toilets. Toilets are usually pit toilets, many of which are on concrete vaults and are accessible to the disabled. Larger campgrounds may offer a designated space for the disabled which will be level but not normally blacktopped. Roads through campgrounds are gravel-based. RV spaces vary in length but tend to be short (25-30 feet) and narrow especially in the northern region of the state. Spaces are usually level but some will require blocking.

Tent campers may or may not have space dedicated for their use; in campgrounds where space is not designated, tenters can park in any available space unless directed to do otherwise. Boat ramps give access to lakes and rivers.

A recent survey of state campgrounds revealed that the greatest user-criticism was lack of level spaces and poorly maintained roads. Overall state campgrounds received favorable ratings and positive approval. Little interest was shown in making Alaskan state campgrounds more commercial by offering concessions. Users in Alaska accept the rustic conditions of their campgrounds and are not seeking radical improvements. However, gradual improvement is taking place throughout the state park system; each year the Division of Parks and Outdoor Recreation upgrades a few campgrounds within the constraints of its budget.

FEES FOR CAMPGROUND USE: Fees are charged for campground use if potable water is on site. An annual camping pass in the form of a windshield decal may be purchased which is good for one calendar year and which allows camp spaces to be occupied from three to fifteen days dependent upon location. Annual passes are available through state park offices in Anchorage, Fairbanks, Juneau, Kodiak, Palmer/Wasilla and Soldotna. They may also be purchased by mail through the State of Alaska, Annual Camping Pass, Division of Parks and Outdoor Recreation, P.O. Box 107001, Anchorage, Alaska 99510-7001.

Boat launching fees are charged at certain state sites which include Finger Lake, Big Lake, Kenai River, Kasilof River, Deep Creek, Quartz Lake, Salcha River, Chena River, Harding Lake, Sitka and Haines.

CAMPERS WITH DISABILITIES: "The Americans With Disabilities Act" is helping to bring change to public campgrounds for campers with disabilities. Most state campgrounds have specially designed latrines and reserved parking for the disabled camper. However, many of the latrines are difficult to get to in a wheelchair.

The Bureau of Land Management is taking the lead in campground design in Alaska and has made major modifications to Sourdough Creek Campground (MP 147.5 Richardson Highway). Wide trails made of finely crushed gravel and latrines throughout the campground are designed for use by disabled campers. A fishing dock is projected which will be accessible by campers in wheelchairs, and two pull-throughs are dedicated for use by the disabled camper. "The disabled camper was foremost in our thinking during all stages of design," according to Gene Keith, District Manager for BLM's Glennallen office.

At Anchor Point a dock-like platform for the elderly and the disabled is available in the Ma Walli Rock Senior Citizen Disabled Fishing Area. The State and local businesses donated time and labor for the project. Another special access fishing pier is available on the Homer Spit.

Permanently disabled persons and senior citizens are eligible for free lifetime access passports to national forests and parks, monuments, historic sites, wildlife refuges, and recreational areas through the National Park Service. However, Golden Eagle Passes, which waive entrance fees to national parks are not issued by the Forest Service in Alaska.

VOLUNTEER CAMPGROUND HOSTS: The Department of Natural Resources' Division of Parks and Outdoor Recreation offers campground host positions each summer in campgrounds throughout the state. Hosts are assigned to a single campground for the season which runs from Memorial Day through Labor Day. Camping space and minimal expenses are provided. Although the commitment varies with the individual applicant, a minimum commitment of four to six weeks is usually required.

Volunteer hosts are given training for their work, free campsites and uniforms. In exchange for free camping, hosts serve as liaisons between campers and state park rangers. Hosts assign spaces and provide information about the area; they do not collect campground fees. Depending upon circumstances, travel expenses for volunteer hosts positions may be tax deductible. Hosting a campground is a personally rewarding experience and hosts frequently return to the same site.

Other volunteer positions include Backcountry Hosts for remote areas, Information Services Volunteers who staff park visitor centers, Trail Crew Members who perform more physically demanding tasks, and Special Projects Volunteers. Volunteer services extend throughout the state and are not restricted to the road system. For further information or an application write to the following addresses:

> Statewide Volunteer Coordinator,
> Division of Parks and Outdoor Recreation,
> P.O. Box 107001, Anchorage, Alaska 99510-7001

> Chugach National Forest
> Seward Ranger District
> PO Box 390, Seward, Alaska 99664

> Kenai National Wildlife Refuge
> (907) 262-7467

DURATION: State operated campgrounds are open throughout the year. This does not mean that they are maintained throughout the year, however. At some campgrounds actual barriers are placed at the entrances during winter months to exclude traffic while, at others, campers can continue to use the sites until snow prevents them from doing so. Roads are not plowed and dumpsters are not tended during winter months. Breakup in early spring leaves campground roads muddy and impassable to most recreational vehicles. Bureau of Land Management and U.S. Fish and Wildlife campgrounds are closed during winter months.

HIKING AREAS: Hiking areas abound throughout Alaska. Many campgrounds have trails which lead from the immediate area to nearby points of interest. Trails are usually well marked but caution is always advised because bears, moose and other animals use them. Hikers should travel in pairs or groups and not use the trails unaccompanied.

Backpackers and persons planning longer trips should advise local authorities such as representatives of the Bureau of Land Management, U.S. Fish and Wildlife Service, U.S. Forest Service, or the National Park Service regarding their plans and estimated times before setting out.

Little Susitna Campground: Susitna Flats State Game Refuge

ANIMALS IN THE WILD

In their eagerness to photograph or to get near wildlife, people can threaten or disrupt the animal's normal existence. Here are some suggestions which can reduce stress in animals. First, avoid getting too close by using binoculars or other spotting devices to watch from a distance. Second, don't chase or follow animals but rather sit or stand quietly in one spot to view them. Third, limit the time spent near animals in the wild and watch for nervous behavior on their part which may be an indication that it is time to leave.

The U. S. Department of the Interior, through divisions such as the Bureau of Land Management and the Fish and Wildlife Service, is responsible for various aspects of National Wildlife Refuge (NWR) management. Of the sixteen wildlife refuges in Alaska, only Tetlin NWR and Kenai NWR are accessible by road.

Both refuges have subarctic environments typical of the central region of the state. They contain wetlands, tundra, mountains and forests and provide homes for Dall sheep, caribou, wolves, bears, small animals and waterfowl. A brochure, "National Wildlife Refuges of Alaska," can be obtained by writing to the Department of the Interior, U.S. Fish and Wildlife Service, 555 Cordova Street, Anchorage, Alaska 99501.

BEARS: The grizzly bear is probably most quickly brought to mind when people think of Alaska. Grizzlies, estimated to number 40,000 in the state, roam throughout much of Alaska and western Canada. They are identifiable by their muscular shoulder humps and massive forelegs; coloration ranges from light brown to near black. Brown bears, which are larger and inhabit the coastal regions, are of the same species as the grizzly. Black bears are smaller than either grizzlies or brown bears but are far more numerous and much more unpredictable in their behavior.

All bears, however, should be treated with respect. Campgrounds frequently have signs noting that bears are known to be in the area. Campers should heed these signs and take appropriate precautions:

- under no circumstances should bears in a campground area be approached or fed;
- food should be stored in tightly sealed containers;
- paper refuse and cans should be burned before being placed in dumpsters or other recepticals;
- domestic animals should be tied securely and not taken away from the campground area or on trails;
- hikers should be alert and make noise through loud talk and other means when on trails.

"The Bears and You" is a brochure available from the Alaska Department of Fish and Game, 1800 Glenn Highway, Suite 4, Anchorage, AK 99504.

CARIBOU: Alaska has an estimated 835,000 caribou which can be encountered almost anywhere along the highway system. They are notable for the size and shape of their antlers and the castanet-like clicking sound they make as they walk. Caribou had disappeared entirely from the Kenai Peninsula by 1913, but herds have gradually been restored through the efforts of the Alaska Department of Fish and Game. Caribou are most frequently seen in the early morning and late evening hours when they are feeding.

DALL SHEEP: All of the major mountain ranges in Alaska are home to Dall sheep. Dall sheep are a species of big horn sheep but have notably smaller horns. Normally elusive animals, they are commonly seen on the hillside along the Seward Highway near Windy Point. Traffic comes to a near standstill along Turnagain Arm when the animals are visible to travelers south of Anchorage.

Dall sheep as viewed from the Seward Highway south of Anchorage

BELUGA WHALES: The distinctive white beluga whale can be seen in Cook Inlet from the Twentymile River to Point Woronzof beginning in mid-April as they feed on hooligan. In late May and June, they can be seen at the mouth of the Kenai River as they pursue salmon. They return to the Cook Inlet and Turnagain Arm in late summer and early October as they feed on silver salmon.

Biologists with the Alaska Department of Fish and Game estimate that there are about 500 belugas in Cook Inlet. The animals are relatively small, about fifteen feet long and 1,500 pounds in weight. They are protected by the Marine Mammal Act but are not considered to be an endangered species.

SHELLFISH AND SALMON

CLAMMING BEACHES: The best clamming in southcentral Alaska occurs along the Sterling Highway from Kasilof to Anchor Point on the west side of the Kenai Peninsula. The first big minus tide in the spring signals the beginning of the season, and clammers head for the beaches. Clam shovels and buckets are filled with razor clams, butter clams (steamers), rednecks, and the larger horseclams (geoducks).

From Memorial Day to the end of summer, owners of motorhomes, fifth wheels, camper trailers and car-top tenters vie for space at Clam Gulch, Deep Creek and Happy Valley in full view of steaming Redoubt Volcano. Park rangers patrol the beaches in pickup trucks as an estimated 3,000-4,000 diggers pursue the elusive mollusks on ebbing tides. An Alaskan sports fisherman's license is required in order to dig clams. Coast Guard auxiliary members check boats for current registrations and the proper number of life jackets.

Tide schedules are essential in order to determine which beaches and dates will be best for clam digging. Tides of minus four and five feet are ideal. Deadly "red tides" are not common but can occur between April and November. Symptoms of paralytic shellfish poisoning will appear within five to thirty minutes after eating toxic shellfish. Precautions should be taken during cleaning and dark parts of the clam (gills and digestive tract) as well as the tip of the neck should be cut away.

ANGLER'S PARADISE: Alaska's streams, rivers, lakes and oceans abound with fish: salmon, steelhead, trout, Arctic char, northern pike, sheefish, whitefish, burbot, and halibut take lures and flies from Sitka to Homer and nearly everyplace in between. The Kenai River is probably the best known salmon river in the state because of its record sized kings (world record 97 pound, 4 ounce king, taken May 17, 1985). It is generally thought of as having two distinct runs, but biologists who count the fish indicate that no significant break occurs between the May–June kings and the July–August kings. The primary difference between the "two runs" appears to be that more six-year-old fish come into the river in July as opposed to the four and five-year-old fish which arrive earlier.

Californians take a salmon on the Kenai River

The Gulkana River in the Copper River basin near Glennallen can also yield big kings. Sixty pounders and above are not unusual. Kings enter the river from mid-June to mid-August. Anglers who fish the river claim that there is more scrappiness to Gulkana River kings than is true of Kenai River kings. They base their argument on the fact that the fish have several hundred miles to swim from the ocean in order to reach their spawning grounds.

Salmon can be taken from many other rivers and streams not the least of them the Anchor River, the Russian River, the Susitna River, Willow Creek, and even Ship Creek in downtown Anchorage. An excellent, yet inexpensive reference book to fishing Alaska's streams and rivers is *Alaska Roadside Salmon Angler's Guide* by Jim and Janet Sumner of Anchorage (Seagrass Publishing, 123 pages). This book gives simple, basic directions on what works, where and why. A number of comprehensive maps showing how to get to the best spots along the road system are offered as are suggestions on when to fish a stream and what gear to use for reds, silvers, chums, kings, and pinks. Suggestions on how to fish salt-water areas such as Seward, Valdez and Homer are also given.

Fishing in Alaska is not restricted to salmon. Halibut charters from Valdez, Seward, and Homer are every bit as popular. Rainbow trout and grayling are taken in Bradley Lake, Kepler Lake, Wishbone Lake and dozens of other lakes in the Matanuska-Susitna valley. Northern Pike in the Minto Flats area west of Fairbanks show their voracious appetites from June to mid-September. Finally, BLM campgrounds on the Denali Highway yield burbot, trout and grayling.

Fishing licenses can be purchased from sporting goods stores throughout the state. Non-resident licenses are issued on either a 3-day or 14-day basis. Contact the Alaska Department of Fish and Game for a copy of the *Alaska Sport Fishing Regulations Summary*. Address requests to Alaska Department of Fish and Game, P.O. Box 3-2000, Juneau, Alaska 99802-2000, telephone (907) 465-4110.

BIRDS AND WETLANDS

Biologists believe that the spectacled eider and Steller's eider, seaducks which commonly nest in the Yukon Delta region, have decreased in numbers by ninety-five percent during the past twenty years. On the other hand, dusky Canada geese which nest in the Copper River Delta have increased from four thousand to 14,000 birds since the mid-eighties. Another dramatic increase is noted in the ranks of the trumpeter swan which have increased by 10,000 birds since 1965.

Canada geese (honkers) abound in Anchorage

Other birds in Alaska whose populations were almost eradicated but which are rising include the Aleutian Canada goose whose nesting grounds follow the remote islands of Alaska toward Asia. Each year hardcore "birders" migrate to the Aleutian and Pribilofs Islands in order to view such rare and exotic birds as the lapland longspur and the narcissus flycatcher decked out in breeding plumage.

One hundred-twenty species of waterfowl, exclusive of birds which winter in Alaska, are known to migrate through the upper Cook Inlet and Anchorage bowl each spring. They come from as far away as North Africa and the tip of South America. The primary routes which they follow take them along the Alaska coastline into Prince William Sound, lead broadly from the Pacific Ocean, or cross from Western Canada through the Copper River basin. From Cook Inlet they continue toward the Alaska Peninsula or into the interior of the state.

Fortunately, it is not necessary to travel to Adak, Attu or St. Lawrence Island in order to observe migratory birds. The Anchorage bowl offers a number of excellent locations for birders. Chester Creek begins in the Chugach foothills and winds seven marshy miles through the city to Westchester Lagoon. Ship Creek, Campbell Creek, Rabbit Creek and Fish Creek also contribute to the wetland's drainage.

Road construction on the Glenn Highway expanded existing wetlands north of Eklutna Flats by 480 acres to the benefit of ducks, birds of prey, geese and other waterfowl. Connors Bog, seven hundred acres of wetlands surrounded by asphalt and concrete in midtown Anchorage, is known to be frequented by eighty-eight species of birds as well as rabbits, muskrats, squirrels and coyotes.

Bird watchers and their vehicles created such congestion along the Seward Highway by the Anchorage Coastal Wildlife Refuge (also known as Potter Marsh State Game Refuge) that a separate parking area and boardwalk were constructed to relieve the problem. Boardwalk signs identify more than fifty species that inhabit or pass through the marsh. Arctic terns travel 11,000 miles to refuel on small fish in the saltwater sanctuary. Canada geese, mallards, widgeons, trumpeter swans, and grebes find time to settle for short periods on the marsh's surface.

The *Kachemak Shorebird Festival* is an annual event celebrated during the second week in May in Homer, Alaska. Each year 100,000 shorebirds migrate through the area and land on the Homer Spit which makes roadside viewing an easy thing to do.

A New, Expanded Guide to the Birds of Alaska by Robert H. Armstrong (Alaska Northwest Publishing) is a popular reference book.

Chapter 3

SOUTHEAST ALASKA

This chapter describes campgrounds and services in Skagway, Haines, and Juneau. Options include the Klondike Highway; the Haines Cutoff Highway; and the Alaska Marine Highway System.

FROM THE ALASKA HIGHWAY

Regardless of the direction, north or south, that RVers are traveling on the Alaska Highway, two alternatives can be considered: the Klondike Highway to Skagway, Alaska; and the Haines Cutoff Highway to Haines, Alaska. Each of these highways connects with the Alaska Marine Highway System, and each offers the opportunity to visit a unique part of the state. A time change from Pacific Daylight Time to Alaska Daylight Time is required at the time of the border crossing.

THE KLONDIKE HIGHWAY

This scenic drive, ninety-eight miles from its junction with the Alaska Highway, presents an opportunity to visit Skagway as well as other points of historic interest. The Carcross Cemetery, where early prospectors and personalities such as Kate Carmacks, Skookum Jim, and Tagish Charlie are buried is at mile 64. The remnants of a stamp mill, mine shafts and a tailings pond can be investigated for several miles along the highway at around mile 51. The tracks and bridges for the White Pass and Yukon Route railroad are visible at a number of points.

THE HAINES CUTOFF HIGHWAY AT HAINES JUNCTION

A word of caution at this point. Drivers who have not driven the Alaska Highway (Highway 1) can become confused at Haines Junction. The Alaska Highway makes a ninety degree turn at the point where the Haines Cutoff Highway (Highway 3) is joined. Signs in both directions indicate the turn and warn drivers.

Yet each year people who do not intend to drive to Haines find that they have done just that. As one Haines resident said, "While they are most assuredly welcome in Haines, if they don't plan to come here, knowledge of the highway can save them 320 miles round trip."

The first highway sign on the Haines Cutoff Highway (#3) reads: "This road to Haines Alaska only connecting with ferry system." The next sign reads: "U.S. Custom hours of service 8:00 a.m. to Midnight, absolutely no entry between Midnight and 8:00 a.m." U.S. and Canadian customs are located at mile 42 which is 116 miles from Highway 1.

SKAGWAY, ALASKA

Skagway is best known for its colorful gold rush period. Founded by a sea captain who staked his claim on its bay in the late nineteenth century, Skagway became the point of departure for men and women seeking their fortunes in the gold fields of the Klondike. Stampeders, as they became known, arrived by ships to trudge nearly forty miles over the Chilkoot Pass from Dyea to Lake Bennett. They were required by the Canadian government to physically transport one ton of supplies over the pass before they could begin the five hundred mile trip down the Yukon River to the actual goldfields.

The remains of Dyea, a town of 10,000 people during the peak of the gold rush, can be visited at nearby Klondike Gold Rush National Historic Park. For the most part, the buildings have crumbled into the past. A cemetery, a wharf, and a few building remnants are all that remain. The Chilkoot Trailhead is also within the park boundaries.

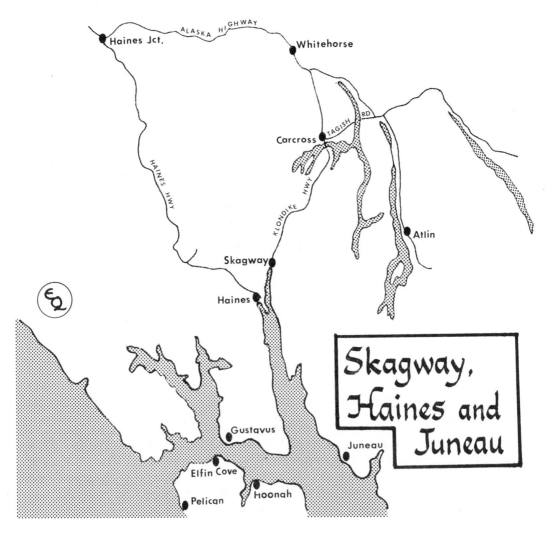

Skagway today retains much of the gold rush atmosphere in its buildings and attractions. The northern terminus for the Alaska Marine Highway System, the town offers visitors a touch of the past with many things of an historic nature to see and do. For example, the Chilkoot Trail, which has its trailhead at Klondike Gold Rush National Historical Park, can be hiked in three to five days. For those persons who are less willing to commit themselves to such an arduous activity, a three-hour trip over White Pass on the narrow-gauge White Pass and Yukon Route railroad may be more appealing.

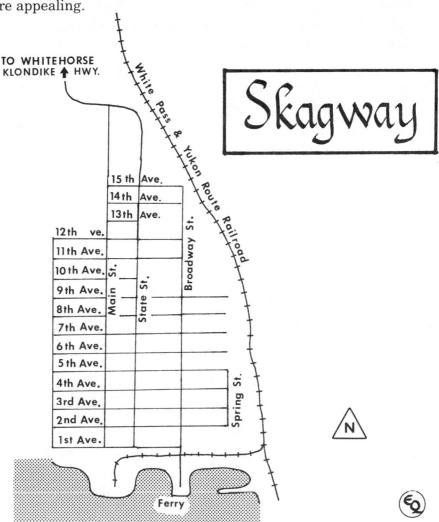

THE WHITE PASS & YUKON ROUTE

Gold was struck in the Klondike in 1897, and Skagway became the gateway into the Yukon. Construction on the railroad began in 1898 by a Canadian railroad contractor. White Pass parallels the Skagway River which stampeders used as an alternative to the steeper Chilkoot Trail on their way to Lake Bennett and the Klondike gold fields. Blasted from granite cliffs by workers hanging by slender ropes, the railroad reached Whitehorse in 1900 as the Klondike's golden era was ending. The line transported materials for the construction of the Alaska Highway during World War II years.

During summer months visitors can ride the historic train on its narrow-gauge (36-inch) track from Skagway to White Pass summit (2,865 feet). The three hour round trip provides panoramic views of Lynn Canal, Mount Harding, the Harding Glacier, and the Chilkat Mountain Range.

THE KLONDIKE GOLD RUSH (NHP) VISITOR CENTER
May 1st—September 30th   Second Avenue and Broadway Street

The center contains historical photographs, national historic park information, a theater featuring films, slide shows and talks, and general details about the Skagway area. Daily walking tours are conducted.

SKAGWAY CONVENTION and VISITORS CENTER   (907) 983-2854
Tourism Director, PO Box 415, Skagway, AK 99840

HEALTH AND EMERGENCY SERVICES

Skagway Health Center	**(907) 983-2255**
Physician's Assistant	**(907) 983-2418**
Fire Department	**(907) 983-2300**
Skagway Police	**(907) 983-2301 or 911**

RV CAMPGROUNDS AT SKAGWAY

PULLEN PARK CAMPGROUND   privately operated
PO Box 324, Skagway, AK 99840   May 1st— October 15th
(907) 983-2768   foot of State Street

Located at the foot of State Street, adjacent to the Alaska Highway ferry dock: 42 spaces; 42 power and water hookups; **sewage dump station**; flush toilets; drinking water; hot showers; laundry facilities; tables; grills; boat launch; fishing; public phone; separate tenting area; no time limit.

Pullen Park Campground has raked gravel throughout the area. Spaces are level but short. The layout is circular with back-in spaces and small trees and decorative grassed areas. Situated next to the small boat harbor and boat ramp, an office is located on site.

HOOVER'S RV PARK   privately operated
PO Box 304, Skagway, AK 99840   open all year
(907) 983-2454   Main Street at Fourth Avenue

Located one block west of State Street on Fourth Avenue: 20 spaces; 6 pull-throughs; 20 power and water hookups; **sewage dump station**; flush toilets, drinking water; hot showers; laundry facilities; public phone; **propane**; no time limit.

Hoover's RV Park has back-in, side-by-side parking with approximately 12 foot separations between spaces. The drive area is gravel-based and spaces are level. The water is turned off during winter months but power and sewer are available all year long.

BACK TRACK CAMPER PARK
PO Box 375, Skagway, AK 99840
(907) 983-3333

privately operated
May 1st—Sept 30th
Broadway Street at Twelfth Avenue

Located one block west of State Street at Twelfth Avenue: 60 spaces; 5 pull-throughs; 30 power and water hookups; 30 w/o hookups; **sewage dump station**; flush toilets; drinking water; hot showers; laundry facilities; tables; public phone; separate tenting area; no time limit.

Back Track Camper Park is level with gravel-based spaces set among alder trees. Larger RVs can be accommodated if arrangements are made ahead of time. The campground is the newest one in Skagway and is walking distance to the historic section of downtown.

HANOUSEK CAMPGROUND
PO Box 324, Skagway, AK 99840
(907) 983-2768

privately operated
May 1st—Sept 30th
Broadway Street at Fourteenth Avenue

Located one block west of State Street at Fourteenth Avenue: 60 spaces; 4 power hookups; 56 w/o hookups; **sewage dump station**; flush toilets; drinking water; hot showers; tables; separate tenting area; no time limit.

Hanousek Campground is lined with alder trees. Spaces are level and of varying lengths. Larger RVs can be accommodated. Plans include power and water.

KLONDIKE GOLD RUSH NATIONAL HISTORIC PARK
U.S. National Park Service

MP 7.0 Dyea Road

The Dyea Road cut-off is located at mile 2.1 where the Klondike Highway makes a sharp turn just past the Highway Department maintenance shops. A gravel road with few pull-outs, it posts a sign warning that it is a "narrow winding road with blind curves—motor homes, trailers and large vehicles use caution." The campground is on the Taiya River at mile seven of Dyea Road. Drivers of large vehicles are not encouraged to use this camp: 22 spaces w/o hookups; pit toilets; no drinking water; tables; grills; separate tenting area; 14 day limit.

The Klondike Gold Rush NHP has a road through the campground which forms two separate loops. RVs must cross a narrow bridge to wooded camp sites. Spaces are level and separated from other campers. Water must be boiled or treated chemically. A fulltime Park Ranger is on site. Interpretive signs, old grave sites and other points of historical interest mark the area. In 1898 Dyea had 10,000 people and was the largest city in the territory. Dyea served to outfit gold prospectors using the Chilkoot Pass. The Chilkoot trailhead is 0.5 mile away.

LIARSVILLE CAMPGROUND
PO Box 398, Skagway, AK 99840
(907) 983-2061

privately operated
May 1st—Sept 30th
MP 2.5 Klondike Highway

Liarsville Campground is located just beyond the point where the Klondike Highway crosses the Skagway River past the Highway Department maintenance shops: 20 spaces; 10 power and water hookups; 10 w/o hookups; pit toilets; drinking water; tables; fire rings; fishing; separate tenting area; no time limit.

The Liarsville Campground is located on the Skagway River. Cottonwood, alder and spruce trees line the site. A gravel road runs through the campground. Gravel-based spaces are level and vary in length.

RV SERVICES AT SKAGWAY

HOOVER'S CHEVRON   (907) 983-2454
Located one block west of State Street at Fourth Avenue: brakes; mufflers; general repairs; emergency road service; towing; **sewage dump station; propane.**

Boarding the M/V Tustumena at Skagway

SKAGWAY OPTIONS

LYNN CANAL FLY-CRUISE   (907) 983-2241
Fly-Cruise tours originate in Skagway or Juneau. Fly one-way and return on a small cruiseboat. Enjoy Alaska's capitol city for a day from Skagway.

HAINES–SKAGWAY WATER TAXI   (907) 766-3395
The owners operate the 42-foot vessel, "Sea Venture," which makes the 15-mile round trip through the Lynn Canal from Haines to Skagway two times a day from June to September. The boat leaves from the small boat harbor and takes an hour to Haines. This is a nice one-day tour which offers the opportunity to see Haines and still spend the night in Skagway.

ALASKA MARINE HIGHWAY SYSTEM   1-800-642-0066
Call the toll free number from anywhere in the continental U.S. for information. In Skagway call locally (983-2229). Reservations must be made as far in advance of the time of departure as possible. Refer to the section on the Alaska Marine Highway System for additional information. Board the ferry in Skagway and take the one hour ride to Haines. Spend some time in Haines, then drive the Haines Cutoff Highway to Haines Junction to join the Alaska Highway.

THE KLONDIKE HIGHWAY
Drive the scenic Klondike Highway to its junction at the Alaska Highway (MP 905) and then on to Whitehorse, Yukon Territory. This will provide the opportunity to spend time in one of the larger cities on the Canadian portion of the highway. The border crossing into Alaska is located at MP 1221.8. There is a one hour time change at the border.

Skagway to Whitehorse	110 miles
Skagway to Dawson City	435 miles
Skagway to Fairbanks	710 miles
Skagway to Anchorage	830 miles

HAINES, ALASKA

Haines is a town of incredible natural beauty. Nestled between the Lynn Canal and the Chilkat Valley, glaciers, fjords and peaks to 6,000 feet from the coastal mountain range surround Haines. Trees include Sitka spruce, Western hemlock, Douglas maple, alder and willow. Photographers, hikers, backpackers and birdwatchers will have difficulty leaving the Alaska Chilkat Bald Eagle Preserve. The Haines Highway, which is one of Alaska's more scenic drives, joins the Alaska Highway at Haines Junction 159 miles away.

A walking tour of Haines includes Fort William H. Seward. The fort was the first U.S. military installation in Alaska and is a National Historic Site. A second National Historic Site is the Government School which was established in 1907 for Native children. The Sheldon Museum and Cultural Center, which has been accredited by the American Association of Museums, has many Tlingit artifacts among its displays.

ALASKA CHILKAT BALD EAGLE PRESERVE

Alaska established the preserve in 1982 in order to protect the habitat and salmon runs necessary to the survival of the bald eagle. Each fall and winter thousands of eagles congregate in the 48,000 acre preserve to feed on spawned-out salmon. Over a seven-year period, the average count was 2,300 birds, but the number has been as high as 4,000 according to aerial surveys performed by the U.S. Fish and Wildlife Service. No evidence has been publicly provided to suggest that the Exxon Valdez oil spill has affected the number of birds in the preserve although eagles do come from Prince William Sound. Unfortunately for summer tourists, the peak viewing period is between October and February.

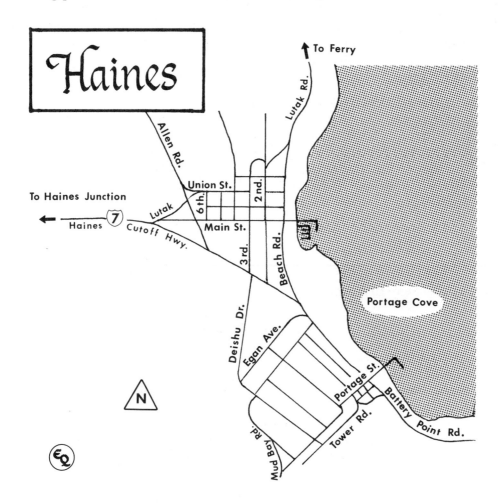

DALTON CITY

Dalton City is an 1890's gold rush town recreated using remnants of the sets erected by Walt Disney Studios for the motion picture, *White Fang*, which was filmed in Haines. It features local artists demonstrating their wares, a Klondike saloon, a turn-of-the-century print shop, and a southeast Alaska logging museum among other things. Performances daily.

THE VISITOR INFORMATION CENTER   **(907) 766-2234**
PO Box 518, Haines, AK 99827   Second Avenue at Willard Street

HEALTH AND EMERGENCY SERVICES

Haines Health Center   **(907) 766-2521**
Haines Police   **(907) 766-2121 or 911**

| Fire Department | (907) 766-2115 or 911 |
| Alaska State Troopers | (907) 766-2552 |

RV CAMPGROUNDS AT HAINES

CHILKOOT LAKE STATE RECREATION SITE   **open all year**
Alaska State Park System   **MP 10 Lutak Road**

Turn right from the ferry dock onto Lutak Road and drive 5.0 miles. Turn left at the State Park sign and continue for 2.1 miles: 32 spaces w/o hookups; 2 pull-throughs; pit toilets; drinking water; picnic sites; boat launch; fishing; trails; 7 day limit.

Chilkoot Lake SRS has a gravel road through Sitka spruce. Spaces vary in length and tend to be long but not level. A number of spaces are at the wrong angle to the road. The campground is secluded and surrounded by mountains. A fish weir used for research and management of the Lynn Canal sockeye salmon fishery is nearby.

Fish wier on the Chilkoot River, Haines

OCEANSIDE RV PARK
PO Box 149, Haines, AK 99827
(907) 766-2444

privately operated
May 1st—Oct 1st
Front Street

Turn left from the ferry dock onto Lutak Road and drive 4.5 miles to Main Street. Turn left to the bottom of the hill, then right on Front Street: 23 spaces with full hookups; drinking water; tables; fishing; public phone; no time limit.

Oceanside RV Park is gravel-based with back-in, side-by-side parking. Narrow areas separate the spaces. Shower and laundry facilities are a block away. The campground overlooks the Lynn Canal with a view of both water and mountains. It is located adjacent to a restaurant, bar and the boat harbor.

PORT CHILKOOT CAMPER PARK
PO Box 1589, Haines, AK 99827
(907) 766-2755   1-800-542-6363

privately operated
May 15th—Sept 30th
Mud Bay Road

Turn left from the ferry dock onto Lutak Road and drive about 4.5 miles to Main Street. Continue through the business district to the Haines Cutoff Highway. Turn left 0.3 mile to Mud Bay Road, then turn right one block. The campground is located halfway up the hill across from the Hotel Halsingland: 60 spaces; 2 full hookups; 50 power hookups; 8 w/o hookups; **sewage dump station**; flush toilets; drinking water; hot showers; laundry facilities; tables; separate tenting area; no time limit.

Port Chilkoot Camper Park is located in a wooded area overlooking the Lynn Canal. The campground is situated on several levels with a gravel-based road throughout. Back-in parking with electric service only.

CHILKAT STATE PARK
Alaska State Park System

open all year
MP 7.0 Mud Bay Road

Turn left from the ferry dock onto Lutak Road and drive about 4.5 miles to Main Street. Continue through the business district to the Haines Cutoff Highway. Turn left 0.3 mile to Mud Bay Road then right to the intersection at the top of the hill. Turn right and drive 1.9 miles on the beach road until a "T" is reached. Then turn right for 1.6 miles. Turn right at the State Park sign: 32 spaces w/o hookups; 14 pull-throughs; pit toilets; drinking water; covered picnic sites; boat launch; fishing; trails; 15 day limit.

Chilkat State Park is heavily wooded with a gravel road through the campground. The final 0.7 mile to the entrance is down a steep, washboard-like gravel road. Medium to large-sized RVs may have difficulty because of the rutted surface. Spaces are not level. A view of the Lynn Canal and several glaciers is available from the campground.

EAGLE CAMPER PARK
PO Box 28, Haines, AK 99827
(907) 766-2335   FAX (907) 766-2339

privately operated
May 1st—Oct 1st
751 Union Street

Turn left from the ferry dock onto Lutak Road and drive about 4.5 miles to Main Street. Continue through the business district to Union Street, turn right six blocks: 84 spaces; 30 full hookups; 22 power and water hookups; 32 w/o hookups; **sewage dump station**; flush toilets; drinking water; hot showers; laundry facilities; tables; grills; **propane**; separate tenting area; no time limit.

Eagle Camper Park is a level, gravel-based campground with back-in, side-by-side pads. Trees border the campground; a separate grass area includes tables and grills. No charge is made for use of the showers and laundry facilities. A senior citizen discount is offered to campers over sixty years of age. Cable TV is included with full hookups. Many RVers return each year to camp for the summer months.

HAINES HITCH-UP RV PARK   **privately operated**
PO Box 383, Haines, AK 99827   **May 1st—Sept 15th**
(907) 766-2882   **Main Street**

Turn left from the ferry dock onto Lutak Road and drive 4.5 miles to Main Street. Turn right for six blocks: 92 full hookups; 20 pull-throughs; flush toilets; drinking water; hot showers; laundry facilities; tables; **propane**; public phone; no time limit.

Haines Hitch-Up RV Park is unique in its design. Three parallel rows of raked, gravel roadways separate areas of trimmed grass. Parking is directly on the grass, not on the gravel. All spaces are level with ample room between rigs. The largest RV can be accommodated. Utilities are underground. Restrooms and showers are clean and well maintained. Decorator shrubs and trees border the campground. A gift shop is located on site. RV storage is available.

EAGLE'S NEST CAMPGROUND   **privately operated**
PO Box 250, Haines, AK 99827   **May 15th—Sept 30th**
(907) 766-2891   **MP 1.0 Haines Highway**

Turn left from the ferry dock onto Lutak Road and drive 4.5 miles to Main Street. Continue through the business district to the Haines Cutoff Highway. Turn right for about 1.0 mile: 20 full hookups; 20 pull-throughs; **sewage dump station**; tables; grills; no time limit.

Eagle's Nest Campground is located next to a city park. Large pull-through spaces with a view of the Cathedral Peaks are featured. The campground is attached to a motel and car rental agency. The owners are helpful in offering directions and bits of local lore.

MOSQUITO LAKE STATE RECREATION SITE   **open all year**
Alaska State Park System   **MP 2.6 Mosquito Lake Road**

Located outside of town. Turn left from the ferry dock onto Lutak Road and drive 4.5 miles to Main Street. Continue through the business district to the Haines Cutoff Highway. Turn right for 27.2 miles. Turn right at the junction of Mosquito Lake Road (at store). Mosquito Lake Road is a state maintained, gravel road in good condition. Go 2.6 miles. Then take a somewhat steep, narrow road sharply branching downhill to the lake: 10 spaces w/o hookups; pit toilets; drinking water; tables; fire rings; boat launch; fishing; 15 day limit.

Mosquito Lake SRS has large Sitka spruce trees throughout the campground. Four back-in, side-by-side parking spaces and six individual sites are provided. A narrow road runs through the campground with a turnaround area. The campground borders the lake. Large RVs can be accommodated but may encounter difficulty entering the campground.

Reflections on Mosquito Lake at Dale's Place

DALE'S PLACE AND RV PARK   privately operated
PO Box 852, Haines, AK 99827   May 15th—Sept 30th
no phone   **MP 3.0 Mosquito Lake Road**

Located outside of town. Turn left from the ferry dock onto Lutak Road and drive 4.5 miles to Main Street. Continue through the business district to the Haines Cutoff Highway. Turn right for 27.2 miles. Turn right at the junction of Mosquito Lake Road (at store). Mosquito Lake Road is a state maintained, gravel road in good condition. Go 3.0 miles to the site: 12 water and sewer hookups; drinking water; tables; grills; boat launch; fishing; trails; no time limit.

Dale's Place and RV Park has back-in, side-by-side level pads which can handle the largest RV. Toilets, showers, and laundry facilities are projected as the campground is developed. The campground is surrounded by state land and a state eagle preserve. This is also the southern-most nesting area for trumpeter swans in Alaska. Nearby mountains reflect on the surface of the lake. Many of the winter scenes for the movie, *White Fang*, were filmed on Mosquito Lake.

RV SERVICES AT HAINES

EAGLE CHEVRON   (907) 766-2328
Turn left from the ferry dock onto Lutak Road and drive 4.5 miles to Second Avenue. Follow Second Avenue to the Haines Cutoff Highway. Turn left on the Haines Cutoff Highway. Located between Second Avenue and Beach Road: **sewage dump station**; **propane**; petroleum products.

HAINES CAR WASH   (907) 766-3122
Turn left from the ferry dock onto Lutak Road and drive 4.5 miles to Main Street. Continue through the business district to the Haines Cutoff Highway. Turn right for six blocks. The Haines Car Wash has two bays which can accommodate RVs of any size. This is a self-service facility.

TOTEM OIL PRODUCTS SUPPLY, INC.   (907) 766-3190
Turn left from the ferry dock onto Lutak Road and drive 4.5 miles to Main Street. Turn right to the junction of the Haines Cutoff Highway: brakes; emergency road service; towing; **sewage dump station**; **propane**. Towing services are available on a 24 hour basis. The sewage dump service is free to campers.

BIGFOOT AUTO SERVICE, INC.   (907) 766-2459
Turn left from the ferry dock onto Lutak Road and drive 4.5 miles to Main Street. Turn right about seven blocks: brakes; tires; mufflers; general repairs; towing; welding. Bigfoot Auto Service, Inc. is a NAPA dealer and parts store. Mechanics are A.S.E. certified. Towing services are available on a 24 hour basis (907) 776-2775.

HAINES OPTIONS

FLIGHTSEEING JUNEAU
Visit Juneau by flying from Haines to the capitol city. A flightseeing trip takes about thirty minutes air time. Reservations can be made locally with little or not advance notice since several carriers maintain regular flight schedules from Haines to Juneau.

HAINES–SKAGWAY WATER TAXI   (907) 766-3395
The owners operate the 42-foot vessel, "Sea Venture," which makes the 15-mile round trip through the Lynn Canal from Haines to Skagway two times a day from June to September. The boat leaves from the small boat harbor and takes an hour to Skagway. This is a nice one-day tour which offers the opportunity to see Skagway and still spend the night in Haines.

ALASKA MARINE HIGHWAY SYSTEM   1-800-642-0066
Call the toll free number from anywhere in the continental U.S. In Haines call locally (766-2113). Reservations must be made as far in advance of the time of departure as possible. Refer to the section on the Alaska Marine Highway System for additional information. Board the ferry in Haines and take the one hour ride to Skagway. This will provide the opportunity to drive the Klondike Highway to its junction

with the Alaska Highway (MP 905) south of Whitehorse, Yukon Territory, as well as to spend some time in Skagway.

THE HAINES CUTOFF HIGHWAY

Drive the scenic Haines Cutoff Highway to Haines Junction, Yukon Territory, and the junction of the Alaska Highway. Before leaving Haines, however, consider spending a few days in the area. A local resident made this wry observation: "The campers get off the ferry in Haines and drive, bumper to bumper, straight to the Canadian border in their hurry to see Alaska and never even stop in one of the most beautiful places Alaska has to offer." A one-hour time change from Pacific Daylight Time to Alaska Daylight Time is necessary at the border.

Haines to Whitehorse	251 miles
Haines to Dawson City	578 miles
Haines to Fairbanks	653 miles
Haines to Anchorage	775 miles

JUNEAU, ALASKA

Juneau is accessible only by air or by water. RVers have not allowed this fact to bother them and each summer several thousand RVers visit Juneau by way of the Alaska Marine Highway System. The number of RV spaces is relatively few, and many of the existing spaces are better suited to mini-motorhomes, pickup trucks and tent campers. RVers who arrive at late hours on the ferries can contact the Juneau Police Department (586-2780) for assistance in finding space.

Alaska's capitol city is an interesting place to visit. The Alaska State Museum features examples of native arts and crafts; a permanent display of an eagle nesting tree; paintings by Alaskan artists; and exhibits from the early Russian period. A walking tour of the downtown area includes the Governor's Mansion and guided tours of the State Capitol Building. A number of old gold mines are in the area.

The most popular attraction in Juneau is the Mendenhall Glacier. The fifth largest ice field in North America carries dozens of glaciers and borders Juneau. Located just fifteen minutes from downtown, the Mendenhall Glacier is just one of the 5,000 glaciers in Alaska. Trails in the area include a 1.5 mile moraine ecology loop. The U.S. Forest Service maintains a visitor center at the glacier.

DAVIS LOG CABIN INFORMATION CENTER   **(907) 586-2201**
134 Third Street, Juneau, AK 99801

RV INFORMATION CENTER   **Nugget Mall**
8745 Glacier Highway, Juneau, AK 99801   **Glacier Sams**

Turn right from the ferry dock onto the Glacier Highway. The Nugget Mall is on the left at the third traffic light. Good Sam volunteers, Juneau Chapter, provide RVers summer information from Mid-May through

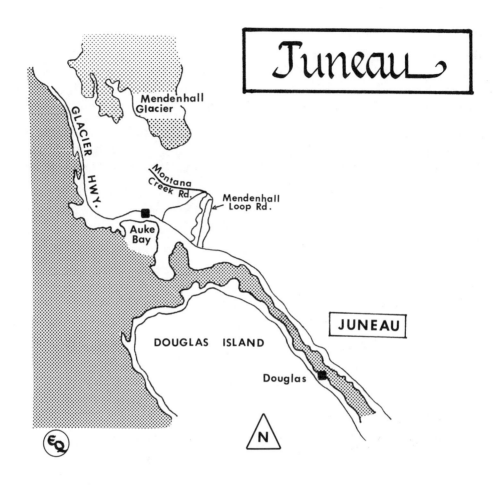

Labor Day: Monday–Friday 10 am–6 p.m; Saturday 10 am–5 pm; Sunday 12 am–4 pm. This service-minded chapter also provides wheelchairs for Alaska Marine Highway System ferries.

SOUTHEAST ALASKA TOURISM COUNCIL　　　　　**(907) 465-2012**
PO Box 20710, Juneau, AK 99802-0710

HEALTH AND EMERGENCY SERVICE

Juneau Police　　　　　　　　　　　　**(907) 586-2780**
Alaska State Troopers　　　　　　　**(907) 789-2161 or 911**
Bartlett Memorial Hospital　　　　　　　**(907) 586-2611**

RV CAMPGROUNDS AT JUNEAU

AUKE VILLAGE CAMPGROUND　　　　**May 15th—Sept 30th**
U.S. Forest Service　　　　　　**MP 15.8 Glacier Highway**

Turn left onto Glacier Highway from the ferry dock. Drive 1.7 miles and turn on gravel-based Point Louisa Road which is not marked by signs on the Glacier Highway: 11 spaces w/o hookups; pit toilets; one flush toilet; drinking water; tables; grills; 14 day limit.

Auke Village Campground has a road which loops through the area. Spaces, some of which are side-by-side, are of varying length but tend to be quite short and are not level. This campground is best suited for mini-motorhomes, travel trailers or fifth wheels up to 22 feet maximum.

AUKE BAY RV PARK
PO Box 210215, Auke Bay 99821
(907) 789-9467

privately operated
Open all year
11930 Glacier Highway

Turn right onto Glacier Highway from the ferry dock. Located 1.5 miles from the ferry dock: 30 spaces; 25 pull-throughs; 5 power and water; flush toilets; drinking water; hot showers; laundry facilities; public phone; no time limit.

Auke Bay RV Park is a clean, gravel-based campground with some decorator plants. It features back-in spaces which are level and can accommodate the largest RV. The campground has city sewer and water. It is walking distance to a small boat harbor. City buses serve downtown Juneau.

AUKE LAKE WAYSIDE
Glacier Highway

Turn right from the ferry dock onto the Glacier Highway. Drive 2.5 miles. This is a wayside park and is not an authorized RV campground. The graded, dirt parking area is not level. The largest RV can be accommodated. Dry parking only.

MENDENHALL LAKE CAMPGROUND
U.S. Forest Service

May 15th—Sept 30th
8465 Old Dairy Road

Turn right onto Glacier Highway from the ferry dock. Drive 4.3 miles (second signal light), turn right on Loop Road. Go 1.4 miles, turn left on Back Loop Road. Drive another 1.5 miles, turn right onto Montana Creek Road for 0.8 mile: 10 spaces w/o hookups; 3 pull-throughs; **sewage dump station**; tables; grills; 14 day limit.

Mendenhall Lake Campground is primarily for tent campers. Gravel-based with back-in spaces, it is best suited for small motorhomes, travel trailers and pickup campers although there are three pull-throughs which can accommodate larger RVs. The campground is heavily wooded with hemlock, spruce and ground cover throughout. A campground host is available at scheduled times of the day.

JUNEAU YACHT CLUB
City and Borough of Juneau

privately operated
Juneau Yacht Club Parking Lot

Turn right onto Glacier Highway from the ferry dock. Drive 12.1 miles. Glacier Highway becomes Egan Drive as it nears the business area. Turn right at the "Aurora Basin" signs. The road to the dry camping area parallels Egan Drive: 10 spaces w/o hookups; 3 day limit.

Juneau Yacht Club's parking area is reserved for RV use only. One chemical toilet and a dumpster are the only amenities provided. The gravel-based parking lot can accommodate the largest RV.

ROBERT SAVIKKO PARK
City and Borough of Juneau

May 1st—Sept 30th
Savikko Road

Turn right onto Glacier Highway from the ferry dock. Drive 12.7 miles. Glacier Highway becomes Egan Drive as it nears the business area. Turn right onto Tenth Street and cross the Juneau-Douglas bridge. Turn left on Harbor Way for 2.0 miles. Parking is restricted to the first lot on the right: 4 spaces w/o hookups; **sewage dump station**; flush toilets; boat launch; 3 day limit.

RV SERVICES AT JUNEAU

VALLEY CHEVRON SERVICE CENTER (907) 789-2880
Turn right from the ferry dock onto the Glacier Highway. Drive 4.3 miles. Turn left at Loop Road (second signal light). Drive one block, turn left at Mendenhall Mall Road at the light: **sewage dump station**; **propane**.

JUNEAU OPTIONS

LYNN CANAL FLY-CRUISE (907) 983-2241
Fly-Cruise tours originate in Skagway or Juneau. Fly one way and return on a small cruise boat. This is an excellent opportunity to visit Skagway especially if you intend to drive the Haines Highway Cutoff to the Alaska Highway junction.

ALASKA MARINE HIGHWAY SYSTEM 1-800-642-0066
If Juneau was your first port of call and you intend to drive the Alaska Highway, you have two choices: Haines and the Haines Cutoff Highway to Haines Junction; or Skagway and the Klondike Highway to Whitehorse.

Flightseeing between Juneau and Haines: Eagle Glacier

RVing in Alaska:

Campgrounds and Services

Section II

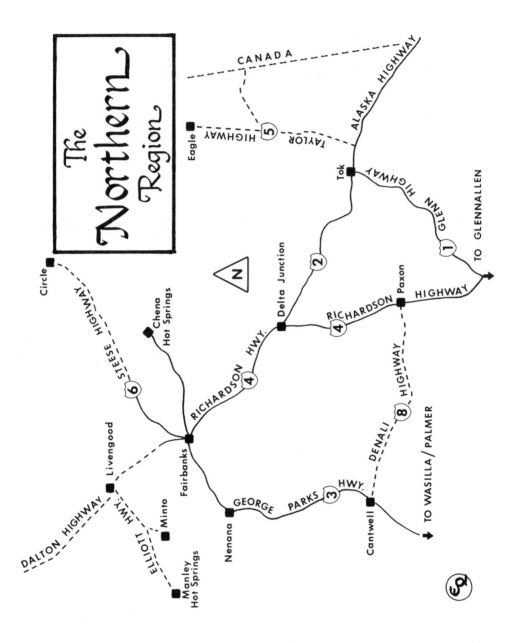

Chapter 4

THE NORTHERN TIER

This chapter describes campgrounds and services on the Alaska Highway between the Canadian Border and Delta Junction including the communities of Tok and Delta Junction. Campgrounds and services on the Richardson Highway between Delta Junction and North Pole are also described. Options include the Taylor Highway to Eagle and Dawson City; the Glenn Highway (Tok Cutoff) to Glennallen; and the Richardson Highway to Glennallen.

THE ALASKA HIGHWAY

United States Customs and Immigration personnel are responsible for inspecting all vehicles entering Alaska. The border crossing for the Alaska Highway is accomplished at MP 1221.8 and for the Yukon Highway/Taylor Highway at MP 105.6. A one-hour time adjustment is necessary at the time of crossing.

The Alaska Department of Transportation and Public Facilities is responsible for maintaining the highways in Alaska's interior, approximating 217,000 square miles. Sub-base failure due to frost heaves is especially pronounced in the interior. The highway between Tok and the Canadian border was graded, and prepared for surfacing in May, 1989. Thirteen months later embankment failures and surface cracks were already evident.

Maintenance crews repair road and highway damage caused by overweight loads, washouts, and sub-base failures during the summer months. Because the working season in Alaska is short, crew-hours are long, and RVers can expect to encounter delays on the highway system.

U.S. border crossing on the Alaska Highway: entering Alaska

TETLIN NATIONAL WILDLIFE REFUGE VISITOR CENTER
MP 1229 Alaska Highway   **(907) 883-5312**

The center is a log building with a sod roof and is open from Memorial Day through mid-September. Tetlin NWR, which is a 930,000 acre refuge, has one of the nation's highest density waterfowl nesting areas. U. S. Fish and Wildlife staff members offer daily nature talks.

HEALTH AND EMERGENCY SERVICES

Northway Fire Department   **(907) 778-2211**

Alaska State Troopers   **(907) 778-2245**

RV CAMPGROUNDS ON THE ALASKA HIGHWAY

DEADMAN LAKE CAMPGROUND   open all year
U.S. Fish and Wildlife Service   **MP 1249.3 Alaska Highway**

Located at MP 1249.3 on a dirt road 1.2 miles from the highway: 15 spaces w/o hookups; pit toilets; no potable water; tables; fire rings; boat launch; fishing; trails; 14 day limit.

Deadman Lake is part of the Tetlin National Wildlife Refuge. Spaces vary in length; at least two pads will accommodate RVs up to 40 feet in length. Most spaces are of moderate length and are not level. The campground is located among heavy stands of spruce and birch trees. The view of the lake is obstructed by trees but the boat launch area is accessible. Water should be boiled or treated chemically.

LAKEVIEW CAMPGROUND   open all year
U.S. Fish and Wildlife Service   **MP 1256.7 Alaska Highway**

Turn onto a dirt road at MP 1256.7. This campground is not recommended for mid-sized RVs or rigs hauling small trailers. Best suited to mini-motorhomes or camper trailers: 10 spaces w/o hookups; pit toilets; no potable water; tables; fire rings; boat launch; fishing; 14 day limit.

Lakeview Campground is part of the Tetlin National Wildlife Refuge. It borders Yarger Lake and is suited to those who like to "rough it outdoors." Spaces are unlevel. Water should be boiled or treated chemically.

WRANGELL VIEW SERVICE CENTER   privately owned
PO Box 395, Northway, AK 99764   **open all year**
(907) 778-2261   **MP 1263 Alaska Highway**

Located at MP 1263 of the Alaska Highway: 20 spaces; 6 full hookups; 14 w/o hookups; **sewage dump station**; flush toilets; drinking water; no time limit.

Wrangell View campground is part of a lodge, cafe and service center. The campground is in a large, open area; spaces are level and gravel-based. Toilets and showers are in the lodge. A table and fire grills are in a separate section. The camping area affords a good view of the river, lakes and the Wrangell Mountains.

NAABIA NIIGN CAMPGROUND
PO Box 476, Northway, AK 99764
(907) 778-2297

privately operated
open all year
MP 1264 Alaska Highway

Turn onto Northway Road for 100 yards at MP 1264: 20 spaces; 16 full hookups; 4 w/o hookups; **sewage dump station**; pit toilets; drinking water; hot showers; laundry facilities; tables; fire rings; no time limit.

Naabia Niign Campground is located at the Northway cutoff in a wooded area behind a small general store. *Naabia Niign*, an Athabaskan term, means "our land by the river." Spaces are not level and the RVer with a large rig may have difficulty. One level concrete pad can serve an RV up to 40-45 feet in length. An area for washing RVs is available.

RV SERVICES

WRANGELL VIEW SERVICE CENTER
Located at MP 1263 of the Alaska Highway. This service center has full-time mechanics on duty who can provide a full range of services. A large bay will accept RVs of any size. **Propane**.

THE TAYLOR HIGHWAY

The Taylor Highway is a misnomer for a gravel road which joins the Alaska Highway at Tetlin Junction, MP 1301.5. This road can be extremely hard on vehicles of all sizes. The RVer must be prepared for washboard-like surfaces and potholes.

Rewards for choosing the Taylor Highway include magnificent views of the rugged and scenic Tanana and Yukon River valleys. The Bureau of Land Management maintains two camps suitable for RVs on the Taylor Highway south of Jack Wade Junction, and one in Eagle, Alaska.

Boaters can float the Fortymile River, which is part of the National Wild and Scenic River System. According to *The Wild and Scenic Rivers Act* an eligible river must have one of the following characteristics:

> "at least one outstanding remarkable scenic, recreational, geologic, fish and wildlife, historic, cultural or ecological value. This value should be a unique or exceptional representation for the area studied."

BLM personnel make frequent float trips on the Fortymile and anyone considering floating this river should contact their offices in Tok (907) 883-5121 or stop at the Chicken field station at MP 68.2 for up-to-date river information.

HEALTH AND EMERGENCY SERVICES

MP 0 to MP 113	Tok Ambulance Service	**(907) (883-2300**
		or 911
MP 113 to MP 161	Eagle EMS, CB Channel 21	**(907) 547-2240**
		or (907) 547-2211

RV CAMPGROUNDS ON THE TAYLOR HIGHWAY

WEST FORK CAMPGROUND   May 15th—Sept 15th
Bureau of Land Management   MP 48.5 Taylor Highway

Located at MP 48.5 south of Jack Wade Junction: 25 spaces w/o hookups; pit toilets; drinking water; fire rings; fishing; 10 day limit.

West Fork Campground was upgraded in 1987. Pit toilets are accessible to the disabled. This is a very scenic area with good fishing possibilities. The Fortymile River can be accessed from the highway at the Dennison Fork Bridge (0.2 mile).

WALKER FORK CAMPGROUND   May 15th—Sept 15th
Bureau of Land Management   MP 82 Taylor Highway

Located at MP 82 south of Jack Wade Junction: 20 spaces w/o hookups; pit toilets; drinking water; tables; fire rings; trails; fishing; separate tenting area; 10 day limit.

Walker Fork Campground is divided by the road into an RV section and a tenting section. Spaces include pull-throughs for larger rigs. A hiking trail leads to the top of a limestone bluff. The Fortymile River can be accessed from the campsite. The gold dredge, Jack Wade No. 1, can be seen from the road at MP 86.1, four miles north of the campground.

EAGLE CAMPGROUND   May 15th—Sept 15th
Bureau of Land Management   MP 160 Taylor Highway

Continue north to Eagle (MP 160.3) from Jack Wade Junction (MP 95.7). The campground entrance is reached by following 4th Avenue. Branch to the left for one mile, then take the second left on the airstrip road: 15 spaces w/o hookups; pit toilets; no drinking water; tables; fire rings; trails; 10 day limit.

Eagle Campground serves both RV users and tent campers. Water must be boiled or treated chemically. The campground is located on a high bluff overlooking a vast area. The Eagle Historical Society assists visitors to locate trails and sights at nearby Fort Egbert which BLM helped to partially restore.

TAYLOR HIGHWAY OPTIONS

THE TAYLOR HIGHWAY: NORTH TO EAGLE
Jack Wade Junction is located at MP 96 of the Taylor Highway. The northern terminus of the Taylor Highway is on the banks of the nearly two thousand mile long Yukon River at Eagle at MP 161. Eagle is home to about 150 people.

TOP OF THE WORLD HIGHWAY
Jack Wade Junction is located at MP 96 of the Taylor Highway. The highway to the east becomes the Yukon Highway in Canada. The section between Jack Wade Junction and Dawson City is usu-

ally referred to as the "Top of the World Highway" because of its terrain. In spite of the ruggedness of the overall road, this route is an alternative to retracing sections of the Alaska Highway. U. S. and Canadian customs stations are open between 9 a.m. and 9 p.m. (Yukon Time) from May until September.

 ### THE ALASKA HIGHWAY: WEST TO TOK
The Taylor Highway joins the Alaska Highway at Tetlin Junction, MP 1301.5. The Alaska Highway leads east to the Canadian border and west to Tok. The Glenn Highway at Tok leads to Glennallen; the Alaska Highway continues to Delta Junction.

TOK, ALASKA

The summer of 1990 found Alaska facing the worst fire season in several decades. Fires burned 3.2 million acres in the state, including 123,300 acres in the Tok area. No lives were lost and damage to tangible property was limited to a few abandoned buildings. The fires did not impact any of the RV campgrounds on the Alaska Highway although the effects of the burn are evident around several of them.

Tok is the first community of any size to greet the RVer in Alaska and is usually a welcome sight with its gift shops, restaurants, motels, and campgrounds. Tok is also the point at which the traveler must choose between continuing to follow the Alaska Highway to Delta Junction and Fairbanks or taking the Glenn Highway to Glennallen and Anchorage.

TOK CHAMBER OF COMMERCE LOG VISITOR'S CENTER
PO Box 389, Tok, AK 99780   **(907) 883-5775**

Located at the junction of the Alaska and Glenn Highways, this is the largest natural Alaskan log structure in the state. Trip planning information, free brochures and other printed materials are provided by Chamber of Commerce volunteers.

ALASKA PUBLIC LANDS INFORMATION CENTER (APLIC)
PO Box 359, Tok, AK 99780   **(907) 883-5667**

The APLIC is located at MP 1314.1 of the Alaska Highway, one block east of the junction with the Richardson Highway. One of three Alaska Public Lands Information Centers, it is sponsored by a consortium of State and Federal agencies. The APLIC shares its building with the Alaska State Troopers. Features include historical material as well as mounted birds and animals (walrus, Dall sheep, owls, and bison). The staff can provide information about highways and campgrounds in Alaska.

BUREAU OF LAND MANAGEMENT   (907) 883-5121
PO Box 309, Tok, AK 99780

BLM's Office is located behind the APLIC. Persons interested in driving the Taylor Highway or in BLM campgrounds on the Richardson or Denali Highways should contact BLM personnel for current information.

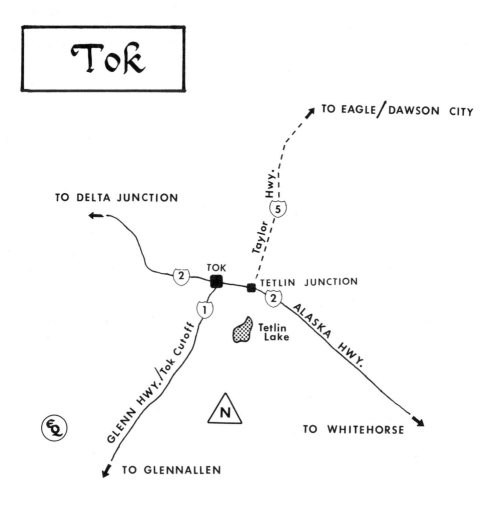

HEALTH AND EMERGENCY SERVICES

Alaska State Troopers	(907) 883-2333
Tok Fire Department	(907) 883-2333

RV CAMPGROUNDS AT TOK

TOK RIVER STATE RECREATION SITE   **open all year**
Alaska State Park System   **MP 1309 Alaska Highway**

Turn onto the gravel road at MP 1309, just east of the steel bridge: 50 spaces w/o hookups; pit toilets; drinking water; tables; fire rings; boat launch; trails; separate tenting area; 15 day limit.

Tok River SRS is a graveled campground with spaces which vary in length but are level. Larger RVs can be accommodated. Pit toilets are accessible to the disabled. Although there is evidence of fire damage nearby, the campground was untouched.

BULL SHOOTER RV PARK
PO Box 553, Tok, AK 99780
(907) 883-5625

privately operated
May 15th—Sept 15th
MP 1313.2 Alaska Highway

Located at MP 1313.2 of the Alaska Highway, east of the Glenn Highway junction: 44 spaces; 24 pull-throughs; 7 full hookups; 17 power and water hookups; 20 w/o hookups; **sewage dump station**; flush toilets; drinking water; hot showers; tables; public phone; no time limit.

Bull Shooter RV Park is a wooded campground located behind a sporting goods store. Grass and trees separate spaces. Gravel-based with diagonal pull-throughs, RVs of any length can be accommodated. Toilets and showers are clean and there is no charge for their use. According to the owner, the Bull Shooter sporting goods store is the "best stocked between Tok, Fairbanks and Anchorage."

Moose and calf grazing by the Alaska Highway

NORTHSTAR TRAVEL CENTER
PO Box 677, Tok, AK 99780
(907) 883-4631

privately operated
May 1st—Oct 1st
1313.3 Alaska Highway

Located at MP 1313.3 of the Alaska Highway, just east of the Glenn Highway junction: 45 spaces; 6 pull-throughs; 15 full hookups; 9 power and water hookups; 21 w/o hookups; **sewage dump station**; flush toilets; drinking water; hot showers; laundry facilities; tables; public phone; **propane**; no time limit.

Northstar Travel Center is located in a wooded area behind a service station, restaurant and gift shop. Spaces are level and gravel-based. Dry parking is free with a full gas fill-up. A high pressure wash station is on site. Western Union services are available. All discounts are honored.

TOK RV VILLAGE
PO Box 739, Tok, AK 99780
(907) 883-5877 1-800- 478-5878 (Alaska)

privately operated
April 1st—Oct 1st
MP 1313.4 Alaska Highway

Located at MP 1313.4 of the Alaska Highway, east of the Glenn Highway junction: 95 spaces; 43 pull-throughs; 49 full hookups; 34 power and water hookups; 12 w/o hookups; **sewage dump station**; flush toilets; drinking water; hot showers; laundry facilities; tables; fire rings; public phone; separate tenting area; no time limit.

Tok RV Village is located in a wooded area with additional decorator trees. Spaces are gravel-based and level with many pull-throughs which can accommodate RVs of any length. Showers are non-metered. Good Sam and KOA discounts are offered. A self-service RV wash is available on site. A mail forwarding service is available. Tok RV Village is a clean, well-managed campground.

TUNDRA LODGE & RV PARK
PO Box 760, Tok, AK 99780
(907)883-7875

privately operated
May 15th—Sept 15th
MP 1315 Alaska Highway

Located at MP 1315 of the Alaska Highway, one mile west of the Glenn Highway junction: 78 spaces; 21 pull-throughs; 30 full hookups; 24 power and water hookups; 24 w/o hookups; **sewage dump station**; flush toilets; drinking water; hot showers; laundry facilities; tables; grills; public phone; separate tenting area; separate playground area; no time limit.

Tundra Lodge and RV Park is one mile west of the main portion of town. It has several roadways through the campground which provide pull-through access. Back-in spaces border the wooded perimeter and the playground area. Showers are non-metered. An area for self-service RV washing is available.

RITA'S CAMPGROUND & RV PARK
PO Box 599, Tok, AK 99780
(907) 883-4342

privately operated
May 15th—Sept 15th
MP 1315.7 Alaska Highway

Located at MP 1315.7 of the Alaska Highway, 1.7 miles west of the Glenn Highway junction: 16 spaces; 7 power only hookups; 7 pull-throughs; 9 w/o hookups; **sewage dump station**; flush toilets; drinking water; hot showers; picnic sites; tables; fire rings; public phone; separate tenting area; no time limit.

Rita's Campground and RV Park is slightly less than two miles west of the main portion of town. It has level, gravel-based spaces and can accommodate RVs of any size but is better suited to small or medium-sized rigs. Flush toilets and hot showers are ramped for the disabled. The owners offer a "relaxing Alaskan camping experience." Three hundred feet of flowers (fireweed, poppies, forget-me-nots) decorate the campground and covered cooking area. They provide a small, clean campground with a comfortable atmosphere.

GLENN HIGHWAY (TOK CUTOFF)

GOLDEN BEAR CAMPER PARK   privately operated
PO Box 276, Tok, AK 99780   May 1st—Sept 30th
(907) 883-2561   MP 124.5 Glenn Highway Cutoff

Located at MP 124.5 of the Glenn Highway (Tok Cutoff) 0.3 mile south of the Alaska Highway junction: 60 spaces; 33 pull-throughs; 15 full hookups; 20 power and water hookups; 25 w/o hookups; **sewage dump station**; flush toilets; hot showers; laundry facilities; tables; fire rings; public phone; separate tenting area; no time limit.

Golden Bear Camper Park offers a wooded setting and level, gravel-based spaces. The pull-throughs will accommodate the largest RVs. The shower building is heated. Part of a motel-gift shop complex, the campground is within walking distance to the center of Tok.

SOURDOUGH CAMPGROUND   privately operated
PO Box 47, Tok, AK 99780   May 15th—Sept 15th
(907) 883-5543   MP 122.8 Glenn Highway Cutoff

Located at MP 122.8 of the Glenn Highway (Tok Cutoff) 1.7 miles south of the Alaska Highway junction: 75 spaces; 18 pull-throughs; 16 full hookups; 21 power and water hookups; 5 power only hookups; 33 w/o hookups; **sewage dump station**; flush toilets; drinking water; hot showers; laundry facilities; tables; no time limit.

Sourdough Campground provides a wooded setting with trees between camping spaces, gravel-based roads and level spaces. The owners take pride in offering "spacious private camp sites – not parking spaces." Each space has a lined garbage can. "Guaranteed" clean restrooms. An RV wash station with a high pressure hose is available. The restaurant could be considered an Alaskan museum since it is filled with authentic Alaskan memorabilia and many old photographs. Discounts are offered to senior citizens, Good Sam, and AAA members.

RV SERVICES AT TOK

WILLARD'S AUTO AND ELECTRIC   (907) 883-5508
Located at MP 1313.2 of the Alaska Highway, 0.3 miles east of the Glenn Highway junction: suspension; carburetion and fuel injection; electrical; brakes; mufflers; general repairs; transmissions; emergency road service; towing; **sewage dump station**. The shop has a full range of electronic diagnostic equipment on site and can handle RVs of any size. Shop policy is to complete a job once it's started, "regardless of the hour." Two wreckers are available to provide 24 hour emergency road service. Free sewage dump service is offered with every gas fill-up.

SHAMROCK HARDWARE   (907) 883-2161
Located at MP 1313.3 of the Alaska Highway, 0.3 miles east of the Glenn Highway junction: hoses, fittings, regulators, electrical adapters and other supplies for the "do-it yourselfer."

YOUNG'S CHEVRON SERVICE (907) 883-2821

Located at the junction of the Alaska and the Glenn Highways: brakes; tires; general repairs; towing; **sewage dump station**; **propane**. The station handles minor repairs and lubrication. The wrecker is available on a 24 hour basis but can handle RVs of moderate size only. The sewage dump station is free with a fuel fill-up.

GRIZZLY AUTO SUPPLY (907) 883-5514

Located at MP 123.5 of the Glenn Highway (Tok cutoff): alignment; brakes; collision repairs; emergency road service; general repairs; muffler repairs; RV parts; spring replacement; tank repairs; towing; welding. Grizzly Auto Repair is a full service center and provides direct factory service for Good Year tires.

NORTHERN ENERGY CORPORATION (907) 883-4251

Located at MP 1314.5 of the Alaska Highway, west of the Glenn Highway junction: tires; car wash; **sewage dump station**; **propane**. Emergency tire service is provided within fifty miles. Miscellaneous propane furnace parts and RV tires are stocked. Use of the car wash and the sewage dump station are free with a fuel fill-up.

TOK OPTIONS

THE ALASKA HIGHWAY: TO THE CANADIAN BORDER

Crossing into Canada can be accomplished from the Alaska Highway at MP 1221.8 or from the Taylor Highway via the Yukon Highway at MP 105.6. The second choice leads to Dawson City and also offers the opportunity to visit the Alaskan town of Eagle on the banks of the Yukon River.

THE ALASKA HIGHWAY: WEST TO FAIRBANKS

West leads to Delta Junction and the terminus of the Alaska Highway. The Richardson Highway continues west to Fairbanks; it connects with the George Parks Highway to Denali Park and Anchorage.

THE GLENN HIGHWAY: SOUTHWEST TO GLENNALLEN

This section of the Glenn Highway is also known as the Tok Cutoff. The more scenic route in terms of the beauty of the Mentasta and Wrangell mountain ranges, the Glenn Highway cutoff offers access to Wrangell–St. Elias National Park and Preserve. It leads to Glennallen which has options to Valdez or Delta Junction (by-way-of the Richardson Highway) or Anchorage and the Kenai Peninsula.

Two RV campgrounds on the Glenn Highway Cutoff were described as part of the Tok region. The remainder of the campgrounds are described in the chapter, "The Copper River Region," under the heading "RV Campgrounds on the Glenn Highway." RVers who choose to drive the Tok Cutoff should *turn to the Copper River Region chapter* for detailed campground descriptions. The first campground to the south is Eagle Trail State Recreation Site.

Eagle Trail SRS	MP 109.5 Glenn Highway Cutoff
Porcupine Creek SRS	MP 64.2 Glenn Highway Cutoff
Sinona Creek RV Campground	MP 34.4 Glenn Highway Cutoff
Chistochina Lodge&Trading Post	MP 32.7 Glenn Highway Cutoff
Gakona RV Park	MP 4.2 Glenn Highway Cutoff
Dry Creek SRS	MP 118 Richardson Highway

RV CAMPGROUNDS ON THE ALASKA HIGHWAY

MOON LAKE STATE RECREATION SITE   **open all year**
Alaska State Park System   **MP 1332 Alaska Highway**

Located at MP 1332 of the Alaska Highway: 15 spaces w/o hookups; pit toilets; drinking water; tables; fire rings; boat launch; trails; 15 day limit.

Moon Lake SRS is set in a wooded area with a view of the Alaska Range and offers back-in spaces which are narrow and not level. Spaces are best suited for RVs up to 26-28 feet in length. However, space is available for longer RVs in a turnaround area. Pit toilets are accessible to the disabled. Recycled birch pellets give evidence of moose in the vicinity. Two float planes were tied nearby when the SRS was visited.

Float planes tied down by Moon Lake State Recreation Site

GERSTLE RIVER WAYSIDE   **open all year**
Alaska State Park System   **MP 1393 Alaska Highway**

Located at MP 1393 of the Alaska Highway, 0.3 miles west of the steel bridge, the wayside is not marked by highway signs. Public picnic areas and toilets are provided but not water. Although this is not a designated campground, RVers frequently use it for overnighting.

CLEARWATER STATE RECREATION SITE   **open all year**
Alaska State Park System   **MP 8.5 Clearwater Road**

Located 8.5 miles north of the Alaska Highway on Clearwater Road at MP 1415, the highway to the campground is paved: 18 spaces w/o hookups; pit toilets; drinking water; tables; fire rings; boat launch; fishing; 15 day limit.

Clearwater SRS is a remote but easily accessed campground with gravel-based spaces. The site is wooded and borders on Clearwater Creek which leads to both the Tanana and Goodpaster rivers. Delta Junction is about seven miles west of Clearwater Road on the Alaska Highway.

CHEROKEE LODGE
privately operated

HC 62 Box 5860, Delta Junction, AK 99737   May 15th—Sept 15th
(907) 895-4814   **MP 1412.5 Alaska Highway**

Located at MP 1412.5 of the Alaska Highway: 9 spaces; 9 power only hookups; **sewage dump station**; flush toilets; hot showers; tables; fire rings; public phones; no time limit.

This rustic campground is located behind a lodge, restaurant and bar and is in the early stages of development. Power only available. Showers and toilets are in the lodge.

BERGSTAD'S TRAVEL AND TRAILER COURT privately operated

PO Box 273, Delta Junction, AK 99737   May 15th—Sept 15th
(907) 895-4856   **MP 1421 Alaska Highway**

Located at MP 1421 of the Alaska Highway, one mile east of the Richardson Highway junction: 104 spaces; 104 full hookups; **sewage dump station**; flush toilets; drinking water; hot showers; laundry; tables; grills; public phone; separate tenting area; no time limit.

Bergstad's Travel and Trailer Court has some mobile homes for permanent occupancy. Short-term parking is available on a large, graveled open area with some back-in spaces. The court can accommodate RVs of any length. A self-service RV wash is available.

DELTA JUNCTION, ALASKA

Delta Junction is located two hundred miles northwest of the Canadian border. The Alaska Highway officially terminates at Delta Junction and the Richardson Highway. Visitors may be confused by signs along the Richardson Highway between Delta Junction and Fairbanks which appear to identify it as part of the original "Alaska Highway." These signs use MP 1523 to suggest that the highway ends in Fairbanks. Milepost 1422, the true end of the Alaska Highway, can be seen at the Visitor Center in Delta Junction.

Milepost numbers on the Richardson Highway reflect the distance from Valdez. The trans-Alaska oil pipeline can be seen near Delta Junction as it parallels the Richardson Highway. The pipeline is suspended by cables at the popular Tanana River view-point (MP 275.3). Bison, occasionally seen from the highway, are descendants from animals which were transplanted from Montana in 1928.

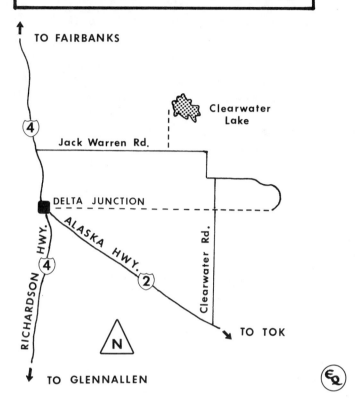

Delta Junction

TO FAIRBANKS

Clearwater Lake

Jack Warren Rd.

DELTA JUNCTION

RICHARDSON HWY.

ALASKA HWY.

Clearwater Rd.

TO TOK

N

TO GLENNALLEN

ALYESKA PIPELINE PUMP STATION 9   **(907) 869-3270**

Alyeska Pipeline Service Company provides free daily tours of Pump Station 9 at MP 258 of the Richardson Highway. Stop at the pump station or telephone (907) 278-1611 for additional information.

MILE 1422 VISITOR INFORMATION CENTER   **(907) 895-9941**
PO Box 987, Delta Junction, AK 99737

Located at the junction of the Alaska and the Richardson Highways, the "End of Alaska Highway Mile 1422" visitor information center displays a section of the 48 inch trans-Alaska oil pipeline with other pipeline para-phernalia. The second floor of the building provides a 360 degree view of the area including portions of the Alaska range.

HEALTH AND EMERGENCY SERVICES

Delta Junction Fire Department   **(907) 895-4600**
Forest Fires   **(907) 895-4227**
Alaska State Troopers   **(907) 895-4800 or 911**

RV CAMPGROUNDS AT DELTA JUNCTION

DELTA STATE RECREATION SITE   open all year
Alaska State Park System   **MP 267 Richardson Highway**

Located at MP 267 of the Richardson Highway next to the Alaska Division of Forestry headquarters. One mile east of the visitor center and the terminus of the Alaska Highway: 24 spaces w/o hookups; pit toilets; drinking water; tables; fire rings; covered picnic area; 15 day limit.

Delta SRS is situated in a wooded area with a graveled road through the campground. Pit toilets on concrete vaults are accessible to the disabled. Spaces have been widened and deepened. There are five side-by-side spaces and three long sites (not pull-throughs) capable of handling 50-60 foot units. Excellent drinking water from faucet's under pressure (unusual for state parks) is available. This campground will provide travelers with a restful pause.

SMITH'S GREEN ACRES   **privately operated**
PO Box 1129, Delta Junction, AK 99737   **May 15th—Sept 15th**
(907) 895-4369   **MP 268 Richardson Highway**

Located at MP 268 of the Richardson Highway, east of Jack Warren Road: 64 spaces; 17 pull-throughs; 34 full hookups; 8 power only hookups; 22 w/o hookups; **sewage dump station**; flush toilets; drinking water; hot showers; laundry facilities; tables; separate tenting area; no time limit.

Smith's Green Acres is in the process of development. Pull-throughs are tree shaded. Permanent mobile homes are located on a portion of the grounds. A playground is on site. Good Sam discounts are offered.

BIG DELTA STATE HISTORICAL PARK   open all year
Alaska State Park System   **MP 275 Richardson Highway**

Located at MP 275 of the Richardson Highway adjacent to Rika's Roadhouse and Landing: 40 spaces w/o hookups; 2 pull-throughs; **sewage dump station**; pit toilets; drinking water; tables; boat launch; fishing; 15 day limit.

Big Delta State Historical Park has back-in, side-by-side spaces. Spaces are gravel-based and level. There is easy access to Rika's Roadhouse and Landing and the banks of the Tanana River. This is an excellent viewing and picture-taking site of the trans-Alaska oil pipeline as it crosses the Tanana River. The sewage dump station is easily accessed. Because this is such a popular place to stay, the earlier in the day that registration is accomplished, the better.

LOST LAKE STATE RECREATION SITE   open all year
Alaska State Park System   **MP 277.8 Richardson Highway**

Located 2.5 miles north of the Richardson Highway at MP 277.8 on Quartz Lake Road: 11 spaces without hookups; pit toilets; drinking water; tables; fire rings; fishing; 15 day limit.

Lost Lake SRS has a graveled road throughout the campground. Spaces are separated by trees in a heavily wooded area. Spaces are graveled but not level. Pit toilets are accessible to the disabled. A trail connects to Quartz Lake SRS. Quartz Lake Road is rough and rutted.

Trans-Alaska oil pipeline crossing at the Tanana River

QUARTZ LAKE STATE RECREATION SITE   **open all year**
Alaska State Park System   **MP 277.8 Richardson Highway**

Located 3.0 miles north of the Richardson Highway at MP 277.8 on Quartz Lake Road: 16 spaces w/o hookups; pit toilets; drinking water; picnic sites; tables; fire rings; boat launch; fishing; swimming; 15 day limit.

Quartz Lake SRS has an open parking area next to the lake. Located side-by-side, spaces are not well differentiated. The largest RV can be accommodated. Pit toilets are accessible to the disabled. The area is surrounded by black spruce and offers an excellent view of the Alaska range. This quiet campground is worth the three mile drive over a rough road. Small boats are available for rent from a private concessionaire.

RV SERVICES AT DELTA JUNCTION

ALASKA MECHANICAL FUEL (TEXACO)   **(907) 895-4067**
Located at 1600 Richardson Highway west of the terminus of the Alaska Highway: petroleum products; alignment; tires; welding; **sewage dump**

station; **propane**. The only place in Delta Junction that does tires of all sizes ("tons of tires") and balancing.

CITY PARK CARWASH   (907) 895-4306
Turn north on Kimball Street from the Richardson Highway by the Delta Diner. Drive two blocks. The carwash has one coin-operated RV bay with a high pressure hose.

DELTA FUEL   (907) 895-4515
Located by the Chevron bulk plant on the Richardson Highway at MP 267.5. **Propane**.

DELTA JUNCTION OPTIONS

THE ALASKA HIGHWAY: EAST TO CANADA
Driving east on the Alaska Highway leads to Tok and the Canadian border. At Tetlin Junction the Alaska Highway joins the Taylor Highway which leads north to Canada and Dawson City.

THE RICHARDSON HIGHWAY: WEST TO FAIRBANKS
Following the Richardson Highway west leads to the trans-Alaska oil pipeline crossing at the Tanana River, Big Delta State Historical Park, North Pole, and Fairbanks.

THE RICHARDSON HIGHWAY: SOUTH TO GLENNALLEN
Turning south on the Richardson Highway from its junction with the Alaska Highway leads to Paxson and the junction with the Denali Highway; continuing south leads to Glennallen with options to Valdez, Anchorage or Tok. MP 123 of the Richardson is a good place to start watching for grazing Bison.

Campgrounds on the Richardson Highway south of Delta Junction are described in the chapter," The Copper River Region," under the heading "RV Campgrounds on the Richardson Highway." RVers who choose to drive south should turn to "The Copper River Region" chapter for detailed campground descriptions. The first campground on that highway is Donnelly Creek State Recreation Site.

Donnelly Creek SRS	MP 238.0 Richardson Highway
Fielding Lake SRS	MP 200.5 Richardson Highway
Paxson Lake Campground	MP 175.0 Richardson Highway
Sourdough Creek Campground	MP 147.5 Richardson Highway
Dry Creek SRS	MP 118.0 Richardson Highway

THE RICHARDSON HIGHWAY WEST TO FAIRBANKS
HEALTH AND EMERGENCY SERVICES

MP 295 to MP 341	Salcha Rescue	(907) 488-4525 or 911
MP 341 to MP 359	North Pole Fire Department	488-2232 or 911

RV CAMPGROUNDS ON THE RICHARDSON HIGHWAY

BIRCH LAKE RECREATION AREA   **(907) 488-6161**
United States Air Force   **MP 305 Richardson Highway**

Birch Lake Recreation Area is available to active or retired military and DOD civilians: 40 power only spaces; flush toilets; drinking water; hot showers; boat launch; fishing; separate tenting area; 14 day limit. Open Memorial Day through Labor Day. Not open to the general public.

BIRCH LAKE STATE RECREATION SITE   **open all year**
Alaska State Park System   **MP 305.5 Richardson Highway**

Located on Birch Road at MP 305.5 of the Richardson Highway: 10 spaces w/o hookups; no drinking water; porta-potty toilet; boat launch; fishing; 15 day limit.

Birch Lake SRS has only minimal amenities. Because spaces are not specified, a large RV can be accommodated. Water should be either boiled or treated chemically.

HARDING LAKE STATE RECREATION AREA   **open all year**
Alaska State Park System   **MP 321.4 Richardson Highway**

Located on Harding Drive at MP 321.4 of the Richardson Highway. Follow the paved road for 1.5 miles: 89 spaces w/o hookups; **sewage dump station**; pit toilets; drinking water; tables; fire rings; boat launch; fishing; swimming; trails; 15 day limit.

Harding Lake State Recreation Area is easily accessed but the road through the campgrounds is narrow. Although spaces vary in length, some can accommodate the larger rigs. Pit toilets are accessible to the disabled. A large recreation field with areas for volleyball and softball is located nearby. This is a popular area for local people who take advantage of the boat launch.

SALCHA RIVER STATE RECREATION SITE   **open all year**
Alaska State Park System   **MP 323.3 Richardson**

Located by the Salcha Marina on Sandshore Drive at MP 323.3 of the Richardson Highway: 25 spaces w/o hookups; pit toilets; drinking water; boat launch; fishing; 15 day limit.

Salcha River SRS features a large parking area for RVs and vehicles with boat trailers. Parking spaces for are not designated. The campground will accommodate the largest RVs. Pit toilets are accessible to the disabled. The Salcha River is a quiet flowing stream at this point.

EIELSON AIR FORCE BASE   **(907) 377-4214**
United States Air Force   **MP 341 Richardson Highway**

Located on Eielson AFB at MP 341 of the Richardson Highway west of the beginning of the divided highway: 24 spaces; **sewage dump station**; pit toilets and flush toilets; hot showers; tables; grills; 14 day limit.

Eielson AFB is available to active or retired military and Department of Defense civilians. Ask to be directed to Recreation Supply. Power and water are available while a few spaces have full hookups. Eligible persons should phone ahead for information regarding space availability.

NORTH POLE, ALASKA

For your own amusement, try to locate these four streets from the Richardson Highway as you approach North Pole from the east: Daniece; Danephew; Damudda; Dafadda.

NORTH POLE VISITOR CENTER   **(907) 488-2242**
Richardson Highway at Mission Road

RV CAMPGROUNDS AT NORTH POLE

NORTH POLE PUBLIC PARK   **Memorial Day to Labor Day**
Fairbanks North Star Borough   **Fifth Avenue from Badger Road**

Turn onto Badger Road at MP 349.2 of the Richardson Highway. Follow the "5th Avenue" signs for 0.7 mile to the park entrance: 9 spaces w/o hookups; 3 pull-throughs; flush toilets; drinking water; two covered picnic sites; tables; grills; 5 day limit.

North Pole Public Park is set in a wooded area with trees separating the individual spaces which are back-in and level. Three pull-throughs can accommodate larger RVs. Two covered picnic areas are available in addition to grills and tables at each site.

SANTALAND RV PARK   **privately operated**
PO Box 55317, North Pole, AK 99705   **open all year**
(907) 488-9123   **St. Nicholas Drive from Badger Road**

Turn onto Badger Road at MP 349.2 of the Richardson Highway. Drive one block and turn east on St. Nicholas Drive, a trunk road paralleling the highway: 137 spaces; 35 pull-throughs; 96 full hookups; 32 power and water hookups; 9 w/o hookups; **sewage dump station**; flush toilets; drinking water; hot showers; laundry facilities; tables; public phone; separate tenting area; no time limit.

Santaland RV Park is located at 125 St. Nicholas Drive, next to the famous Santa Claus House. Spaces are level, wide, graveled, and separated by grassed areas. The campground is surrounded by birch and spruce trees. It features full private bathrooms which are disabled accessible and exceptionally clean. A shuttle bus service is available to downtown Fairbanks. Good Sam and senior discounts are offered.

RIVERVIEW RV PARK   **privately operated**
PO Box 72618, Fairbanks, AK 99707   **May 1st—Sept 7th**
(907) 488-6281   **1316 Badger Road**

Turn onto Badger Road at 349.2 of the Richardson Highway. Follow Badger Road to the right for 8.2 miles (Badger Road forms an eleven mile loop and returns to the Richardson Highway): 59 spaces; 18 pull-throughs; 52 full hookups; 7 power and water hookups; **sewage dump station**; flush toilets; drinking water; hot showers; laundry facilities; tables; fishing; public phone; no time limit.

Riverview RV Park has several parallel roads through the campground. Trees surround the perimeter. Spaces are mostly back-ins, level, gravel-based and separated by grass. The campground is on the banks of the Chena River and behind a Quik Stop and gas station. An unusual feature is a nightly seafood and barbeque cookout in an enclosed recreation room overlooking the river.

THE RICHARDSON HIGHWAY (continued)

CHENA LAKE RECREATION AREA　　　　May 23rd—Sept 23rd
Fairbanks North Star Borough　　MP 346.7 Richardson Highway

Turn onto Laurence Road at MP 346.7 of the Richardson Highway: 78 spaces w/o hookups; 12 pull-throughs; **sewage dump station**; pit toilets; drinking water; covered picnic sites; tables; fire rings and grills; boat launch; fishing; swimming; public phone; separate tenting areas; dumpsters; trails; 5 day limit.

Chena Lake Recreation Area is located by the Chena River with stands of birch and spruce trees throughout. Non-motorized boats use its large lake. Group-use picnic shelters, excellent walking trails, boat rentals and other recreational activities are provided. Roads into the many designated parking sites are graveled and easily accessed. Parking areas are graveled and level. Spaces designated for the disabled are blacktopped and level. This is an excellent municipal campground.

ROAD'S END RV PARK　　　　　　　　privately operated
1463 Westcott Lane, North Pole, AK 99705　　May 1st—Sept 1st
(907) 488-0295　　　　　　　MP 356 Richardson Highway

Turn north from the Richardson Highway at MP 356 onto Westcott Lane: 94 spaces; 46 full hookups; 16 power hookups; 32 w/o hookups; **sewage dump station**; flush toilets; drinking water; hot showers; no time limit.

Road's End RV Park is easily accessed from the Richardson Highway in either direction. It has level back-in spaces in a graveled open area surrounded by trees. No other RV campgrounds are available between this point and the City of Fairbanks.

RV SERVICES

NORTH POLE PLAZA MALL
Turn onto Badger Road at MP 349.2 of the Richardson Highway and drive to the mall parking lot. RV services on the mall grounds include a self-service, coin-operated wash facility with six large bays and a Tesoro service station with a **sewage dump station** and **propane**.

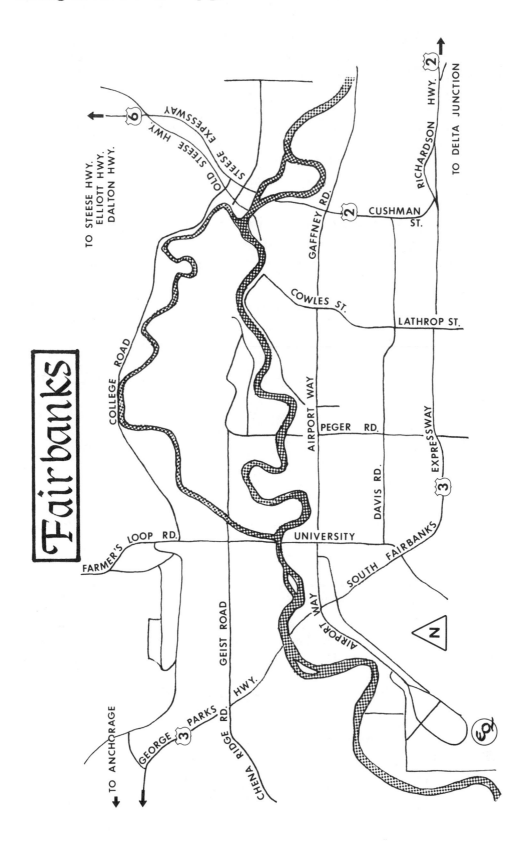

Fairbanks

Chapter 5

THE FAIRBANKS REGION

This chapter describes campgrounds and services in Fairbanks. It also describes campgrounds along Chena Hot Springs Road; the Steese Highway; the Elliott Highway; and the Dalton Highway. Options include the Richardson Highway from Fairbanks to Delta Junction and the George Parks Highway from Fairbanks to Denali National Park.

FAIRBANKS, ALASKA

Fairbanks originated during the time of the gold rush as the transportation hub of interior Alaska which it remains today. Much of the gold rush period is reflected in its architecture. The "tailings" from gold dredges can be seen from highways in and around Fairbanks. The second largest of the five gold dredges that worked the area can be seen at Chatanika, Alaska, on the Old Steese Highway across from the Chatanika Lodge. Between 1928 and about 1962-64, Dredge #3, operated by the U.S. Smelting, Mining and Refining Company, extracted $125 million dollars worth of gold at $35 an ounce.

RVers may be attracted to the Chena River State Recreation Area in addition to the normal tourist attractions such as the University of Alaska Museum, the old section of downtown Fairbanks, and sternwheeler cruises on the Chena River.

Float trips on the Chena and Chatanika rivers provide an opportunity to do something out-of-the-ordinary. The Alaska Division of Parks and Outdoor Recreation (451-2695) can provide maps and specific information for both novice and experienced boaters.

ALASKA PUBLIC LANDS INFORMATION CENTER (APLIC)
250 Cushman Street, Suite 1A, Fairbanks, AK 99701 (907) 451-7352

The center is located in Courthouse Square at the corner of Cushman Street and Third Avenue, two blocks from the Fairbanks Convention and Visitor Center. One of three Alaska Public Lands Information Centers sponsored by a consortium of State and Federal agencies, the center features educational films, book and map sales, trip planning assistance, and information on state and national parks, wildlife refuges, and recreation areas. The building is accessible to the disabled.

Guaranteed reservations for a limited number of RV spaces or bus seats at Denali Park can be made through the APLIC. Reservations must be made in person at the APLIC counter. Reservations for parking or bus seating can be made from seven to twenty-one days in advance.

LOG CABIN VISITOR INFORMATION CENTER   (907) 456-5774
550 First Avenue, Fairbanks, AK 99701   1-800-327-5774

This center is located on the Chena River at First Avenue and Cushman Streets next to Golden Heart Park. Information about Fairbanks and the surrounding region as well as self-guided driving tours is available. The center also offers a 24 hour recorded telephone message service for daily activities in Fairbanks.

BUREAU OF LAND MANAGEMENT   (907) 474-2350
1150 University Avenue, Fairbanks, AK 99709

BLM can provide the traveler up-to-the-minute information regarding road conditions in the area especially on the Dalton Highway (trans-Alaska oil pipeline haul road). Although the author does not encourage RVers to put their rigs on the Dalton Highway, those who do consider such a trip should check with BLM for current road condition information before leaving Fairbanks.

HEALTH AND EMERGENCY SERVICES

Alaska State Troopers	**(907) 452-1527 or 911**
Fairbanks Police	**(907) 452-1313**
Fairbanks Memorial Hospital	**(907) 452-8181**
Fairbanks Clinic	**(907) 452-1761**
Doctor's Medical & Surgical Clinic	**(907) 452-4646**
evenings	**(907) 452-1611**

RV CAMPGROUNDS AT FAIRBANKS

CLUB RV PARK   privately operated
747 Old Richardson Highway, fairbanks, Ak 99701   open all year
(907) 452-6801   FAX (907) 456-5961   Old Richardson Highway

Take the "Old Richardson Highway" exit from the Richardson Highway when headed to the west. Located next door to the Fairbanks Athletic Club at the corner of the Old Richardson Highway and Easy streets: 31 power and water spaces; **sewage dump station**; flush toilets; drinking water; hot showers; laundry facilities; covered picnic sites; tables; grills; recreation facilities; public phone; no time limit.

Club RV Park provides level, graveled side-by-side spaces which are quite close together. Fees, although somewhat higher for the area, include admittance to the Fairbanks Athletic Club for two adults and two children. The facility has tennis and racquetball courts, a running track, fitness center, weight room, and swimming pool.

GLASS PARK, FORT WAINWRIGHT   (907) 353-2706
United States Army   Steese Highway junction with Airport Way

The Richardson Highway turns into the Steese Expressway. Turn east at the junction of the Steese Highway with Airport Way. Check in with the

Outdoor Recreation Director upon arrival. The campground is available to active or retired military and Department of Defense civilians.

Glass Park is an open area without designated spaces and without hookups. It offers restroom facilities, grills, covered pavilions, and access to a golf course. A **sewage dump station** is available at the gas station on post. Fourteen day limit. Eligible persons should phone ahead for information regarding space availability.

TRAIL'S END
906 Old Steese Highway, Fairbanks, AK
(907) 456-8838

privately operated
May 15th—Sept 15th
Old Steese Highway at Trainor Gate Road

The Richardson Highway turns into the Steese Expressway. Drive west on Trainor Gate Road to the intersection with the Old Steese Highway: 167 spaces w/o hookups; 137 pull-throughs; **sewage dump station**; flush toilets; drinking water; tables; public phone; no time limit.

Trail's End has level spaces separated by aspen trees. Dry camping only. This campground is under development. Good Sam discounts are offered.

PIONEER RV AND TRAILER COURT
2201 Cushman, Fairbanks, AK
(907) 452-8788

privately operated
open all year
Cushman at 22nd

Turn south from Airport Way on South Cushman for seven blocks: 40 spaces with full hookups; 10 pull-throughs; public phone; no time limit.

The Pioneer RV and Trailer Court is basically intended for fulltime residents. It serves short term users on a day-to-day basis. It offers full hookups on level gravel spaces; tables, grills, and other amenities are lacking.

ALASKALAND
Fairbanks North Star Borough

open all year
Airport Way and Peger Road

The parking lot is located on the north side of Airport Way between Moore and Peger Road: 80 spaces w/o hookups; chemical toilets; covered picnic sites; playground; public phone; 4 day limit.

Alaskaland is a Pioneer Theme Park sponsored by the Fairbanks North Star Borough. Although the RV parking area is used during the entire year, it is fully operational only between Memorial Day and Labor Day. The parking area is for dry camping, self-contained RVs only. Chemical toilets are located on the grounds as is a children's playground area. The city maintains a sewage dump station and potable water one block away (where Moore turns into 2nd Avenue).

NORLIGHT CAMPGROUND
1660 Peger Road, Fairbanks, AK 99709
(907) 474-0206   (1-800-478-0206)

privately operated
May 15th—Sept 15th
1660 Peger Road

Turn south on Peger Road from Airport Way: 290 spaces; 77 pull-throughs; 48 full hookups; 217 power and water hookups; 25 w/o hookups;

sewage dump station; flush toilets; drinking water; hot showers; laundry facilities; covered picnic sites; tables; public phone; separate tenting area; no time limit.

Norlight Campground is located in a semi-wooded metropolitan area with level, gravel RV spaces in several separate divisions of the grounds. A restaurant, limited grocery and liquor store, and an area for washing RVs are on site. The owners take seriously their statement: "We love tourists and we try to make your trip a vacation to remember." If Sara Sears can't get a chuckle out of you, no one can.

RIVER'S EDGE RV PARK & CAMPGROUND   privately operated
4140 Boat Street, Fairbanks, AK 99709   May 15th—Sept 15th
(907) 474-0286   (1-800-288-9799)   4140 Boat Street

Turn north from Airport Way onto Sportsman's Way, one block west of University Avenue. Turn west onto Boat Street which parallels Airport Way: 152 spaces; 77 pull-throughs; 93 full hookups; 41 power and water hookups; 18 w/o hookups; **sewage dump station**; flush toilets; drinking water; hot showers; laundry facilities; picnic sites; grills; boat launch; fishing; separate tenting area; no time limit.

Gold dredge across from Chatanika Lodge on the old Steese Highway

River's Edge RV Park and Campground features a quiet location over-looking the Chena River. Birch, cottonwood and spruce trees are throughout the grounds. Graveled spaces, up to 60 feet in length and diagonal in design, provide easy access for the largest RVs. Staff members at the gift shop will book tours in the area. Paved bike trails lead into the downtown section of Fairbanks.

CHENA RIVER STATE RECREATION SITE open all year
Alaska State Park System University Avenue

Located on the east side of University Avenue 0.4 mile north of Airport Way: 59 spaces w/o hookups; **sewage dump station**; flush toilets; drinking water; tables; grills; boat launch; fishing; trails; 5 day limit.

Chena River SRS borders the Chena River among birch and spruce trees. Wide and deep gravel-based spaces are easily accessed. Flush toilets are accessible to the disabled. The campground is walking distance to a shopping mall. A playground area is provided for children.

JOHN ALFONI MEMORIAL CAMPGROUND open all year
(907) 474-7355 University of Alaska

Located on the UAF campus: 15 spaces w/o hookups; drinking water. The John Alfoni Memorial Campground gives first priority to UAF students. No reservations are taken. Call UAF for information.

TANANA VALLEY STATE FAIRGROUNDS privately operated
1800 College Road, Fairbanks, AK May 15th—Sept 15th
(907) 456-3750 or 456-9756 1800 College Road

Turn north onto University Way from Airport Way; drive to the signal light at College Road, then turn east to the signal light at Aurora Drive: 36 spaces; 31 power hookups; 5 w/o hookups; **sewage dump station**; flush toilets; drinking water; hot showers; tables; grills; no time limit.

Tanana Valley State Fairground is in a wooded area. A narrow road leads to the spaces which are level but hard to access with larger RVs. A separate overflow area can accommodate the largest RVs. A campground host is on-site. The campground is clean and people using it are expected to maintain their immediate areas. A Good Sam discount is offered.

CHENA MARINA RV PARK privately operated
1145 Shypoke Drive, Fairbanks, AK 99709 May 1st—Sept 15th
(907) 479-4653 Shy Poke Drive at Chena Pump Road

Take the Anchorage exit to the Parks Highway from Airport Road. Turn west at the Chena Ridge exit. Turn left on Chena Pump Road, then right on Grebe to Shypoke Drive: 40 spaces; 23 pull-throughs; 23 power only hookups; 17 w/o hookups; **sewage dump station**; flush toilets; drinking water; hot showers; tables; grills; boat launch; fishing; no time limit.

Chena Marina RV Park is a large, open grassed area on the banks of Chena Marina float plane pond. Spaces are wide and graveled with a view of the mountains. Water is trucked in from mountain wells at near-by Ester and is excellent. Attention is given to senior citizens and inter-national tourists. A free "Klondinental" breakfast is offered each morn-ing. Discounts are available to senior citizens and veterans. The Chena Marina RV Park is a pleasant alternative to larger campgrounds.

(nearby RV campgrounds)

The following two RV campgrounds are located on the George Parks Highway but are within driving distance. They are listed here as part of the Fairbanks RV campgrounds as well as in the section on the Parks Highway.

GOLDHILL RV PARK	privately operated
PO Box 60769, Fairbanks, AK 99706	May 5th—Sept 30th
(907) 474-8088 1-800-428-8303	MP 355.2 Parks Highway

Located 0.5 mile from the Parks Highway at MP 355.2. Drive 0.5 mile on an entry road to the gravel and turn right: 36 spaces; 5 pull-throughs; 20 power hookups; 16 w/o hookups; **sewage dump station**; flush toilets; drinking water; laundry facilities; tables; grills; public phone; separate tenting area; no time limit.

Goldhill RV Park is located in a secluded, wooded area on the outskirts of Fairbanks. Most of the back-in spaces are level and on gravel bases; some may require blocking. Power hook-ups only but water is on the premises.

CRIPPLE CREEK RV PARK AND HOTEL	privately operated
PO Box 109, Ester, AK 99725	open all year
(907) 479-2500 1-800-676-6925	MP 351.7 Parks Highway

Turn onto the Old Nenana Highway from the Parks Highway at MP 351.7. Drive 0.4 mile, then turn right onto Village Road. Turn left on Main Street: 16 spaces w/o hookups; **sewage dump station**; flush toi-lets; drinking water; hot showers; tables; public phone; no time limit.

Cripple Creek RV Park is a level, dirt area adjacent to the hotel which offers dry camping only. The resort is approximately seven miles from Fairbanks. Evening transportation to Fairbanks is available. Cripple Creek Resort is home of the famous "Malemute Saloon," a popular night-time tourist entertainment attraction.

RV SERVICES AT FAIRBANKS (listed alphabetically)

ALASKA CHEVRON SERVICE	(907) 456-3438

petroleum products, **sewage dump station; propane**.

AMERICAN TIRE	(907) 452-5145

alignment, brakes, tune-ups, shocks and struts.

CRAIG TAYLOR EQUIPMENT SALES & SERVICE	(907) 452-1192

Kohler Generator Set repairs.

DISCOUNT TRUCK STOP   (907) 456-1122
petroleum products, **sewage dump station; propane**.

FAIRBANKS CAMPER SALES &SERVICE   (907) 452-4531
large supply of RV parts and accessories: Fleetwood; Pace Arrow; Tioga.

FAIRBANKS MUFFLER&AUTO REPAIR   (907) 452-2511
alignment; brakes; mufflers; spring repair; welding.

FAIRBANKS RV SERVICE CENTER   (907) 452-4279
complete body shop; Itasca, Winnebago, Jamboree service.

THE FRONT END SHOP   (907) 479-7550
alignment; brakes.

GENERATOR SYSTEMS   (907) 456-2624
ONAN Generator Set repairs.

HAPPY HOOKER TOWING   (907) 451-7226
24 hour emergency road service, AAA sponsored (479-4503 nights)

INTERIOR CUSTOM TOPPER&RV CENTER   (907) 451-8356
RV parts and accessories; general repairs; electrical.

L&L RV SERVICE   (907) 474-9260
complete appliance repair; generator repair; electrical repair; brakes; holding tank replacement; oil and lubrication; RV parts.

LEE'S MOBILE SUPPLY&SERVICE   (907) 456-7502
collision repairs; general repairs; RV parts.

MIDAS MUFFLER SHOP   (907) 479-6262
alignment; brakes; mufflers; spring replacement; catalytic converters.

MIKE'S UNIVERSITY CHEVRON   (907) 479-4616
alignment; brakes; general repairs; air conditioning; electrical; tune-ups; **sewage dump station; propane**; authorized U-Haul dealer.

MOBAT TIRE COMPANY   (907) 452-7131
alignment; brakes; transmissions; tires.

MOTOR INN TRANSMISSION   (907) 456-1603
alignment; brakes; towing; transmissions.

PHILLIPS FIELD EQUIPMENT&REPAIR   (907) 479-5865
tires; shocks; struts; brakes; tune-ups; windshields; GM warranty work.

R&R SMALL ENGINE   (907) 456-1693
air conditioning; refrigeration; propane systems; electrical; plumbing; welding; complete RV services.

RON'S SERVICE&TOWING   (907) 456-4224
sewage dump station; emergency road service; towing.

TRAILERCRAFT   **(907) 451-0333**
RV parts and accessories.   Alaska 800 number **1-800-478-0513**

INDEPENDENT RENTAL   **(907) 456-6595**
2020 South Cushman, Fairbanks, AK 99701
Persons interested in floating creeks and rivers in the Fairbanks area can rent inflatable boats, canoes, tents, backpacks, camp stoves and other camping items through Independent Rental.

RV DUMP STATION LOCATIONS

ALASKA CHEVRON SERVICE	**333 Illinois Street**
CHENA RIVER SRS	**University Avenue north of Airport Way**
DISCOUNT TRUCK STOP	**3569 South Cushman Street**
MIKE'S UNIVERSITY CHEVRON	**3245 College Road**
RON'S SERVICE&TOWING	**First Avenue and Nobel Street**
UNIVERSITY AVENUE...CAR WASH	**3701 Cameron Street**

CHENA HOT SPRINGS ROAD

The Chena River is rated as a Class I and II river in terms of difficulty and is suitable for canoes and rubber rafts. U. S. Coast Guard approved flotation devices should be worn at all times. Obstacles such as sweepers and log-jams can create minor difficulties. Popular small craft put-in places on the Chena Hot Springs Road:

Fourth bridge	MP 48.9	exercise caution
Third bridge	MP 44.0	exercise caution
Second bridge	MP 39.5	exercise caution
First bridge	MP 37.8	easier going
Rosehip Campground	MP 27.0	easier going

EMERGENCY SERVICES

MP 0.0 to MP 52   Alaska State Troopers   (907) 452-1313 or 911

ROSEHIP CAMPGROUND   **open all year**
Alaska State Park System   MP 27 Chena Hot Springs Road

Follow the Steese Expressway north to "Chena Hot Springs Road" cut-off. Turn east for twenty-seven miles: 38 spaces w/o hookups; pit toilets; drinking water; tables; fire rings; boat launch; fishing; trails; dumpster; 15 day limit.

Rosehip Campground is part of the larger Chena River State Recreation Area which begins at mile twenty-six. Heavily wooded with birch trees and dotted with forget-me-nots, the campground is on the bank of the Chena River. Spaces at the campground are gravel-based and level. Paired side-by-side with some single sites, spaces vary in size. A few spaces can accommodate larger RVs. Campers with larger RVs may prefer to camp on the sandbars. Pit toilets are accessible to the disabled.

TORS TRAILHEAD CAMPGROUND   **open all year**
Alaska State Park System   MP 39 Chena Hot Springs Road

Follow the Steese Expressway north to "Chena Hot Springs Road" cut-off. Turn east to mile thirty-nine: 18 spaces w/o hookups; pit toilets; drinking water; tables; fire rings; fishing; trails; 15 day limit.

Tors Trailhead Campground is part of the larger Chena River State Recreation Area which begins at mile twenty-six. The gravel-based and level spaces will accommodate the largest RVs. Pit toilets are accessible to the disabled. The campground is set on the Chena River against a quarry with a white-rocked hillside.

CHENA HOT SPRINGS RESORT   **privately operated**
PO Box 73440, Fairbanks, AK 99707   **open all year**
(907) 452-7867   **MP 57 Chena Hot Springs Road**

Follow the Steese Expressway north to "Chena Hot Springs Road" cut-off. Turn east to MP 57: flush toilets; **sewage dump station**; showers; picnic tables; grills; fishing; trails. An undetermined number of spaces with some electric hookups are available for self-contained RVs.

A close-up view of the trans-Alaska oil pipeline

STEESE HIGHWAY

EMERGENCY SERVICES

MP 2.0 to MP 162   **Alaska State Troopers**   **(907) 452-1313 or 911**
CB Channels 2, 19, or 22; ask for relay to troopers

UPPER CHATANIKA STATE RECREATION SITE   **open all year**
Alaska State Park System   **MP 39 Steese Highway**

Take the Steese Expressway north until it becomes the Elliott Highway. Turn east at Fox to MP 39 of the Steese Highway: 25 spaces w/o hookups; pit toilets; drinking water; tables; fire rings; boat launch; 15 day limit.

73

Upper Chatanika SRS is set in a wooded area on the bank of the river. Spaces vary in length. Larger RVs can park on the sandbars if necessary. This is a popular place to launch canoes and rubber rafts for an all-day float trip to the take-out point at mile 11 (Whitefish Campground) of the Elliott Highway.

CRIPPLE CREEK CAMPGROUND
Bureau of Land Management

June 1st—Nov 1st
MP 60.5 Steese Highway

Take the Steese Expressway north until it becomes the Elliott Highway. Turn east at Fox to MP 60.5 of the Steese Highway: 12 spaces w/o hookups; pit toilets; drinking water; tables; fire rings; fishing; separate tenting area; 7 day limit.

Cripple Creek Campground is a remote campground which provides for both tent camping and RV spaces. Located on the bank of Cripple Creek, it gives canoe and rubber raft launch access to the Upper Chatanika River. A nature trail is in the area.

THE ELLIOTT HIGHWAY

EMERGENCY SERVICES

MP 0.0 to MP 152   Alaska State Troopers   (907) 452-1313 or 911
CB Channels 9, 14, or 19; ask for relay to troopers

OLNES POND
Alaska State Park System

open all year
MP 10.5 Elliott Highway

Take the Steese Expressway north until it becomes the Elliott Highway at the junction with the Steese Highway at Fox. Turn left at MP 10.5 and follow the gravel road 0.7 mile: 50 spaces w/o hookups; pit toilets; drinking water; picnic sites; tables; grills; boat launch; fishing; swimming; dumpster; 15 day limit.

Olnes Pond Campground is part of the Lower Chatanika State Recreation Area. The pond is man-made in a quiet, scenic setting. The area is level with spaces placed around the pond. Spaces are undesignated and can accommodate the largest RV. There is a swimming area for children.

WHITEFISH CAMPGROUND
Alaska State Park System

open all year
MP 11.4 Elliott Highway

Take the Steese Expressway north until it becomes the Elliott Highway at the junction with the Steese Highway at Fox. Turn left into the campground just past the bridge: 15 spaces w/o hookups; pit toilets; drinking water; picnic sites; tables; fire rings; boat launch; fishing; 15 day limit.

Whitefish Campground is part of the Lower Chatanika State Recreation Area. Gravel-based roads lead through the campground which borders on the river. Some spaces require backing down slight inclines for access. Large RVs will have problems unless they are parked in the turnaround areas which are not designated for camping. Pit toilets are accessible to the disabled. People with canoes and rubber rafts often launch their crafts at the Upper Chatanika SRS (MP 39 Steese Highway) and return to this campground.

MANLEY HOT SPRING RESORT　　　　　　privately operated
PO Box 28, Manley Hot Springs, AK 99756　　　　open all year
(907) 672-3611　　　　　　　　　　　**MP 151 Elliott Highway**

Take the Steese Expressway north until it becomes the Elliott Highway at the junction with the Steese Highway at Fox. Continue to MP 151. An RV area with a **sewage dump station**, hot showers, laundromat, plus a restaurant, rooms and service station is located at the resort. The feature attraction is swimming in the mineral hot springs pool. The junction road to the village of Minto (11 miles) is at MP 42 of the Elliott Highway.

THE DALTON HIGHWAY
EMERGENCY SERVICES

MP 0.0 to MP 100　　　　　　　　　　**Alaska State Troopers**

1. CB Channel 19; ask for relay to troopers

2. Ask for a message to be relayed to the guard facility at any Alyeska facility or at any Department of Transportation facility.

MP 100 to MP 250　　　**Coldfoot Area Rescue Emergency Squad**
An Alaska State Trooper is stationed at Coldfoot year-round.

1. CB Channels 5, 9, or 19.

2. Phone Alaska State Troopers　　　　　　　　**(907) 452-1313**

The Dalton Highway is the official name now given to the road which was referred to as the "North Slope Haul Road" or the "Trans-Alaska Pipeline Haul Road" or merely "the haul road" during the years when it was used to transport materials overland to Prudhoe Bay. Built by the oil companies in the 1970's, title was later transferred to the state after the pipeline was completed.

Although the State of Alaska owns and maintains the Dalton Highway, a number of different agencies manage land through which it passes. The Bureau of Land Management (BLM) is responsible for a strip of land, ranging from six to twenty-four miles in width on both sides of the highway. The Gates of the Arctic National Park and Preserve is managed by the U.S. National Park Service, and the U.S. Fish and Wildlife Service manages the Yukon Flats National Wildlife Refuge. The state opened the Dalton Highway to Deadhorse in July, 1991.

From Fairbanks, take the Steese Expressway to the junction with the Elliott Highway (11.5 miles). Follow the Elliott to MP 73.5 just beyond Livengood. MP 73.5 marks mile 0.0 of the Dalton. In another 416.6 miles, the road reaches the Arctic Ocean and the northern limit of the highway. The first point-of-special-interest on the Dalton Highway is the Yukon

River which is the fifth largest river in North America. The bridge (MP 56) is wooden-decked and 2,290 feet in length; this is the only bridge in Alaska across the Yukon River.

Crossing the Yukon River on the Dalton Highway

The next point-of-interest is north latitude 66 degrees, 33 minutes, or the Arctic Circle at MP 115. A pull-out for off-road parking and picture taking is provided. At this point the sun stays above the horizon for one 24 hour period on the day of summer solstice. Conversely, it does not rise for one 24 hour period on the day of winter solstice.

Any RVer considering putting a rig on the Dalton Highway should be warned that it is a scenic but extremely rugged road which, in the words of one trucker, "just eats tires." Extra tires and extra containers of fuel are essential since only three places on the Dalton Highway offer tire and emergency repairs, or gasoline and diesel fuel: MP 56.6 north of the Yukon River; Coldfoot (MP 175) and Deadhorse (MP 416).

Wrecker service is available at Coldfoot, but if repairs cannot be accomplished, the expense of bringing a Ford 600 wrecker from Fairbanks and return is $80 for the call and $4 per mile. An alternative to driving the highway is taking a packaged tour over part or all of the road. Three companies provide commercial round-trip tours to Prudhoe Bay: Northern Alaska Tour Company; Gray Line of Alaska; and Princess Tours.

The primary purpose for maintaining the Dalton Highway is to provide truckers access to the Prudhoe Bay oil fields. Recreational interests are secondary The road is slick under rainy conditions and dusty otherwise. Driving protocol is to slow down and pull over to the right side of the highway *when trucks are passing in either direction.*

The section of road from Disaster Creek to Prudhoe Bay is closed except for industrial traffic and others with special permits. Drivers without permits whose vehicles break down north of Disaster Creek are subject to citations and fines.

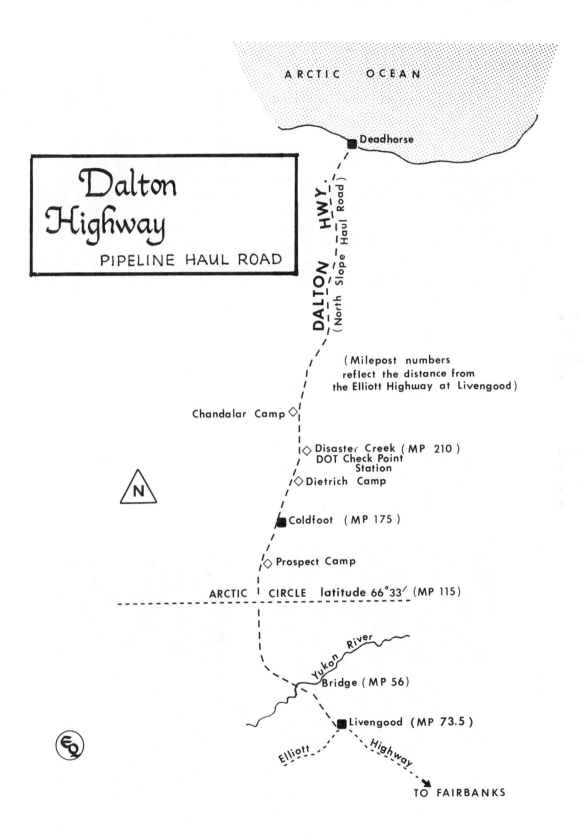

ARCTIC OCEAN

■ Deadhorse

Dalton
Highway
PIPELINE HAUL ROAD

DALTON HWY.
(North Slope Haul Road)

(Milepost numbers
reflect the distance from
the Elliott Highway at Livengood)

◇ Chandalar Camp

◇ Disaster Creek (MP 210)
DOT Check Point
Station
◇ Dietrich Camp

N

■ Coldfoot (MP 175)

◇ Prospect Camp

ARCTIC CIRCLE latitude 66°33' (MP 115)

Yukon River

Bridge (MP 56)

■ Livengood (MP 73.5)

Elliott   Highway

TO FAIRBANKS

DALTON HIGHWAY CAMPGROUNDS

To repeat an earlier statement: *the author does not encourage putting RVs on the Dalton Highway especially beyond the Arctic Circle.* RVers who are considering such a trip should check with BLM personnel for recreational opportunities (474-2300) and the Department of Transportation (451-2200) for current road condition information .

Construction camps on the Dalton Highway are being dismantled and provide excellent overnight dry camping possibilities. Old Man Camp, Prospect Creek and Sixty Mile Camp are examples. BLM has plans to increase recreational opportunities, especially for the RVing public, and to construct five new recreational campgrounds, three visitor centers, eighteen interpretive sites and at least two sewage dump stations in three phases over a period of ten years. BLM campgrounds are maintained from mid-May through mid-September.

BLM did a study which indicated that fifty percent of recreational drivers turn around at the Yukon River; twenty-five percent turn around at the Arctic Circle; twelve and-a-half turn around at Coldfoot and Marion Creek; the remaining twelve and-a-half percent drive north of the Department of Transportation check point at Disaster Creek.

Points of interest include a single spruce tree north of Disaster Creek with a BLM sign which identifies it as the "farthest north spruce tree." Finger Rock (MP 97.5) is one of many granite tors which can be seen in the area for several miles (a tor is granite that remains after softer rock surrounding it has eroded away). An excellent spot for picture taking.

The Arctic Circle: north latitude 66 degrees, 33 minutes

The Kanuti River (MP105.8) offers a view of the pipeline crossing. The Arctic Circle (north latitude 66, degrees 33 minutes) has a wayside stop and interpretive signs which is a popular spot for picture taking.

MP 56: The Yukon River. There is a commercial complex operated under BLM permit that includes a restaurant, automotive services, and lodging. BLM maintains an information center and a picnic site at the Yukon River. There is no overnight parking at this point.

MP 60: Sixty Mile Camp. This is an old construction camp five miles north of the Yukon River. It offers dry camping only. Artesian water is on site. The campground is not maintained but is available for overnighters.

MP 115: The Arctic Circle. Just east of the wayside interpretive site is a dry camping area. There is no water but there are fifteen spaces, concrete vault pit toilets, fire rings and tables. Fourteen day limit.

MP 135: Prospect Creek–Jim Creek. This is another old construction camp. It is located on the bank of the Jim River which offers excellent fishing. There is a pit toilet, no water, and it is not maintained.

MP 175: Coldfoot Services. Located at Coldfoot is a store, restaurant, lounge, motel and automotive services. Their motto: "Coldfoot Is What Alaska Was!" RVers who overnight here will put up with truck noise all night long. **Sewage dump station**. Spaces are located in the parking lot by the restaurant. There are 10-15 spaces with power and water hookups.

MP 180: Marion Creek. Located five miles north of the Visitor Center at Coldfoot, Marion Creek is a BLM campground (fee charged). There are 28 spaces, all pull-throughs, with some trees. Pit toilets are on concrete vaults. Potable water is available.

MP 275: Galbraith Lake. This is a former construction camp. It is a large gravel pad by a lake in the Brooks Range. Dry camping only. There is a pit toilet on site. The one-half mile hike to the lake is difficult. There are no camp sites north of Galbraith Lake.

FAIRBANKS OPTIONS

PARKS HIGHWAY SOUTH TO DENALI NATIONAL PARK
The George Parks Highway leads to Denali National Park and to Anchorage. At Cantwell the Denali Highway leads east to the Richardson Highway and Paxson where options are north to Delta Junction or south to Glennallen.

THE RICHARDSON HIGHWAY EAST TO CANADA
East on the Richardson highway leads to Delta Junction which offers two options: continuing to follow the Richardson Highway south to Glennallen or joining the Alaska Highway east to Tok and the Canadian border.

George Parks Highway

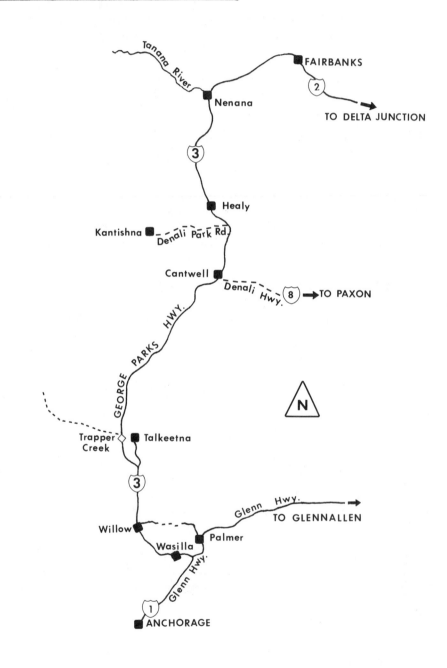

Tanana River

FAIRBANKS

②

TO DELTA JUNCTION

Nenana

③

Healy

Kantishna ■ — Denali Park Rd.

Cantwell

Denali Hwy. ⑧ ➤ TO PAXON

GEORGE PARKS HWY.

Ⓝ

Trapper Creek ◇ ■ Talkeetna

③

Glenn Hwy. TO GLENNALLEN

Willow

Wasilla

Palmer

Glenn Hwy.

①

ANCHORAGE

Chapter 6

FAIRBANKS TO DENALI

This chapter describes campgrounds on the George Parks Highway from Fairbanks to Denali National Park. Campgrounds inside the park are also described. Options include the George Parks Highway north to Fairbanks and south to Anchorage. The Denali Highway is also offered as an option leading east to Paxson and the Richardson Highway.

THE ROAD TO DENALI PARK

The easiest access to the George Parks Highway is to drive west on Airport Way and enter the highway at the cloverleaf. RVers may wish to drive directly to Denali National Park and bypass the Fairbanks business area altogether. The Richardson Highway enters an expressway to the east of the city which becomes the George Parks Highway.

Milepost markers on the George Parks Highway are numbered in descending order from Fairbanks (MP 358) where the highway ends to the Glenn Highway where it begins. Milepost numbers accrue from Anchorage thirty-five miles west of the junction at the Glenn Highway; in other words, the Parks Highway is 323 miles in length, but milepost numbers (358) represent the distance between Anchorage and Fairbanks.

The drive between Fairbanks and Nenana is scenic with panoramic views on both sides of the highway. Northeast of Nenana at MP 318.7 is a pull-out overlooking the Minto Flats area, an expanse of meandering waterways, interior marshes and lakes. Boggy terrain and conifer-covered hills provide a prime nesting area. An estimated 12 million mallard ducks, bald eagles, sandhill cranes, trumpeter swans and other migratory birds pass through the Minto Flats each spring and summer. Freshwater fish and wildlife, including beaver, muskrat, otter, moose, and bear also inhabit the marshes.

The only legal 65 MPH section of highway in Alaska begins at Nenana and ends at the Susitna River bridge. The original Usabelli mine buildings and the "tipple" (turn-over) which dumped coal onto gondola railroad cars can be viewed by following Healy Spur Road from its junction with the Parks Highway in Healy.

NENANA VISITOR CENTER   **Memorial Day to Labor Day**
Nenana, Alaska (MP 303.7)   **A Street and the Parks Highway**

The center is located on a triangular lot at the junction of A Street with the Parks Highway. The center is next to the riverboat, *Taku Chief*.

HEALTH AND EMERGENCY SERVICES

MP 326 to MP 358   Chena ... Fire and Rescue (907) 474-1911 or 911

MP 289 to MP 325   Nenana Public Safety   (907) 832-5632 or 911

MP 276 to MP 290   Anderson Volunteer Fire Department   911

MP 224 to MP 276   Alaska State Troopers   (907) 683-2222
                                          or (907) 683-2232

RV CAMPGROUNDS ON THE GEORGE PARKS HIGHWAY

GOLDHILL RV PARK   privately operated
PO Box 60769, Fairbanks, AK 99706   May 5th—Sept 30th
(907) 474-8088 1-800- 428-8303   MP 355.2 Parks Highway

Located 0.5 mile from the Parks Highway at MP 355.2. Drive 0.5 mile on an entry road to the gravel and turn right: 36 spaces; 5 pull-throughs; 20 power hookups; 16 w/o hookups; **sewage dump station**; flush toilets; drinking water; laundry facilities; tables; grills; public phone; separate tenting area; no time limit.

Goldhill RV Park is located in a secluded, wooded area on the outskirts of Fairbanks. Most of the back-in spaces are level and on gravel bases; some may require blocking. Power hook-ups only but water is on the premises.

CRIPPLE CREEK RV PARK AND HOTEL   privately operated
PO Box 109, Ester, AK 99725   open all year
(907) 479-2500 1-800- 676-6925   MP 351.7 Parks Highway

Turn onto the Old Nenana Highway from the Parks Highway at MP 351.7. Drive 0.4 mile, then turn right onto Village Road. Turn left on Main Street: 16 spaces w/o hookups; **sewage dump station**; flush toilets; drinking water; hot showers; tables; public phone; no time limit.

Cripple Creek RV Park is a level, dirt area adjacent to the hotel which offers dry camping only. The resort is approximately seven miles from Fairbanks. Evening transportation to Fairbanks is available. The Cripple Creek Resort is home of the famous "Malemute Saloon," a popular night-time tourist entertainment attraction.

LAST RESORT RV PARK   privately operated
PO Box 419, Nenana, AK 99760   May 20th—Sept 20th
(907) 582-2776   MP 305 Parks Highway

Located behind the Nenana Visitor Center next to the riverboat, *Taku Chief*: 15 spaces; 4 power and water hookups; 7 w/o hookups; **sewage dump station**; flush toilets; drinking water; tables; no time limit.

Last Resort RV Park is in an open area adjacent to the Nenana Visitor Center. Spaces are level and can accommodate the largest RVs.

NENANA VALLEY RV PARK   privately operated
PO Box 38, Nenana, AK 99760   May 15th—Sept 15th
(907) 832-5431   4th Street east of A Street

Turn north from the Parks Highway at the Visitor Center "Y." Turn right on 4th Street. Drive two blocks: 40 spaces; 30 pull-throughs; 30 power only hookups; 10 w/o hookups; **sewage dump station**; flush toilets; drinking water; hot showers; laundry facilities; covered picnic sites; tables; fire rings; public phone; no time limit.

Nenana Valley RV Park is a large, level graveled area with grass separated spaces. Each space has its own birch, spruce or tamarack decorator tree. Private shower rooms adjacent to the laundry are included in the camp fee. There are two covered picnic areas. Fences screen nearby streets from view. This is a pleasant campground in a quiet area.

SUMMER SHADES CAMPGROUND **privately operated**
HC 66, Box 28980, Nenana, AK 99760 **May 15th—Sept 15th**
(907) 582-2798   1-800- 478-2798 **MP 289.8 Parks Highway**

Located at MP 289.8 of the Parks Highway: 30 spaces; 5 power and water hookups; 25 w/o hookups; **sewage dump station**; flush toilets; drinking water; hot showers; fishing; no time limit.

Summer Shades Campground is located on a five acre lake amid aspen, birch and spruce trees. There is a covered pavilion for picnicking and a play area for children. Ideally suited for families, the owner aptly described the campground as ". . . kind of a restful little place."

Lynx Creek Campground

ANDERSON RIVERSIDE PARK **City of Anderson**
PO Box 3100, Anderson, AK 99744 **May 1st—Sept 15th**
(907) 582-2798 **MP 283 Parks Highway**

Turn from the Parks Highway at MP 283. Turn right at the first street and follow the road signs to the City of Anderson. Do not continue from the highway toward Clear Air Force Base which is located directly ahead after the turn from the Parks Highway: 22 spaces; 10 power only hookups; 12 w/o hookups; **sewage dump station**; flush toilets; drinking water; hot showers; covered picnic site; no time limit.

Anderson Riverside Park is located in an eighty acre wooded area on the bank of the Nenana River. The ten power hookups are adjacent to the covered pavilion and fireplace while the twelve spaces without hookups are scattered throughout the park. All spaces are level and graveled. An honor system with envelopes is used. The annual "Anderson Bluegrass Festival" is celebrated during the last week of July.

TATLANIKA TRADING COMPANY   privately operated
PO Box 40179, Clear, AK 99704   May 15th—Sept 15th
(907) 582-2341   MP 276 Parks Highway

Located at MP 276 of the Parks Highway, on the northeast side of the Nenana River bridge: 11 spaces; 3 pull-throughs; 11 full hookups; **sewage dump station**; flush toilets; drinking water; hot showers; tables; fire rings; no time limit.

Tatlanika Trading Company campground is located behind a gift shop amid birch, aspen and spruce trees. Trees separate the spaces. The near-by river is too silty for good fishing. A unique fish wheel is displayed in the parking area.

A typical Alaska state campground

WAUGAMAN VILLAGE RV PARK   privately operated
PO Box 78, Healy, AK 99743   open all year
(907) 683-2737   MP 248.8 Parks Highway

Turn on Healy Spur Road at its junction with the Parks Highway by the Totem Pole Cafe. Drive 3.7 miles to the Golden Valley Power House: 25 spaces; 9 full hookups; 12 w/o hookups; remainder unknown; flush toilets; drinking water; hot showers; laundry facilities; fire rings; no time limit.

Waugaman Village RV Park is an isolated, primitive campground with level, gravel-based spaces. RVs of any size can be accommodated. It is walking distance to the Nenana River where there is fishing.

Continue on the gravel-based road to reach the site of the original mine buildings and the railroad "tipple" which was used to overturn railroad cars to empty their contents.

KOA McKINLEY KAMPGROUND   privately operated
PO Box 340, Healy, AK 99743   May 1st—Sept 15th
(907) 683-2379   1-800-478-AKOA   **MP 248.5 Parks Highway**

Located 0.3 mile south of the Healy Spur Road junction with the Parks Highway: 88 spaces; 33 pull-throughs; 13 full hookups; 20 power and water hookups; **sewage dump station**; flush toilets; drinking water; hot showers; laundry facilities; tables; grills; recreation room; public phone; no time limit.

KOA McKinley Kampground is the only KOA facility in Alaska. The campground is located below the level of the Parks Highway. Spaces are level and can accommodate the largest RVs. A recreational facility is available as are areas for volleyball and horseshoes. Films on Alaska are shown each evening. Discounts are offered to KOA members.

DENALI RV PARK   privately operated
PO Box 155, Denali Park, AK 99755   May 15th—Sept 15th
(907) 683-1500   1-800- 478-1501   **MP 245.1 Parks Highway**

Located at MP 248.5 of the Parks Highway: 90 spaces; 10 pull-throughs; 49 power and water hookups; 41 power only hookups; **sewage dump station**; flush toilets; drinking water; hot showers; tables; recreation room; public phone; no time limit.

Denali RV Park is a large, open graveled area set on a slope. Spaces are level and graveled but some small blocking may be required. Shower and toilets are clean, self-contained and private. A small motel is located toward the back of the property. There are three hiking trails in the area. The setting is lovely with mountains to be seen in all directions.

THE LAST RESORT AT DENALI   privately operated
MP 240.2 Parks Highway

Located at MP 240, north of Hornet Creek bridge: undetermined number of spaces; no hookups; porta-potties; no time limit.

The Last Resort at Denali is a large, open area that has been filled with dirt in order to widen a roadside pull-out. Situated on a bluff that over-looks the Nenana River, spaces are not designated. Dry camping only.

LYNX CREEK CAMPGROUND   privately operated
825 West 8th Ave, Anchorage, AK 99501   May 12th—Sept 15th
(907) 276-7234   **MP 238.6 Parks Highway**

85

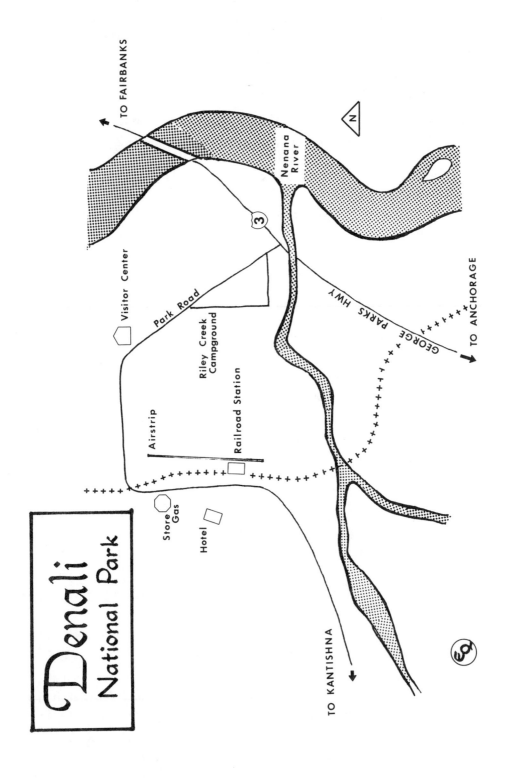

Denali National Park

TO FAIRBANKS

Nenana River

Visitor Center

Park Road

Riley Creek Campground

Railroad Station

Airstrip

Store Gas

Hotel

GEORGE PARKS HWY

TO ANCHORAGE

TO KANTISHNA

Located at MP 238.6, north of the McKinley National Park entrance: 25 spaces; 8 pull-throughs; 12 power hookups; 13 w/o hookups; **sewage dump station**; flush toilets; drinking water; hot showers; tables; fire rings; trails; public phone; separate tenting area; no time limit.

Lynx Creek Campground is set in a wooded area walking distance to the Nenana River. Spaces are gravel-based and best suited to motorhomes or travel trailers up to 27 feet. However, pull-throughs can accommodate larger RVs. A grocery store and service station are located on site.

DENALI NATIONAL PARK AND PRESERVE

A gold prospector is credited with being the first non-Native person to see the tallest peak in North America which he named for President William McKinley in 1896. The name immediately created controversy because the U.S. Board on Geographic Names had a policy against commemorating living persons in such a manner. When President McKinley was assassinated in 1901, the board gave the mountain his name. However, the controversy had not ended.

A large number of Alaskans supported the name given to the mountain by the Athabasken Indians: *Denali*, meaning "The Great One." The controversy continued until 1975 when the Alaska legislature officially requested that the name be changed. Pressure was immediately applied to the Committee on Domestic Names to retain McKinley as the mountain's name by a U.S. Representative from Ohio which was President McKinley's home state.

Mount McKinley National Park was established as part of the National Park Service in 1917. When President Jimmy Carter expanded the park in 1980, the name was officially changed to the Alaskan preference, "Denali National Park and Preserve."

Denali Visitor Information Center

DENALI NATIONAL PARK VISITOR CENTER   (907) 683-1266
Mile 1, Denali Park Road, Denali, AK 99755

The Visitor Center is located in a new building with paved parking adjacent to the facility. It received a Merit Award for its design from the Alaska Chapter of the American Institute of Architects and for its integration with the natural setting. The center contains a viewing room for park-related films, a gift shop, and informational displays.

Reservations for camp sites are made with park rangers at the center on a first-come, first-served basis. The center opens at 7 a.m., but lines begin to form before that. Reservations can be made only two days in advance. Usually there is a two day waiting list which requires campers to use public campgrounds in the area until park openings become available.

The first fifteen miles of road into Denali National Park and Preserve is open to private traffic. Visitors can reserve space on converted school buses operated by the Park Service at the visitor center, or reserve space on the "Tundra Wildlife Tour" motorcoaches operated by ARA, a private concessionaire (907) 683-2215. To make ARA reservations more than forty-eight hours in advance, call (907) 276-7234.

Reservations for a limited number of campsites and bus seats can be made seven to twenty-one days in advance in person through the Fairbanks (907) 451-7352 and Anchorage (907) 271-2737 Alaska Public Lands Information Centers (APLIC).

RILEY CREEK CAMPGROUND   open all year
U.S. National Park Service   MP 1 Denali Park Road

Located 0.3 mile from the Parks Highway entrance: 102 spaces w/o hookups; **sewage dump station**; flush toilets; drinking water; tables; fire rings; separate tenting area; 14 day limit.

Riley Creek Campground is open all year, but water is not available during winter months. Spaces are blacktopped, level and can accommodate RVs of any length. Toilets are accessible to the disabled. Showers and firewood are available at a nearby Mercantile. Registrations are made at the Visitor Center for the present day and following day only to a maximum of fourteen days.

SAVAGE RIVER CAMPGROUND   May 25th—Oct 1st
U.S. National Park Service   MP 13 Denali Park Road

Located 12 miles west from the Parks Highway entrance: 34 spaces w/o hookups; flush toilets; drinking water; tables; grills; fishing; trails; dumpster; 14 day limit.

Savage River Campground spaces are short but can accommodate RVs to about 25-27 feet in length. Toilets are accessible to the disabled. Fires in designated areas only. Registrations are made at the Visitor Center.

TEKLANIKA RIVER CAMPGROUND   May 27th—Sept 15th
U.S. National Park Service   MP 29 Denali Park Road

Located 29 miles west from the Parks Highway entrance: 50 spaces w/o hookups; pit toilets; fire rings; 3-14 day limit.

Teklanika River Campground has restricted use. In order to reduce travel on the road, spaces must be reserved for a minimum of three days and a maximum of fourteen days. Shuttle buses can be used to move freely around and through Denali National Park. Registrations are made only through the Visitor Center.

Savage River Campground: Denali National Park and Preserve

GEORGE PARKS HIGHWAY (continued)

DENALI GRIZZLY BEAR ... CAMPGROUND   privately operated
PO Box 7, Denali, AK 99755   May 15th—Sept 15th
(907) 683-2696   MP 231 Parks Highway

Located at MP 231 of the Parks Highway south of the Nenana River Bridge: 65 spaces; 15 power hookups; 9 water hookups; 41 w/o hookups; **sewage dump station**; pit toilets; flush toilets; drinking water; hot showers; tables; fire rings; **propane**; public phone; separate tenting area; no time limit.

Denali Grizzly Bear Cabins and Campground is located in heavy stands of spruce on the bank of the Nenana River. Roads through the campground have a number of inclines. Spaces are not level and will accommodate RVs to about 30 feet although some spaces may handle larger rigs. A separate level area by the office can easily accommodate the largest RVs. The shower and toilet area are accessible to the disabled.

CARLO CREEK LODGE   privately operated
HC 2, Box 1530, Healy, AK 99743   June 1st—Sept 15th
(907) 683-2576   MP 224 Parks Highway

Located at MP 224, just south of Carlo Creek bridge: 25 spaces w/o hookups; flush toilets; drinking water; hot showers; **sewage dump sta-**

tion; tables; fire rings; fishing; trails; public phone; separate tenting area; **propane**; no time limit.

Carlo Creek Lodge offers dry camping in a large open area nestled in the mountains with tent camping among the trees. A graveled road runs through this rustic setting. Cabins are also available.

HIGHWAY OPTIONS FROM DENALI

THE GEORGE PARKS HIGHWAY: NORTH TO FAIRBANKS

Fairbanks is 120 miles northeast from Denali Park on the George Parks Highway. Towns include Healy and Nenana. From Nenana the highway follows a series of ridges over the mountains which provide excellent views of migratory bird breeding grounds.

THE GEORGE PARKS HIGHWAY: SOUTH TO ANCHORAGE

Anchorage is 237 miles south from Denali Park on the George Parks Highway. This route offers a number of interesting places to camp or visit including Talkeetna, the Nancy Lake Recreation Area, and Big Lake. The Parks Highway ends at the junction of the Glenn Highway.

THE DENALI HIGHWAY: EAST TO PAXSON

The Denali Highway joins the Parks Highway at Cantwell. It extends east to the Richardson Highway at Paxson. The Bureau of Land Management maintains one RV campground on the west side of the Denali Highway and two campgrounds on the east side.

Last seen on Alaska's highways

Chapter 7

DENALI TO WASILLA

This chapter describes campgrounds and services on the George Parks Highway from Denali National Park south to Wasilla. Campgrounds on the Denali Highway east to Paxson and the Richardson Highway are also described. A side trip to Talkeetna is suggested as an option. Other options are the George Parks Highway north to Fairbanks or south to Anchorage.

THE DENALI HIGHWAY

The junction of the Denali Highway with the Richardson Highway is at MP 188.5 at Paxson. At one time the road was the only access to Denali National Park because the George Parks Highway had not been completed. The one hundred thirty-four miles of gravel road is narrow and rutted but offers unmatched views of scenic wilderness.

The posted maximum speed is 35 MPH but prudent RVers will probably travel at much slower speeds. One couple who drove the road reported that they "took it easy all the way." Their only damage was two broken casserole dishes. Extra tires and a full tank of fuel are essential.

There are two lodges on the Denali Highway where dry RV parking is permitted. The first, Maclaren River Lodge, is located at mile 42 from the Paxson side. The second, Gracious House Lodge, is located at mile 82 from the Paxson side. Each lodge has a restaurant and bar. Gracious House Lodge also has gasoline available.

The Bureau of Land Management has five exhibits on the Denali Highway. Orientation panels are located at miles 13 and 115; an archaeology exhibit is located at Tangle Lakes, mile 22; a wildlife exhibit is located at mile 50; a geology exhibit is located at mile 94.

BLM has an excellent brochure, *Denali Highway: Points of Interest*, which describes the terrain. Archaeological studies of the area reveal four hundred sites in the Tangle Lakes Archaeological District. Ancient peoples occupied the area for a period of more than ten thousand years. These prehistoric sites lie between miles fifteen and forty-five.

EMERGENCY SERVICES

MP 78 to MP 135	**Cantwell Volunteer Ambulance**	**(907) 768-2982**
	Alaska State Troopers	**(907) 786-2202**
	Fire Department	**(907) 768-2240**
MP 0 to MP 78	**Copper River EMS/Glennallen**	**(907) 822-3203**
	Alaska State Troopers	**(907) 786-2202**

RV CAMPGROUNDS ON THE DENALI HIGHWAY

BRUSHKANA CREEK CAMPGROUND	**May 1st—Oct 1st**
Bureau of Land Management	**MP 104.3 Denali Highway**

The campground is located at MP 104.3 on the Denali Highway or 29.8 miles from the junction of the George Parks Highway (MP 209.9). At this point the Denali Highway is rough and sections are washboard-like: 17 spaces w/o hookups; pit toilets; drinking water; covered picnic site; tables; fire rings; fishing; 7 day limit.

Brushkana Creek Campground is bordered by spruce. It has back-in spaces which are not level. An overflow area can accommodate the largest RVs. Pit toilets on concrete vaults and a group picnic shelter are provided. Fish include dolly varden, lake trout, burbot and grayling. The camp is within walking distance to the Brushkana River.

TANGLE RIVER CAMPGROUND	**May 1st—Oct 1st**
Bureau of Land Management	**MP 21.7 Denali Highway**

Located at the eastern end of the Denali Highway or 21.7 miles before the junction of the Richardson Highway at Paxson (MP 188.5). Blacktop begins just past the campground entrance: 7 spaces w/o hookups; pit toilets; drinking water; tables; boat launch; fishing; 7 day limit.

Tangle River Campground is near the Tangle Lakes Campground but on the opposite side of the road. The campground is narrow and parallels the river which allows road access at either end. This small campground will accommodate RVs of any size and should be considered before taking a big rig into the Tangle Lakes Campground side.

The boat launch is widely used as a put-in location for Delta River float trips as well as fishing.

Fishing west of Montana Creek bridge

TANGLE LAKES CAMPGROUND	May 1st—Oct 1st
Bureau of Land Management	MP 21.5 Denali Highway

Located at the eastern end of the Denali Highway or 21.5 miles before the junction of the Richardson Highway at Paxson (MP 188.5). Blacktop begins just past the campground entrance: 27 spaces w/o hookups; pit toilets; drinking water; tables; fire rings; boat launch; fishing; 7 day limit.

Tangle Lakes Campground is rough. Spaces are not level and require some blocking. The campground is surrounded by hills and mountains and is situated on a shallow, fast moving creek. Some scrub brush and small trees are in the area. Pit toilets are on concrete vaults and are accessible to the disabled. A handwritten comment on the bulletin board read "fishing good in creeks between lakes (grayling, trout)."

DENALI HIGHWAY OPTIONS AT PAXSON

THE RICHARDSON HIGHWAY: NORTH TO DELTA JUNCTION CONNECTING WITH THE ALASKA HIGHWAY
The Denali Highway joins the Richardson Highway at MP 188.5. North from Paxson leads to Delta Junction where the Richardson Highway connects with the Alaska Highway to the east.

THE RICHARDSON HIGHWAY: SOUTH TO GLENNALLEN
The Denali Highway joins the Richardson Highway at MP 188.5. South from Paxson leads to the Glenn Highway (Tok Cutoff) at Gulkana. The Richardson Highway continues to Glennallen and terminates in Valdez.

THE GEORGE PARKS HIGHWAY

HEALTH AND EMERGENCY SERVICES

MP 174 to MP 224	Cantwell Volunteer Ambulance	(907) 768-2982
	Alaska State Troopers	(907) 768-2232
MP 91 to MP 200	Trapper Creek Ambulance	(907) 733-2256
	Alaska State Troopers	(907) 733-2256 or 911
MP 64 to MP 91	Willow Ambulance Service	911
MP 52 to MP 64	Houston Ambulance Service	911

McKINLEY VIEWING AREAS

MP 135.2	McKinley and Ruth, Eldridge and Buckskin Glaciers
MP 147.1	McKinley and the Moose's Tooth up the Coffee River
MP 158.1	McKinley's top and Buckskin Glacier Valley
MP 162.3	McKinley and the Moose's Tooth
MP 170.1	McKinley and Eldridge Glacier

RV CAMPGROUNDS ON THE GEORGE PARKS HIGHWAY

EAST FORK REST AREA	open all year
Alaska State Park System	MP 185.6 Parks Highway

Located 0.4 mile south of the East Fork Chulitna bridge at MP 185.6 of the Parks Highway: 25 spaces w/o hookups; **sewage dump station**; pit toilets; drinking water; picnic site; tables; fire rings; 15 day limit.

East Fork Rest Area has a blacktopped loop road approximately 0.5 mile in length with back-in, side-by-side spaces for RVs up to 25 feet. An inner-loop road borders the east fork of the Chulitna River. A blacktopped area parallel to the Parks Highway can accommodate larger RVs parked one behind the other.

BYERS LAKE CAMPGROUND

Alaska State Park System

open all year

MP 147 Parks Highway

Located at MP 147 on a gravel road 0.7 mile east of the Parks Highway: 66 spaces w/o hookups; 9 pull-throughs; pit toilets; drinking water; 15 picnic sites; tables; fire rings; boat launch; fishing; swimming; trails; separate tenting area; 15 day limit.

Byers Lake Campground has four separate, wooded, camp areas descending to the lake. Three tiers have level back-in spaces while the outside perimeter has pull-throughs. There is also a large overflow parking area near the upper level which can accommodate the largest RVs. A separate parking area for boat trailers is provided. The campground features a small, non-staffed, log cabin visitor information center and a large amphitheater. This is one of the more prominent campgrounds on the Parks Highway. It is walking distance to the Alaska Veterans' Memorial.

LOWER TROUBLESOME CREEK CAMPGROUND

Alaska State Park System

open all year

MP 137.2 Parks Highway

Located at MP 137.2 of the Parks Highway: 20 spaces w/o hookups; pit toilets; drinking water; sheltered picnic sites; tables; fire rings; fishing; trails; 15 day limit.

Lower Troublesome Creek Campground is more of a wayside park or pull-off rest area than a campground in the true sense. Paved and shaped somewhat like a half-moon, no specific spaces are designated; parking is back-in, side-by-side facing the Parks Highway. The area can accommodate the largest RVs. A short hike leads to the Chulitna River. The parking area offers a clear view of Mt. McKinley.

TRAPPER CREEK TRADING POST

PO Box 13167, Trapper Creek, AK 99683
(907) 733-2315

privately operated
May 1st—Oct 30th
MP 115.5 Parks Highway

Located north of the junction of the Petersville Road with the Parks Highway: 15 spaces; 6 full hookups; 9 w/o hookups; **sewage dump station**; pit toilets; flush toilets; hot showers; laundry facilities; fishing; **propane**; public phone; no time limit.

Trapper Creek Trading Post is located by a stream. A small store and a welding shop are also on the grounds. Spaces are on gravel bases. This undeveloped site is best suited to last-minute, overnight parking.

MOOSE CREEK CAMPGROUND   privately operated
PO Box 13463, Trapper Creek, AK 99683   May 15th—Sept 15th
(907) 733-1345   MP 7.1 Petersville Road

Located at MP 7.1 of the Petersville Road, west of the Parks Highway at MP 114.9: 6 spaces w/o hookups; flush toilets; picnic area; boat launch; fishing; no time limit.

Moose Creek Campground offers dry camping only beside Moose Creek. A store and cabins are on site. Salmon and grayling fishing.

PETRACACH, INC.   privately operated
PO Box 13209, Trapper Creek, AK 99683   May 1st—Oct 1st
(907) 733-2302   FAX (907) 733-1002   MP 114.8 Parks Highway

Located at the junction of the Petersville Road with the Parks Highway: 32 spaces; 9 pull-throughs; 18 full hookups; 14 w/o hookups; **sewage dump station**; flush toilets; drinking water; hot showers; laundry facilities; covered picnic site; tables; grills; public phone; no time limit.

Petracach, Inc. campground offers level, graveled spaces separated by trees. A covered gazebo provides a sheltered eating area. Approximately one mile east of the campground is a public boat launch for the Susitna River. Fishing licenses available at the gift shop. An airstrip is located on the grounds; flightseeing charters to Mount McKinley can be booked.

H & H RESTAURANT   privately operated
(907) 733-2415   MP 99.5 Parks Highway

Located 0.5 north of the junction with Talkeetna Spur Road and the Parks Highway. H & H Restaurant offers dry camping spaces on a lake behind the restaurant. A picturesque and wooded area, parking is far enough removed from the highway to eliminate traffic noise. Float planes land on the lake and are frequently tied nearby.

TALKEETNA SPUR ROAD

The junction of the Talkeetna Spur Road is located at MP 98.7 of the Parks Highway. Round trip to Talkeetna is twenty-nine miles. Talkeetna is included in this section as an option because it offers RVers a variety of river float-trips and fishing trips as well as flightseeing opportunities.

The Talkeetna Historical Society and Museum is open daily during the summer months and features historical displays from Talkeetna's gold mining past. There is also a mountain climbing exhibit with a scale model of Mount McKinley and Bradford Washburn photographs displayed.

The Moose Dropping Festival is celebrated on the second Saturday in July. This annual event features a 5-K run, a parade, and free entertainment in the park. Not the least of the events is the "moose toss," where contestants throw recycled moose pellets at a table covered with numbers. There seems to be no limit to the number of creative ways moose pellets can be used.

Four flightseeing services are available in Talkeetna. They provide scenic, charter aerial tours of Mount McKinley. Landings on Ruth Glacier at 5,000 feet or Kahiltna Glacier at 7,000 feet can be arranged. This is one way to view Mount McKinley that is unequalled.

Doug Geeting Aviation	PO Box 42, Talkeetna, AK 99676	(907) 733-2366
Hudson Air Service	PO Box 82, Talkeetna, AK 99676	(907) 733-2321
K-2 Aviation	PO Box 545, Talkeetna, AK 99676	(907) 733-2291
Talkeetna Air Taxi	PO Box 73, Talkeetna, AK 99676	(907) 733-2218

TALKEETNA RIVER PARK City of Talkeetna

Located at the end of the Talkeetna Spur Road: dry camping only. Seven day limit. Small RVs can camp in the town park which has a limited number of spaces for RVs and tent campers. Overnight camping is permitted on the road paralleling the river.

TALKEETNA RIVER RV CAMPGROUND privately operated

Follow the gravel spur road adjacent to the airport. Turn left at the first road past the tracks. Drive one block and turn right at Mahay's Riverboat Service. This small, level, graveled area provides dry camping only.

TALKEETNA BOAT LAUNCH & PARK Chamber of Commerce

Follow the gravel spur road adjacent to the air strip. Turn left at the first road past the tracks: dry camping only; pit toilets; tables; covered picnic sites; potable water; boat launch; no time limit.

Talkeetna Boat Launch and Park has an undetermined number of spaces amid heavy stands of aspen and birch. Some pull-throughs are available. The largest RV can be accommodated. A boat launch provides access to the river. A separate parking area for boat trailers is provided.

THREE RIVERS TESORO (907) 733-2620

Located next to the Fairview Inn in the center of Talkeetna: general repairs; **sewage dump station**; **propane**.

Driving the Talkeetna Spur Road

RV CAMPGROUNDS ON THE PARKS HIGHWAY
(continued)

MONTANA CREEK CAMPGROUND   privately operated
Susitna Recreational Camps, Inc.   MP 97.6 Parks Highway

Located at MP 97.6 of the Parks Highway on the north side of the bridge
at Montana Creek: 50 spaces w/o hookups; porta-potties; tables; garbage
cans; no time limit.

This campground is located on the bank of Montana Creek. Dry camping
only. Spaces are gravel-based, back-ins, separated by aspen and spruce
trees. There is an overflow area at the entrance to the campground that
will accommodate the largest RV.

MONTANA CREEK STATE RECREATION SITE   open all year
Alaska State Park System   MP 97.6 Parks Highway

Located at MP 97.6 of the Parks Highway on the south side of the bridge
at Montana Creek: 89 spaces w/o hookups; pit toilets; drinking water;
tables; fire rings; fishing; trails; separate tenting area; 15 day limit.

Montana Creek SRS is located on Montana Creek and has back-in, side-
by-side parking spaces which vary in length; campers with larger RVs
may find the spaces confining. Pit toilets are accessible to the disabled.

CHANDALAR RV CAMPER PARK   privately operated
HC 89-PO Box 399, Willow, AK 99688   June 1st—Oct 1st
(907) 495-6700   FAX (907) 495-5840   MP 90.8 Parks Highway

Located at MP 90.8 of the Parks Highway: 48 spaces with full hookups;
sewage dump station; flush toilets; drinking water; hot showers; laundry facilities; tables; grills; public phone; separate tenting area; dumpster; no time limit.

Chandalar RV Camper Park is set back from the highway. An attached
grocery, liquor store and plumbing supply outlet are located on site.
Spaces are set in an open area, side-by-side style with pull-through
capacity for easy turn around. Grills are used in designated areas.
Charter fishing trips can be arranged.

HATCHER PASS ROAD (MP 71.3)

DECEPTION CREEK STATE RECREATION SITE   open all year
Alaska State Park System   MP 48 Hatcher Pass Road

Drive east on Hatcher Pass Road 1.2 miles from the junction with the
Parks Highway (MP 71.3): 7 spaces w/o hookups; pit toilets; drinking
water; picnic shelter; tables; fire rings; fishing; 15 day limit.

Deception Creek SRS is located on shallow, slow-flowing Deception Creek.
This is an older state campground which requires making a complete loop
in order to properly back in and park. Spaces are gravel-based but not

level. Pit toilets are accessible to the disabled. The campground is not recommended for RVs much longer than 27-28 feet.

GEORGE PARKS HIGHWAY (continued)

WILLOW CREEK STATE RECREATION AREA   **open all year**
Alaska State Park System   **MP 70.8 Parks Highway**

Turn west from the Parks Highway at MP 70.8. Drive 3.8 miles on a gravel-based road: 138 spaces w/o hookups; pit toilets; drinking water; tables; fire rings; fishing; 15 day limit.

Willow Creek SRA is located on the creek in a wooded area with both side-by-side spaces and back-in spaces. Pit toilets are on concrete vaults and are accessible to the disabled. This is a very nice campground.

WILLOW ISLAND RESORT RV PARK . . .   **privately operated**
PO Box 85, Willow, AK 99688   **May 1st—Sept 30th**
(907) 495-6343   FAX (907) 495-6343   **MP 71.5 Parks Highway**

Located at MP 71.5 of the Parks Highway north of Willow Creek bridge: 37 spaces; 16 full hookups; 21 power and water hookups; **sewage dump station**; flush toilets; drinking water; hot showers; laundry facilities; tables; fire rings; boat launch; fishing; public phone; separate tenting area; no time limit.

Willow Island Resort RV Park and Campground is attractively designed and located directly on the bank of Willow Creek. The gravel-based spaces are level and easily accessed by RVs of any length. Willow Creek, which is not glacial-fed, offers excellent clearwater salmon and trout fishing. A permanent fish-cleaning area juts out over the river. Fishing tackle and licenses can be purchased at the small store.

PIONEER LODGE, INC.   **privately operated**
PO Box 1028, Willow, AK 99688   **May 1st—Sept 30th**
(907) 495-6883   **MP 71.4 Parks Highway**

Located at MP 71.4 of the Parks Highway south of Willow Creek bridge: 33 spaces; 10 full hookups; 15 power and water hookups; 8 w/o hookups; 4 pull-throughs; **sewage dump station**; flush toilets; porta-potties; drinking water; hot showers; laundry facilities; tables; fire rings; boat launch; fishing; public phone; no time limit.

Pioneer Lodge, Inc. has a rough, graveled road through the campground by the creek. Spaces are back-ins, separated by trees. The lodge has a gift and tackle shop.

WILLOW TRADING POST LODGE RV PARK   **privately operated**
PO Box 49, Willow, AK 99688   **May 15th—Sept 15th**
(907) 495-6457   **MP 69.5 Parks Highway**

Turn east on Willow Station Road directly across from Willow Elementary School at MP 69.5 of the Parks Highway (marked by signs). Follow the road until it crosses the railroad tracks. Turn left 0.2 mile: 16 spaces; 8 power and water hookups; 8 w/o hookups; flush toilets; drinking water; showers; laundry; no time limit.

Willow Trading Post Lodge RV Park has guest cabins, a gift shop, and a bar and liquor store in addition to camping. Spaces are gravel-based, level and separated from one another and from the larger complex by lattice fences. The largest RV can be accommodated. A covered picnic area and a wood-fired sauna are available. Hanging baskets and flowers are planted throughout the area.

SOUTH ROLLY LAKE CAMPGROUND
Alaska State Park System

open all year
MP 6.5 Nancy Lake Parkway

Nancy Lake Parkway forms a junction at MP 67.2 with the Parks Highway: 98 spaces w/o hookups; pit toilets; drinking water; 20 picnic sites; boat launch; fishing; trails; 15 day limit.

Rolly Lake Campground is part of the Nancy Lake State Recreation Area. The 6.5 mile gravel road into the campground is marked by many small lakes and stands of birch and spruce trees. The heavily wooded campground has separate cul-de-sac camping areas, some of which have pull-throughs. Larger RVs can be accommodated. The Little Susitna River flows through the campground.

More than 130 small lakes and ponds, which offer a variety of recreational opportunities, are connected by creeks and short portages in this 22,000 acre park. Canoes can be rented at designated lake sites.

NANCY LAKE STATE RECREATION SITE
Alaska State Park System

open all year
MP 66.5 Parks Highway

Turn at MP 66.5 from the Parks Highway onto Buckingham Palace Road on the north side of the railroad tracks. Drive 0.3 mile and turn right: 30 spaces w/o hookups; pit toilets; drinking water; picnic shelters; boat launch; fishing; trails; separate tenting area; 15 day limit.

Nancy Lake SRS is a wooded area located on Nancy Lake. Spaces are short and best suited to mini-motorhomes or small travel trailers. Separate picnic areas, tenting areas and dumpsters are located on site. Pit toilets are accessible to the disabled.

NANCY LAKE MARINA RESORT
(907) 495-6284

privately operated
MP 64.5 Parks

Located at MP 64.5 of the Parks Highway: 50 spaces w/o hookups; flush toilets; hot showers; tables; grills; boat launch; fishing; **propane**.

Nancy Lake Marina Resort is not available to overnight, drop-in campers. RV camp signs on the highway are misleading in this regard. Do not stop if prior reservations have not made through the travel services in Anchorage (907) 495-6284.

RIVERSIDE CAMPER PARK
PO Box 87, Houston, AK 99694
(907) 892-9020

privately operated
May 1st—Sept 1st
MP 57.5 Parks Highway

Located at MP 57.5 of the Parks Highway: 56 full hookups; 12 pull-throughs; **sewage dump station**; flush toilets; drinking water; hot showers; laundry facilities; covered picnic sites; tables; boat launch; fishing; separate tenting area; no time limit.

Riverside Camper Park is located on the bank of the Little Susitna River. Gravel, back-in campsites are wide enough that awnings can be opened. One toilet and shower for men and one toilet and shower for women are available in the main office building. Discounts are offered to Good Sam members and to active or retired military persons. A convenience store is within walking distance.

MILLER'S PLACE
(907) 892-6129

privately operated
MP 57.5 Parks Highway

Located at MP 57.5 of the Parks Highway: 50 spaces w/o hookups; pit toilets; flush toilets; drinking water; hot showers; laundry facilities; boat launch; fishing; no time limit.

Miller's Place is located on the Little Susitna River. The campground is little more than an unlevel, open field without designated spaces. Miller's Place is primarily a river charter fishing service with a small store.

LITTLE SUSITNA RIVER CAMPGROUND
City of Houston

open all year
MP 57.3 Parks Highway

Turn from the Parks Highway at MP 57.3 by the Houston Fire Station: 85 spaces w/o hookups; pit toilets; drinking water; covered pavilion; tables; fire rings; fishing; separate tenting area; 15 day limit.

Little Susitna River Campground is a heavily wooded area designed in the form of four interlocking rings. Some of the spaces are not level but the largest RVs can be accommodated. A covered pavilion and access to the river for fishing are provided. This is a quiet campground away from highway traffic noise.

ALASKA HISTORICAL & TRANSPORTATION MUSEUM
(907) 745-4493   MP 40 Parks Highway
Artifacts from Alaska's industrial and transportation past are displayed. Guided tours are available. Closed Sunday and Monday.

RV SERVICES BETWEEN DENALI AND WASILLA

CANTWELL CHEVRON   (907) 768-9342
Located 0.5 mile north of the Denali Highway junction at MP 210.5 of the Parks Highway: **sewage dump station**; general repairs; towing.

CACHE CREEK CHEVRON   (907) 733-2799
Located on the Parks Highway at the intersection with the Petersville Road: general repairs; towing; **propane**.

TIPPECANOE RENTALS   **(907) 495-6688**
PO Box 1175, Willow, AK 99688

Tippecanoe Rentals offers free pickup and delivery at designated spots within a fifteen mile radius of Willow. This includes both Nancy Lake Recreation Area and Willow Creek Recreation Area. Personalized guided float trips for small groups are offered.

THE GEORGE PARKS HIGHWAY OPTIONS

 THE GEORGE PARKS HIGHWAY: NORTH TO FAIRBANKS
Fairbanks is 317 miles north of Wasilla on the Parks Highway. Places to camp or visit include Big Lake, Nancy Lake State Recreation Area, and the town of Talkeetna. Denali National Park and Preserve is at MP 237.3.

 THE GEORGE PARKS HIGHWAY: SOUTH TO ANCHORAGE
Anchorage is 41 miles from Wasilla on the Parks and Glenn Highways. The terminus of the Parks Highway is 35 miles from Anchorage at its junction with the Glenn Highway.

 THE DENALI HIGHWAY: EAST TO PAXSON
The Denali Highway joins the Parks Highway at MP 209.9 by Cantwell. It extends east 134 miles to the Richardson Highway at Paxson. One campground on the west side of the Denali Highway and two on the east side are maintained by BLM.

 THE TALKEETNA SPUR ROAD
The junction of the Talkeetna Spur Road is located at mile 98.7 of the Parks Highway. Talkeetna offers float trips, fishing, and flightseeing to Mount McKinley. Round trip from the highway is twenty-nine miles.

Alaska Veterans Memorial: MP 147.2 George Parks Highway

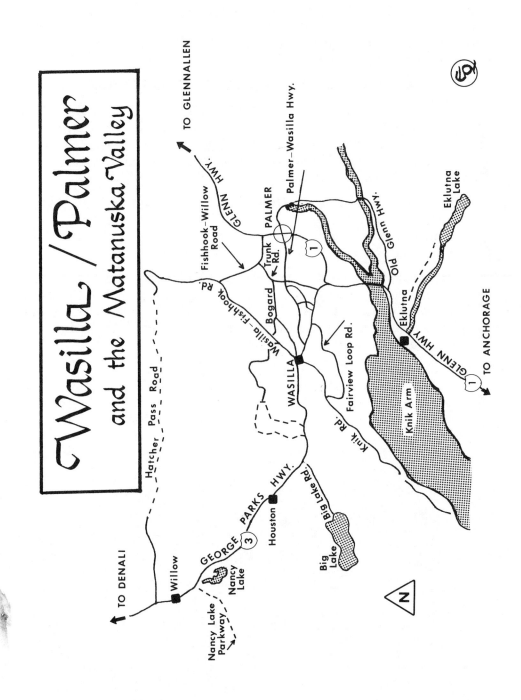

Wasilla/Palmer and the Matanuska Valley

Chapter 8

THE WASILLA/PALMER REGION

This chapter describes campgrounds and services in Big Lake, Wasilla and Palmer. Options include the George Parks Highway north to Fairbanks; the Glenn Highway leading west to Anchorage and the Kenai Peninsula; or the Glenn Highway leading east to Glennallen, Valdez, and Tok.

THE MATANUSKA-SUSITNA VALLEY

The Matanuska-Susitna Valley extends north on the George Parks Highway for several hundred miles, but this chapter is limited to the valley as encompassed by the cities of Big Lake, Wasilla and Palmer. The valley is probably best-known for the huge vegetables (record cabbage, ninety-eight pounds; record turnip, fifty-one pounds) which grow in its volcanic soil during twenty-hour summer days.

President Roosevelt's administration proposed developing the Matanuska Valley early in 1935 by allowing farmers from Michigan, Wisconsin and Minnesota to homestead Federal land. The economically troubled farmers and their families were given free transportation, forty acres of land, a home, farm buildings, livestock and equipment for which they agreed to pay $3,000 plus three percent interest over a thirty-year period. Unfortunately, there was little market for the crops they raised; within ten years, only twenty-five percent of the original Palmer farming community remained on the land.

INDEPENDENCE MINE STATE HISTORIC PARK   (907) 745-2827
Alaska Division of Parks and Outdoor Recreation

The Palmer–Fishhook Road branches from the Glenn Highway north of Palmer and ends at the junction with the Parks Highway at Wasilla. This Hatcher Pass drive has many hairpin turns and may be difficult for larger vehicles to negotiate. The Visitor Center highlights mining activities in the 1930s and 1940s. Tours are conducted several times each day.

MAT-SU VALLEY VISITOR CENTER   (907) 746-5000
HC01, Box 6166 J 21, Palmer, AK 99645   MP 35.5 Parks Highway

Turn onto Welcome Way from the Parks Highway by the entrance to the Best View RV Park. In addition to visitor information, the Cook Inlet and Chugach mountain range can be seen from the center's main level.

PALMER VISITOR INFORMATION CENTER   (907) 745-2880
PO Box 45, Palmer, AK 99645   South Valley Way

Turn east from the Glenn Highway at the signal light at Evergreen Avenue. The Matanuska-Susitna Experimental Garden is a walk-through garden located on the visitor center grounds.

IDITAROD HEADQUARTERS   **(907) 376-5155**
PO Box 870800, Wasilla, AK 99687   **Mile 2.2 Knik Road**

From the signal light at Main Street in Wasilla, turn west for 2.2 miles. This outstanding museum of Iditarod history and memorabilia displays dog sleds, harnesses and gear; videos for on-site viewing; trail photographs and information about the annual, thousand mile sled-dog race to Nome on the Iditarod Trail.

ALASKA STATE FAIR   **(907) 745-FAIR**
2075 Glenn Highway, Palmer, AK 99645

The Alaska State Fair opens on the fourth Friday of August and runs for eleven days through Labor Day. Displays and exhibits include agricultural products, farm animals, and homemaker demonstrations. Outdoor musical presentation, a rodeo and carnival are also featured.

HEALTH AND EMERGENCY SERVICES

MP 52.3 to MP 64.5	Houston Ambulance Service	911
	Wasilla Fire Department	(907) 376-5320
	Valley Hospital	(907) 745-4813
	Alaska State Troopers	(907) 745-2131

RV CAMPGROUNDS AT BIG LAKE

ROCKY LAKE STATE RECREATION SITE   **open all year**
Alaska State Park System   **MP 3.5 Big Lake Road**

Turn west onto Big Lake Road from the junction of the Parks Highway at MP 52.4. Drive 3.5 miles, then turn onto Beaver Road for 1.0 mile: 10 spaces w/o hookups; pit toilets; drinking water; boat launch; fishing; dumpster; 7 day limit.

Rocky Lake SRS is a wooded campground with lake access. A narrow road with short spaces at right angles makes access difficult. This campground is best suited to people driving small RVs, small travel trailers or tent campers. Tables, grills and other amenities are lacking.

SAIL 'N' FUN RESORT   **privately operated**
PO Box 520129, Big Lake, AK 99652   **May 1st—Sept 15th**
(907) 892-6298   **MP 1.5 North Shore Drive**

Turn west onto Big Lake Road from the junction of the Parks Highway at MP 52.4. Drive 3.5 miles, then turn right at Fisher's "Y" onto North Shore Drive for 1.5 miles. Turn left on the gravel road and follow signs: 20 spaces; 6 power hookups; 14 w/o hookups; chemical and pit toilets; tables; grills; boat launch; fishing; swimming; no time limit.

Sail 'N' Fun Resort has a steep hill and rough road for the final 0.2 mile. An open area has been set aside which can accommodate larger RVs. Chemical and pit toilets. A recreational area offers miniature golf, volleyball, horseshoes and badminton in addition to water sports. Two covered BBQ areas are available.

BIG LAKE NORTH STATE RECREATION SITE   open all year
Alaska State Park System   MP 5 North Big Lake Road

Turn west onto Big Lake Road from the junction of the Parks Highway at MP 52.4. Drive 3.5 miles, then turn right at Fisher's "Y" onto North Shore Drive for 1.5 miles: 60 spaces w/o hookups; pit toilets; drinking water; picnic shelters; tables; fire rings; boat launch; fishing; swimming; dumpster; 7 day limit.

Big Lake SRS offers a swimming area protected by roped, buoy markers. The designated RV area is open and has back-in, side-by-side parking. The 60 space estimate by the park service is more realistically 30-35. Nonetheless, the area can accommodate the largest RV. A parking area for boat trailers is provided. Pit toilets are accessible to the disabled.

BIG LAKE SOUTH STATE RECREATION SITE   open all year
Alaska State Park System   MP 5.2 South Big Lake Road

Turn west on Big Lake Road from the junction of the Parks Highway at MP 52.4. Drive 3.5 miles, then turn left at Fisher's "Y" onto South Big Lake Road. Drive 1.6 miles: 20 spaces w/o hookups; pit toilets; drinking water; 10 picnic sites; tables; fire rings; boat launch; fishing; 7 day limit.

Big Lake South SRS is a small, open campground with an easily accessed boat launch. Spaces are short and cannot accommodate a large RV. However, campers driving larger RVs might "eyeball" this attractive campground and, if it is not overcrowded, park in a manner which suits the rig. Pit toilets are accessible to the disabled.

Lions Club Sewage Dump Station   **Mile 3.4 Big Lake Road**

RV CAMPGROUNDS AT WASILLA

RAINBOW ACRES RV PARK   **privately operated**
PO Box 870989, Wasilla, AK 99687   **May 15th—Oct 1st**
(907) 376-8897   **MP 49.4 Parks Highway**

Located at MP 49.4 of the Parks Highway: 20 spaces with full hookups; **sewage dump station**; flush toilets; drinking water; hot showers; laundry facilities; tables; grills; trails; public phone; separate tenting area; no time limit.

Rainbow Acres RV Park is located near a small pond. It offers two fenced playgrounds for toddlers and small children. The graveled parking spaces are back-in and have no size limits. Open fires are prohibited. A two-day limit is placed on the designated tenting area.

Iditarod Trail Race Headquarters: Wasilla

LAKE LUCILLE RV PARK
open all year
Mat-Su Borough Parks and Recreation **access Knik Road**

Turn west at the signal light at the junction of Main Street and the Parks Highway. This becomes Knik Road. Drive 2.1 miles then turn at the sign before the Iditarod Trail Race Headquarter's building: 56 spaces w/o hookups; 2 pull-throughs; pit toilets; drinking water; covered pavilion; tables; grills; no time limit posted.

Lake Lucille RV Park is heavily wooded with narrow, back-in spaces which are not level and may require blocking. They vary in length but some can accommodate RVs to 35 feet. At least two pull-throughs are available. Lake Lucille can be reached by foot but has no boat launch. Pit toilets are located inside a concrete block building and are accessible to the disabled.

LITTLE SUSITNA CAMPGROUND
open all year
Alaska Department of Fish and Wildlife **Burma Road**

Turn west at the signal light at the junction of Main Street and the Parks Highway. Main Street becomes Knik Road. Drive 17.7 miles, then turn right on a 40 foot wide gravel road marked by a "Susitna Flats State Game Refuge" sign. Drive 7.6 miles until the road forms a "T". Turn right for 2.8 miles. Take the right fork at the "Y" for 3.0 miles: 130 spaces w/o hookups; **sewage dump station**; pit toilets; drinking water; picnic sites; tables; fire rings; boat launch; fishing; trails; 15 day limit.

Little Susitna Campground is a joint venture between the Alaska Department of Fish and Wildlife and the Alaska Division of Parks and Outdoor Recreation. The last miles into the campground are quite rough. Set on two levels with gravel throughout and numerous small stands of trees for aesthetic purposes, it features level campsites on gravel bases with easy turnaround maneuverability. RVs of any size can be accommodated. The lower level borders a salmon and trout fishing stream. A launch and parking area is reserved for boats. Toilets, inside sheltered buildings set on concrete slabs, are accessible to the disabled. Two full-time campground hosts are on site.

FINGER LAKE STATE RECREATION SITE
Alaska State Park System

open all year
MP 0.7 Bogard Road

Turn east at the signal light at the junction of Main Street and the Parks Highway. Drive three blocks then turn right onto Bogard Road for 6.6 miles: 41 spaces w/o hookups; pit toilets; drinking water; tables; fire rings; boat launch; fishing; trails; 7 day limit. (*note: a different set of driving instructions is given from Palmer*).

Finger Lake SRS is formed around two separate loops. The first loop has short, back-in spaces which are not level and may require blocking. The second loop forms a large, level turnaround area and will accommodate the largest RVs. Extensive reconstruction has improved lake access. The boat launch has an area set aside for boat trailer parking.

The Palmer/Wasilla office of the Division of Parks and Outdoor Recreation has headquarters near the entrance to this campground and rangers are responsive to questions.

WOLF LAKE STATE RECREATION SITE
Alaska State Park System

open all year
MP 2.5 Engstrom Road

Turn east at the signal light at the junction of Main Street and the Parks Highway. Drive three blocks and turn right onto Bogard Road for 6.8 miles to Engstrom Road. Turn left for 3.5 miles: 4 spaces without hookups; pit toilets; no drinking water; fishing; 7 day limit. (*note: a different set of driving instructions is given from Palmer*).

Wolf Lake SRS has four back-in, side-by-side spaces which are very short. Not set on the lake, it does offer lake access. Water must be boiled or treated chemically.

GREEN RIDGE CAMPER PARK
1130 Vicki Way, Wasilla, AK 99654
(907) 376-5899

privately operated
May 1st—Oct 1st
MP 39.5 Parks Highway

Turn east from the Parks Highway at MP 39.5 onto Seward Meridian Parkway: 35 spaces with full hookups; flush toilets; drinking water; hot showers; laundry facilities; tables; grills; public phone; no time limit.

Green Ridge Camper Park is a clean, well-maintained campground with large, grassed areas. A graveled, circular area with back-in spaces is featured. RVs of any size can be accommodated. Decorator trees in the area won't interfere with parking or the use of awnings. A youth playground area has swings and teeter-totters for small children.

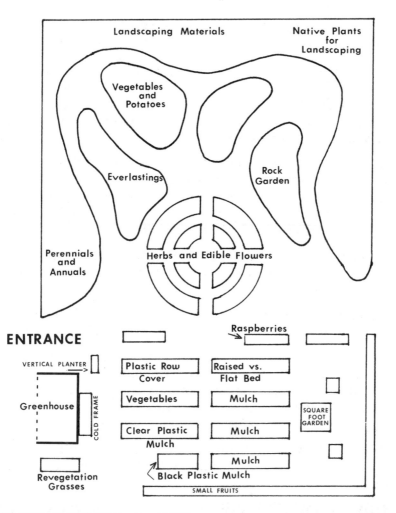

BEST VIEW RV PARK   privately operated
PO Box 872001, Wasilla, AK 99687   May 1st—Oct 30th
(907) 745-7400   1-800- 478-6600   MP 35.6 Parks Highway

Turn east from the Parks Highway onto one of two streets: Best View Street and Welcome Way: 64 spaces with full hookups; 14 pull-throughs; **sewage dump station**; flush toilets; drinking water; hot showers; laundry facilities; picnic sites; fire rings; public phone; separate tenting area; no time limit.

Best View RV Park has blacktopped roads throughout the campground with side-by-side parking. A section set aside for permanent mobile home residents is screened by a decorator fence. The campground offers an unsurpassed, panoramic view of the Chugach mountain range and the Cook Inlet. Good Sam discounts.

RV CAMPGROUNDS AT PALMER

THE HOMESTEAD RV PARK   privately operated
PO Box 354, Palmer, AK 99645   May 15th—Sept 15th
(907) 745-6005   MP 36 Glenn Highway

Located 0.5 mile northeast of the junction of the George Parks Highway with the Glenn Highway: 64 power and water hookups; 53 pull-throughs; **sewage dump station**; flush toilets; drinking water; hot showers; laundry facilities; tables; grills; public phone; no time limit.

The Homestead RV Park overlooks the Matanuska River valley and the Chugach mountain range. Pull-throughs can accommodate rigs up to 70 feet in length. Individual sites are separated by birch and cottonwood trees. An enclosed recreation center is available. Restrooms, built on concrete floors covered with dry deck, have ceramic tile in the showers, ivy plants as decor, hooks for clothing, and classical background music. Showers are clean and there is no charge for their use. Discounts are offered to Good Sam members.

KEPLER PARK CAMPGROUND   privately operated
Star Route B, Box 7810, Palmer, AK 99645   May 1st—Sept 15th
(907) 745-3053   MP 37.3 Glenn Highway

Located at MP 37.3 of the Glenn Highway, 1.8 miles northeast of the junction of the George Parks Highway and the Glenn Highway. Kepler Drive, the gravel road into the campground, doubles back to parallel the Glenn Highway which makes access difficult when driving east: 15 spaces w/o hookups; pit toilets; drinking water; tables; fire rings; fishing; swimming; trails; public phone; separate tenting area; no time limit.

Kepler Park Campground is located on Kepler Lake with access to Harriet and Bradley Lakes. A small wooden bridge, with weight restrictions, must be crossed to the designated camping area. Drivers with RVs longer than 25 feet should not consider camping here, not only because spaces are short, but also because little room is available for turning around. Lakes are stocked with trout and boat rentals are available.

WOLF LAKE STATE RECREATION SITE
Alaska State Park System

open all year
MP 2.5 Engstrom Road

Turn north at the signal light at the junction of the Glenn Highway and Evergreen Avenue. Drive approximately four miles to Trunk Road, turn right for 1.0 mile to the four-way stop at Bogard Road. Turn left for 0.3 mile to Engstrom Road. Then turn right for 3.5 miles: 4 spaces w/o hookups; pit toilets; no drinking water; fishing; 7 day limit. (*note: a different set of driving instructions is given from Wasilla*).

Wolf Lake SRS has four back-in, side-by-side spaces which are very short. Not set on the lake, it does offer lake access. Water must be boiled or treated chemically.

FINGER LAKE STATE RECREATION SITE
Alaska State Park System

open all year
MP 0.7 Bogard Road

Turn north at the signal light at the junction of the Glenn Highway and Evergreen Avenue. Drive approximately four miles to Trunk Road, turn right 1.0 mile to the four-way stop at Bogard Road. Turn left for 0.7 mile: 41 spaces w/o hookups; pit toilets; drinking water; tables; fire rings; boat launch; fishing; 7 day limit. (*note: a separate set of driving instructions is given from Wasilla*).

Finger Lake SRS is formed around two separate loops. The first loop has short, back-in spaces which are not level and may require blocking. The second loop forms a large, level turnaround area and will accommodate the largest RVs. The boat launch has an area set aside for boat trailer parking. The Palmer/Wasilla office of the Division of Parks and Outdoor Recreation has headquarters near the entrance; the rangers are quite responsive to questions.

MATANUSKA RIVER PARK
Mat-Su Borough Parks and Recreation

open all year
East Arctic Avenue

Turn onto West Arctic Avenue from the signal light at the intersection of the Glenn Highway. Drive 0.9 mile. Turn north on the gravel road marked by signs: 26 spaces; **sewage dump station**; flush toilets; drinking water; hot showers; covered picnic sites; limit for camping not known.

Matanuska River Park has a loop road which runs through the campground. Spaces are back-in, dry parking. Restrooms are located in a concrete block building. Four covered, pavilion-style picnic areas plus recreational areas including a children's' playground are provided. A small office registration building is adjacent to the campground host's trailer.

MOUNTAIN VIEW RV PARK
PO Box 2521, Palmer, AK 99645
(907) 745-5747

privately operated
open all year
Smith Road/Old Glenn Highway

Turn onto West Arctic Avenue from the signal light at the intersection of the Glenn Highway. Follow this road, which is the Old Glenn Highway, 1.3 miles past the Matanuska River bridge. Turn onto Smith Road for 0.6 mile until the road makes a right angle turn. Access from Anchorage can be made from the Old Glenn Highway cut off north of Eklutna Flats: 58 spaces; 23 full hookups; 10 power hookups; 25 w/o hookups; **sewage dump station**; flush toilets; drinking water; hot showers; covered pavilion; tables; public phone; separate tenting area; no time limit.

Mountain View RV Park offers a large open area with trees as windbreaks on three sides. A gravel-based road encircles the larger campground with four parallel roads leading to grassed pull-throughs. This campground is secluded and offers the Chugach mountains as a backdrop. Discounts are offered to Good Sam members. Mail can be forwarded to the above address for registered guests.

RV SERVICES IN THE MAT-SU AREA

CACHE CAMPER MANUFACTURING, INC.   **(907) 745-4061**
Located at mile 3.5 of the Palmer–Wasilla Highway: custom built truck campers are the primary function of Cache Camper. Motorhome chassis repairs are also performed.

WASILLA CHEVRON . . . SERVICE CENTER   **(907) 376-5900**
Located on the Parks Highway north of the signal light at the intersection of Main Street: alignment; electrical repair; brakes; tires; mufflers; general repairs; transmissions; emergency road service; welding; **sewage dump station**; **propane**. RV repairs are a specialty.

GOODYEAR HOUSE OF TIRES   **(907) 376-5279**
Located on the Parks Highway, 0.5 mile south of the signal light at the intersection by the Cotton Creek Mall: alignment; brakes; tires; mufflers; general repairs; emergency road service; towing; welding. They are authorized to provide 24-hour towing service for AAA, Allstate, and Good Sam members. A senior citizen discount is offered.

NORTHERN RECREATION RV PARTS   **(907) 376-8087**
Located on the east side of the Parks Highway, 1.0 mile south of the signal light at the intersection by the Cotton Creek Mall: RV parts and accessories; general repairs. Northern Recreation provides services and a full line of parts (hitches, plumbing and electrical).

NYE RV CENTER   **(907) 376-8923**
Located on the Parks Highway, 1.0 mile south of the Cotton Creek Mall: body repairs; electrical; parts and accessories; brakes; mufflers; general repairs; transmissions; tank repairs; emergency road service; towing; **propane**. Nye RV Center is a Ford dealership and an authorized representative for Jayco and Georgie Boy motorhomes.

VALLEY R/V   **(907) 745-5771**
Located on the east side of the Parks Highway at MP 36.5: body repairs; mufflers; general repairs; tank repairs; emergency road service; welding;

propane. Valley R/V provides service and repairs on most models. A discount is offered to senior citizens and active or retired military.

PALMER CHEVRON   (907) 746-6363
Located at the signal light at the intersection of the Glenn Highway and Evergreen Avenue: alignment; tires; general repairs; towing; **sewage dump station; propane**.

EAGLE VIEW CAR WASH
Turn onto Evergreen Avenue toward the Carr's Mall from the signal light at the intersection of the Glenn Highway. Drive 3.0 miles to the corner of 49th Street: This car wash has two bays: self-service, coin-operated.

DEE'S TRUCK & EQUIPMENT PARTS   (907) 745-1900
Turn onto West Evergreen Avenue from the signal light at the intersection of the Glenn Highway. Cross the railroad tracks and turn right. Turn left onto East Elmwood Avenue to 1226 South Chugach. A full selection of RV and trailer parts is available.

WASILLA/PALMER OPTIONS

THE GEORGE PARKS HIGHWAY: NORTH TO FAIRBANKS
Fairbanks is 323 miles north of the junction of the George Parks Highway and the Glenn Highway. Camping opportunities include Big Lake, the Nancy Lake Recreation Area, and Denali National Park and Preserve. The Denali Highway junction east to Paxson and the Richardson Highway is at Cantwell.

THE GLENN HIGHWAY: WEST TO ANCHORAGE
Anchorage is thirty-five miles west of the junction of the George Parks Highway. Anchorage is the largest city in Alaska and affords a number of cultural as well as recreational opportunities. The Seward Highway, leading to the Kenai Peninsula, is accessed through Anchorage.

THE GLENN HIGHWAY: EAST TO GLENNALLEN
The Glenn Highway leads east to Glennallen. The Glenn Highway is interrupted by the Richardson Highway leading north from Glennallen but continues once again from the junction at Gakona to Tok and the Canadian border.

Chapter 9

THE MUNICIPALITY OF ANCHORAGE

This chapter describes campgrounds and services in Anchorage. Options include the Glenn Highway which forms a junction with the George Parks Highway to Fairbanks west of Anchorage, and the Seward Highway which leads south to the Kenai Peninsula and forms a junction with the Sterling Highway.

ANCHORAGE, ALASKA

Anchorage is an urban community and home to more than forty percent of Alaska's people. Because of its large population and its sprawling location between Cook Inlet and the Chugach mountain range, it is factiously described as "a big city close to Alaska." One community on the George Parks Highway has the audacity to describe itself as the point where the "real Alaska begins."

Anchorage is not only the state's population center, it is also the state's transportation hub. Freight is transported by highway, railroad, sea and air carriers. Parallel to Helsinki, Finland to the north and Honolulu, Hawaii to the west, Anchorage serves international air carriers to Europe and the Orient. Both Federal Express and United Parcel Service maintain cargo redistribution terminals at Anchorage International Airport. Domestic and international airlines process nearly 4.5 million passengers through the terminal each year.

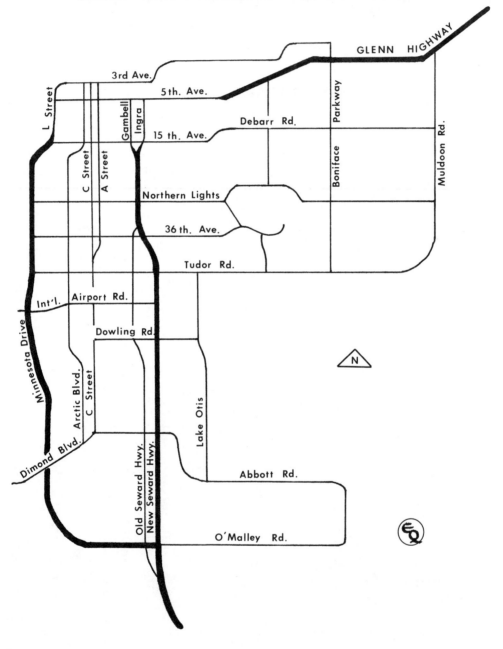

Anchorage caters to its young, active population. Cyclists use nearly ninety miles of bike trails during the summer and cross-country skiers use the same trails during the winter. Lakes attract swimmers even though water temperatures rarely exceed sixty-eight degrees during summer months. The half million acres in Chugach State Park draw back-packers to the old Iditarod Trail and Flattop Mountain, the park's most frequently climbed peak. Even Turnagain Arm has wet suited windsurfers and jet skiers who test their skills against the power of its unpredictable tides.

Not all activities are out-of-doors, however. Students can choose to attend the University of Alaska or Alaska Pacific University. Nearly 900,000 readers are attracted each year to the stacks in the Loussac Library and its branches. Geneologists have 28,000 rolls of microfilmed documents and other historical data from Alaska's past which can be perused in the regional office of the "National Archives and Records Administration."

The Anchorage Museum of History and Art features exhibitions by contemporary Alaskan artists, craft exhibits such as "Earth, Fire, and Fibre," and Native dance performances throughout the year. Each November the Sullivan Sports Arena hosts college basketball teams for the "Great Alaska Shootout." The concert association, the opera company, and the symphony share three stages at the Anchorage Center for Performing Arts with their productions, and the Egan Convention Center attracts a variety of national organizations. There seems to be something for each of the 226,338 people identified by the 1990 census who call Anchorage their home.

ACVB LOG CABIN VISITOR INFORMATION CENTER
546 West Fourth Avenue, Anchorage, AK 99501   (907) 274-3531

The Anchorage Convention Visitor Bureau (ACVB) Visitor Information Center is located at the corner of Fourth Avenue and F Streets. It provides general information about Anchorage: things to do; things to see; places to go. Maps and brochures describe current activities in the Anchorage bowl area.

A daily recording of events and activities to enjoy in Anchorage is provided by Anchorage Convention Visitor Bureau.   (907) 276-3200

ALASKA PUBLIC LANDS INFORMATION CENTER (APLIC)
605 West Fourth Avenue, Anchorage, AK 99501   (907) 271-2737

The center is located in the Old Federal Building at the corner of Fourth Avenue and F Streets, diagonally across the street from the Anchorage Visitor Information Center. One of three APLICs sponsored by a consortium of State and Federal agencies, the center features educational films, book and map sales, trip planning assistance, and information on state and national parks, wildlife refuges, and recreation areas. Mounted wildlife is displayed.

Guaranteed reservations for a limited number of RV parking spaces or bus seats at Denali National Park can be arranged through the APLIC.

Reservations must be made in person at the APLIC counter. Reservations can be made from seven to twenty-one days in advance.

NATIONAL ARCHIVES: ALASKA REGION
654 West Third Avenue, Anchorage, AK 99501   **(907) 271-2441**

The archives are located behind the Old Federal Building at the corner of Fourth Avenue and F Streets, diagonally across the street from the Anchorage Visitor Information Center. Nearly 53,000 rolls of microfilm as well as historically valuable federal paper records are available to the public. Geneologists will find Federal population censuses for all states from 1790-1920 as well as for Alaska's Territorial years.

ANCHORAGE CONVENTION AND VISITOR'S BUREAU
1600 "A" Street, Anchorage, AK 99501   **(907) 276-4118**

Write or FAX (907) 278-5559 ACVB and request a complimentary copy of the "Anchorage Visitors Guide" which describes activities and services not only in Anchorage but Southcentral Alaska and the Kenai Peninsula as well.

ALASKA AVIATION HERITAGE MUSEUM   **(907) 248-5325**
Located on the south shore of Lake Hood at 4721 Aircraft Drive, the Air Museum offers a rare collection of historical photographs and films from early flight services, photos and memorabilia of items used by Alaska's first bush pilots, plus a large collection of rare historical Alaskan aircraft.

THE ALASKA ZOO   **(907) 346-2133**
Located at 4731 O'Malley Road, the zoo provides visitors with the opportunity to see most native Alaskan animals such as bears, moose, wolves, and eagles.

EAGLE RIVER VISITOR CENTER   **(907) 694-2108**
Located at MP 12 Eagle River Road. Exit the Glenn Highway at the Eagle River overpass and turn onto Eagle River Road at the signal light. The road is blacktopped to the visitor center. Geology and wildlife displays are featured at the center. Video films on indigenous wildlife and the aurora borealis are shown hourly. Park rangers offer guided hikes and nature programs in Chugach State Park.

POTTER SECTION HOUSE
Located south of the Anchorage Coastal Wildlife Refuge at MP 115 of the Seward Highway. This historic building is operated by the Kenai Peninsula Borough's Economic Development District as a visitor center describing the attractions on the Kenai Peninsula. A snow plow and section car are displayed as part of the state historic site.

HEALTH AND EMERGENCY SERVICES

Anchorage Police Dept/Fire Dept/Paramedics	**(907) 276-7232**
Alaska State Troopers – Seward Highway/Girdwood	**(907) 783-2525**
Providence Hospital	**(907) 562-2211**
Alaska Regional Hospital	**(907) 276-1131**

Overlooking Westchester Lagoon toward downtown Anchorage

RV CAMPGROUNDS IN THE GREATER ANCHORAGE AREA

EKLUTNA LAKE CAMPGROUND   **Memorial Day to Labor Day**
Alaska State Park System   **MP 26.5 Glenn Highway**

Exit the Glenn Highway at the Eklutna overpass then turn right at the "T" for 0.4 mile. Turn onto the paved road (which becomes gravel in two miles) and continue for a total of ten miles: 50 spaces w/o hookups; 1 pull-through; pit toilets; 32 picnic sites; tables; fire rings; boat launch; fishing; trails; public phone; separate tenting area; 15 day limit.

Eklutna Lake Campground is set on the lake against a back-drop of rugged mountains. Spaces are wide, level and set on gravel bases. Space lengths vary but the largest RVs can be accommodated. An overflow area is also available. Pit toilets are accessible to the handicapped. An unusual feature is the use of all terrain vehicles (ATVs) which is allowed. A full-time host is on site. Birch, cottonwood and aspen trees abound as do grizzly bears, Dall sheep and moose. The beauty of the area compensates for the long, difficult drive into the campground.

EKLUTNA LODGE AND RESTAURANT   **privately operated**
PO Box 670789, Chugiak, AK 99567   **May 1st—Sept 30th**
(907) 688-3150   **MP 26.0 Glenn Highway**

Exit the Glenn Highway at the Eklutna overpass and turn left at the "T". Follow the blacktop road which parallels the Glenn Highway north for 0.6 mile: 20 spaces; 15 full hookups; 5 no hookups; **sewage dump station**; flush toilets; drinking water; hot showers; laundry facilities; tables; grills; no time limit.

Eklutna Lodge and Restaurant operates a small motel, liquor store and bar as well as the camping area. Spaces are level and set back from the road. Tent space is available.

PETERS CREEK PETITE CAMPER PARK   privately operated
20940 Old Glenn Highway, Chugiak, AK 99567   May 15th–Oct 15th
(907) 688-2487   MP 21.5 Old Glenn Highway

Exit the Glenn Highway at the South Peters Creek exit. Turn south on the Old Glenn Highway: 32 spaces; 12 full hookups; 10 power and water hookups; 10 power only hookups; **sewage dump station**; drinking water; no time limit.

Peters Creek Petite Camper Park is located, in part, on a level, graveled lot behind an apartment house and on an uneven grassed field among trees. The grassed area offers a view of the Chugach mountain range. The owner described the campground as "a small, friendly, hard-to-find place."

EAGLE RIVER CAMPGROUND   Memorial Day to Labor Day
Alaska State Park System   MP 12.6 Glenn Highway

Exit the Glenn Highway at Hiland Road overpass. Turn north on the black-topped, frontage road which parallels the Glenn Highway for 0.7 mile. A sign is located at the point where the road becomes gravel: 50 spaces w/o hookups; 3 pull-throughs; pit toilets; flush toilets; drinking water; picnic sites; tables; fire rings; fishing; trails; 4 day limit.

Eagle River Campground is tiered on a hillside with two major, circular gravel roads. Three dead-end roads branch from the main ones. Spaces vary in length and can accommodate RVs to about thirty feet in length. Trees between sites serve as visual barriers. At least three pull-throughs can accommodate longer RVs. Pit toilets are located throughout the campground; flush toilets are in an enclosed building constructed on a concrete slab. Toilets are accessible to the handicapped. A full-time campground host is on site.

FORT RICHARDSON ARMY BASE   (907) 384-1480
United States Army   Fort Richardson Main Gate

Exit the Glenn Highway at the Fort Richardson/Arctic Valley overpass. Ask for directions at the main gate to I.T.R. (International Travel Reservations) in Building 600: 23 spaces with full hookups; **sewage dump station** flush toilets; drinking water; hot showers; laundry facilities; tables; grills; separate tenting area. 14 day limit.

Black Spruce Campground is open to active duty personnel and their families including National Guard and Army Reserves, and Department of Defense personnel. A playground is provided for children. Reservations should be made as far in advance as possible. The campground is open from mid-May to mid-September. An alternate number is (907) 384-1110 for the main switchboard.

CENTENNIAL CAMPER PARK   **Municipality of Anchorage**
Department of Parks & Recreation   **Memorial Day to Labor Day**
(907) 248-4346   FAX (907) 278-6595   **8300 Glenn Highway**

Exit the Glenn Highway at the Muldoon Road overpass. Turn north on Boundary Avenue, the first street. Drive one block, turn left, then follow the frontage road which parallels the Glenn Highway (0.5 mile): 83 spaces w/o hookups; 3 pull-throughs; **sewage dump station**; flush toilets; drinking water; hot showers; tables; fire rings; trails; public phone; separate tenting area; 14 day limit.

Centennial Camper Park is sponsored by the Anchorage Department of Parks and Outdoor Recreation and is located in a heavily wooded area with interconnecting, blacktopped roads throughout the campground. Spaces are level and vary in length but some can accommodate RVs up to 40 feet. The camper park has access to the Anchorage bike trail system and is walking distance to a nearby baseball diamond and covered picnic area. TTY phone contact is also available (907) 343-6457. Discounts are offered to "Golden Age Pass" holders.

ELMENDORF AIR FORCE BASE (907) 552-4015
United States Air Force   Main Gate/Boniface Parkway Entrance

Exit the Glenn Highway at Boniface Parkway. Ask for directions at the main gate to FAMCAMP: 39 spaces with water and electricity; flush toilets; drinking water; hot showers; laundry facilities; **sewage dump station**; tables; grills; playground for children; 14 day limit.

FAMCAMP requires that advance telephone reservations be made through the campground coordinator in the billeting office. However, campers without prior reservations may be accepted on a "space available" basis. Priority is given to active duty air force personnel and their families. Secondary consideration is given to retired military, reservists and members of the National Guard. The campground is open from mid-May to mid-September. An alternate number is (907) 552-1110 for the main switchboard.

EAST ANCHORAGE CAMPER PARK   privately operated
5800 Glenn Highway, Anchorage, AK 99504   May 1st—Sept 1st
(907) 333-1533   5800 Glenn Highway

Exit the Glenn Highway at the Boniface Parkway overpass. Turn north on the frontage road which parallels the Glenn Highway (0.3 mile): 30 spaces with full hookups; flush toilets; drinking water; hot showers; laundry facilities; public phone; no time limit.

East Anchorage Camper Park is located next to a motel/apartment complex. Spaces are not set on gravel pads. Utilities are at the rear of each space. Although there is no recreation in the immediate area, the camper park is easy driving distance to downtown Anchorage as well as to tourist points of interest.

RUSSIAN JACK . . . LIONS' PARK   Municipality of Anchorage
Department of Parks & Recreation   Memorial Day to Labor Day
(907) 248-4346   FAX (907) 278-6595   800 Boniface Parkway

Exit the Glenn Highway at the Boniface Parkway overpass. Drive 0.5 mile south: 50 spaces; flush toilets; drinking water; hot showers; picnic sites; public phone; separate tenting area; trails; 14 day limit.

Russian Jack Springs–Lions' Park is sponsored by the Anchorage Department of Parks and Outdoor Recreation and is located by Russian Jack Park. The maximum recommended RV length is thirty feet. Facilities at the adjacent Russian Jack Springs Park include a nine hole golf course, softball fields, tennis courts and picnic areas. Discounts are offered to "Golden Age Pass" holders.

JOHN'S MOTEL AND RV PARK
privately operated
3543 Mountain View Drive, Anchorage, AK 99508   **open all year**
(907) 277-4332   **1-800-478-4332**   **3543 Mountain View Drive**

Turn north from the Glenn Highway at the signal light onto Bragaw Street. Drive one block then turn left at the signal light at Mountain View Drive: 60 spaces; 46 full hookups; 10 power and water hookups; 4 w/o hookups; **sewage dump station**; flush toilets; drinking water; hot showers; laundry facilities; tables; public phone; no time limit.

John's Motel and RV Park is an adult park. Pets are welcome. Spaces are level in a large, open area. Some spaces are not available for short term use. The park is near a major mall and is 2.5 miles to downtown Anchorage. Discounts are offered to Good Sam members and to senior citizens. Reservations are encouraged using the Alaska 800 number.

GOLDEN NUGGET RV PARK
privately operated
4100 DeBarr Road, Anchorage, AK 99508   **May 15th—Sept 30th**
(907) 333-2012   **FAX (907) 333-1016**   **4100 DeBarr Road**

Turn south from the signal light at Bragaw Street. Drive to the signal light at DeBarr Road then turn east one block to Hoyt Street: 112 spaces with full hookups; 6 power and water hookups; 13 power only hookups; 1 pull-through; flush toilets; drinking water; hot showers; laundry facilities; tables; grills; public phone; separate tenting area; no time limit.

Golden Nugget Camper Park is screened from the road by fences. Spaces are level and easily accessed. Cable TV and telephone hookups are available. A separate picnic area and a fenced play area for children is provided. The camper park is walking distance to Russian Jack Park and to buses serving downtown Anchorage.

SHIP CREEK LANDING
privately operated
PO Box 200947, Anchorage AK 99520-0947   **May 15th–Sept 15th**
(907) 277-0877   **FAX (907) 277-3808**   **Ingra Street at East First Ave**

The Glenn Highway becomes East Fifth Avenue as it nears Anchorage. Turn north on Ingra Street from East Fifth Avenue. Stay in the center lane and cross Third Avenue. Continue down the hill and turn left on East First Avenue: 81 spaces w/o hookups; **sewage dump station**; drinking water; no time limit.

Ship Creek Landing is a partially developed campground which parallels the railroad tracks. A chain-link fence separates the grounds from the railroad tracks. Spaces are level, gravel-based, side-by-side, back-ins. Ship Creek has a summer salmon run. The campground is close to downtown Anchorage. Anticipate noise at night.

HILLSIDE MOTEL AND RV PARK
privately operated

2150 Gambell Street, Anchorage, AK 99509 — May 1st—Oct 15th

(907 258-6006   1-800- 478-6008 Alaska   2150 Gambell Street

The Glenn Highway becomes East Fifth Avenue as it nears Anchorage. Turn south at the signal light onto Gambell Street. Located halfway up the hill past the Sullivan Sports Arena: 78 spaces; 59 full hookups; 19 w/o hookups; **sewage dump station**; flush toilets; drinking water; hot showers; laundry facilities; picnic sites; **propane**; public phone; no time limit.

Hillside Motel and RV Park is centrally located in the midtown section of Anchorage. Spaces are back-in, side-by-side on paved surfaces. The largest RV can be accommodated. An additional graveled, overflow area is available. Nearby municipal bicycle trails are easily accessed. Reservations are encouraged using the Alaska 800 number.

HIGHLANDER CAMPER PARK
privately operated

2706 Fairbanks Street, Anchorage, AK 99503   May 1st—Sept 30th

(907) 277-2407   2706 Fairbanks Street

The Glenn Highway becomes East Fifth Avenue as it nears Anchorage. Turn south at the signal light onto Gambell Street. Drive south to the signal light at Northern Lights Boulevard. Turn west one block to Fairbanks Street: 52 spaces; 48 full hookups; 4 w/o hookups; **sewage dump station**; flush toilets; drinking water; hot showers; laundry facilities; no time limit.

Highlander Camper Park has a large, fenced area with level, gravel-based spaces. Parking is back-in, side-by-side. The largest RV can be accommodated. The camper park is on city water and sewer and is walking distance to a major shopping mall.

BIRD CREEK CAMPGROUND
Alaska State Park System

Memorial Day to Labor Day

MP 101.5 Seward Highway

Located south of Anchorage at MP 101.5 of the Seward Highway: 25 spaces w/o hookups; pit toilets; drinking water; covered picnic sites; tables; fire rings; fishing; trails; 7 day limit.

Bird Creek Campground has several roads through stands of Sitka spruce. Spaces are level back-ins with trees separating spaces. Most large RVs can be accommodated. An overflow area is located directly across the highway. Pit toilets are set on concrete vaults and are accessible to the disabled. A fulltime campground host is on site. Although the trees shelter the area from normal traffic noise, there could be problems with noise at night since the Alaska Railroad tracks parallel the campground.

RV SERVICES IN ANCHORAGE (listed alphabetically)

AAMCO   1-800-478-2627   **(907) 563-2626**
automatic and manual transmission repair; towing in Anchorage area.

ABC TOWING   **(907) 522-1456**
twenty-four hour towing service available.

ALASKA MUFFLER   **(907) 276-4021**
muffler repairs and welding.

ALASKA SPRING   1-800-478-3802   **(907) 563-3802**
alignment, brakes, springs, suspension.

AL'S CARBURETION   **(907) 344-4384**
alignment, brakes, carburetor repairs, emission control repairs, tuneups.

ARCTIC ALIGNMENT AND M/H REPAIRS   **(907) 276-2727**
alignment, brakes, collision repairs, **propane**, general repairs, springs, tank repairs, towing, welding.

AURORA TOWING   **(907) 338-1979**
emergency road service, 24 hour towing.

B & B TRANSMISSIONS   **(907) 349-3573**
automatic transmission repairs, free towing in the Anchorage area, ATRA certified mechanics.

CALL EARL CHEVRON #1   **(907) 562-2414**
petroleum products, general repairs, towing, **sewage dump station**, **propane**.

CALL EARL CHEVRON #2   **(907)337-2512**
petroleum products, general repairs, sewage dump station.

CALL EARL RV SERVICE CENTER   **(907) 562-0133**
alignment, brakes, general repairs, generator sets, carbueration, electrical repairs, parts and accessories, mufflers, transmissions, welding.

CLINE'S TEXACO   **(907) 277-3241**
petroleum products, **sewage dump station**.

CRAIG TAYLOR EQUIPMENT SALES & SERVICE   **(907) 276-5050**
Kohler generator set repairs.

CUMMINS NORTHWEST   **(907) 279-7594**
ONAN generator set repairs.

DEAN'S AUTOMOTIVE SERVICE CENTER   **(907) 276-5731**
alignment, brakes, electrical, alternators, radiator repairs, welding.

EDDIE'S CHEVRON   **(907) 277-7424**
petroleum products, **sewage dump station**, **propane**.

FIFTH AVENUE AUTO AND RV CENTER   **(907) 272-8228**
alignment, brakes, collision repair, generator sets, mufflers, parts and accessories, spring repair, tank repair, welding.

FOUNTAIN CHEVRON   **(907) 272-4142**
petroleum products, **sewage dump station**.

G.E.M. CAMPER AND AUTOBODY REPAIR   (907) 694-2885
complete collision repairs (located in Eagle River).

HEGEDUS & SONS   (907) 274-6602
alignment, brakes, general repairs, Firestone tires.

INDIAN HILLS CHEVRON   (907) 333-9000
petroleum products, **sewage dump station**, **propane**.

JOHNSON'S TIRE SERVICE   (907) 349-8000
alignment, brakes, mufflers, (full size RV hoist) RV wheels and tire sizes.

JOHNSON'S TIRE SERVICE/EAGLE RIVER   (907) 694-5055
alignment, brakes, mufflers, tires.

MAPCO # 8   (907) 272-6701
petroleum products, **sewage dump station**.

MOBILE TRAILER SUPPLY, INC.   (907) 277-1811
parts/accessories, furnace parts, general repairs, **sewage dump station**.

MOUNTAIN VIEW CAR WASH   (907) 279-4819
large bays, self-service, **sewage dump station**.

N & S TEXACO   (907) 277-8331
trailer hitches, wiring, brake controls, tow bars, air springs, welding.

RV ELECTRIC   (907) 349-1808
alternators, ONAN generator sets, refrigerators, water heaters, furnaces.

SOURDOUGH CAMPER VILLAGE   (907) 563-3277
parts/accessories, general repairs, tire service.

TRAILER CRAFT   (907) 563-3238
brakes, general repairs, collision repairs, wiring, lights, wheels, welding.

TRANSMISSION WORLD   (907) 276-2112
automatic and standard transmission repairs, ATRA certified mechanics.

TRAVELWELL OF ALASKA FAX (907) 344-0644   (907) 349-8845
body repairs, generator sets, carbueration and fuel injection, electrical repairs, repairs of a general nature. Ford warranty service center.

TRIPLE A SERVICE   (907) 277-0723
petroleum products, **sewage dump station**.

RV DUMP STATION LOCATIONS

CALL EARL CHEVRON #1	**815 West International Airport Rd**
CALL EARL CHEVRON #2	**415 Muldoon Rd**
CLINE'S TEXACO	**422 Gambell Blvd**
EDDIE'S CHEVRON	**832 East Fifth Ave**
FOUNTAIN CHEVRON	**3608 Minnesota Dr**
INDIAN HILLS CHEVRON	**6470 DeBarr Rd**
MAPCO #8	**717 East Northern Lights Blvd**
MOBILE TRAILER SUPPLY	**3150 Mountain View Dr**
MOUNTAIN VIEW CAR WASH	**3433 Commercial Dr**
TRIPLE A SERVICE	**1304 Airport Heights Dr**

ANCHORAGE OPTIONS

THE GLENN HIGHWAY: EAST TO GLENNALLEN

The Glenn Highway east from Anchorage to Glennallen offers options to Delta Junction, Tok and Valdez. Thirty-five miles west of Anchorage, the highway forms a junction with the George Parks Highway which leads north to Denali National Park and Fairbanks.

Anchorage to Denali National Park	237 miles
Anchorage to Fairbanks	358 miles
Anchorage to Haines	775 miles
Anchorage to the Matanuska Glacier	102 miles
Anchorage to Palmer/Wasilla	42 miles
Anchorage to Skagway	830 miles
Anchorage to Tok	328 miles
Anchorage to Valdez	304 miles

THE SEWARD HIGHWAY: SOUTH TO SEWARD

The Seward highway south from Anchorage to Seward offers options to Portage Glacier, the Hope cut-off, and the Sterling Highway to Kenai, Soldotna and Homer.

Anchorage to Homer	226 miles
Anchorage to Kenai/Soldotna	136 miles
Anchorage to Portage Glacier	53 miles
Anchorage to Seward	127 miles

Eagle River Campground

Chapter 10

THE SOUTHERN TIER

This chapter describes campgrounds and services on the Glenn Highway between Anchorage and Glennallen. The single option offered from the Glenn Highway is the junction with the George Parks Highway which leads north to Denali National Park and Fairbanks.

THE GLENN HIGHWAY TO GLENNALLEN

The beginning of the Glenn Highway in Anchorage can be identified as the corner of Merrill Field at the signal light marking the junction with Airport Heights and Mountain View Drives. Points of interest on the Glenn Highway to Glennallen include Palmer, Sutton, the Matanuska Glacier, and Lake Louise.

RVers who are interested in plant and vertebrate fossils will find Sutton a fascinating place. Leaf and petrified wood fossils, deposited fifty million years ago, are common in the area; vertebrate fossils are less common but have been found. Because of Sutton's coal mining history, many of the fossils have been located in the area's abandoned mines. Petrified wood can occasionally be found near Moose Creek Campground. For additional information contact the Chugach Gem and Mineral Society in Anchorage.

EAGLE RIVER VISITOR CENTER   (907) 694-2108

Located at MP 12 Eagle River Road. Exit the Glenn Highway at the Eagle River overpass and turn onto Eagle River Road at the signal light. The road is blacktopped to the visitor center. Geology and wildlife displays are featured and video films on indigenous wildlife and the aurora borealis are shown hourly. Park rangers offer guided nature programs in Chugach State Park.

PALMER VISITOR INFORMATION CENTER   (907) 745-2880
PO Box 45, Palmer, AK 99645   South Valley Way

Turn onto Evergreen Avenue at the Glenn Highway signal light. In addition to printed materials describing attractions in the Matanuska-Susitna Valley, the visitor center has a walk-through garden on the grounds which contains a variety of flowers and vegetables.

HEALTH AND EMERGENCY SERVICES

Alaska State Troopers		(907) 745-2131 or 911
Valley Hospital		(907) 745-4813
MP 52 to MP 120	Sutton Ambulance Service	911
MP 120 to MP 189	Copper River EMS (Glennallen)	(907) 822-3203

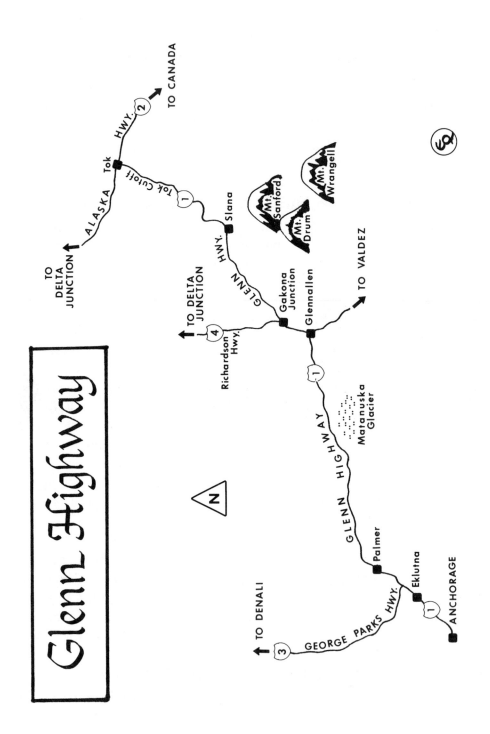

Glenn Highway

VIEWING AREAS FROM THE GLENN HIGHWAY

MP 101	Matanuska Glacier as seen from the Mat-Su SRS
MP 102	Matanuska Glacier as seen from the Glacier Park Resort
MP 102	Matanuska Glacier as seen from the Long Rifle Lodge
MP 113	Sheep Mountain as seen from Sheep Mountain Lodge
MP 128	Matanuska Glacier as seen from the Eureka Lodge
MP 175-89	Wrangell Mountains as seen toward Glennallen

RV CAMPGROUNDS ON THE GLENN HIGHWAY

EAGLE RIVER CAMPGROUND   **open all year**
Alaska State Park System   **MP 12.6 Glenn Highway**

Exit the Glenn Highway at Hiland Road overpass. Turn north on the blacktopped, frontage road which parallels the Glenn Highway for 0.7 mile. A sign is located at the point where the road becomes gravel: 50 spaces w/o hookups; 3 pull-throughs; pit toilets; flush toilets; drinking water; picnic sites; tables; fire rings; fishing; trails; 4 day limit.

Eagle River Campground is tiered on a hillside with two major, circular gravel roads. Three dead-end roads branch from the main ones. Spaces vary in length and can accommodate RVs to about thirty feet in length. Trees between sites serve as visual barriers. At least three pull-throughs can accommodate longer RVs. Pit toilets are located throughout the campground; flush toilets are in an enclosed building constructed on a concrete slab. Toilets are accessible to the disabled.

PETERS CREEK PETITE CAMPER PARK   **privately operated**
20940 Old Glenn Highway, Chugiak, AK 99567   **May 15th–Oct 15th**
(907) 688-2487   **MP 21.5 Old Glenn Highway**

Exit the Glenn Highway at the South Peters Creek exit. Turn south on the Old Glenn Highway: 32 spaces; 12 full hookups; 10 power and water hookups; 10 power only hookups; **sewage dump station**; drinking water; no time limit.

Peters Creek Petite Camper Park is located, in part, on a level, graveled lot behind an apartment house and on an uneven grassed field among trees. The grassed area offers a view of the Chugach mountain range. The owner described the campground as "a small, friendly, hard-to-find place."

EKLUTNA LODGE AND RESTAURANT   **privately operated**
PO Box 670789, Chugiak, AK 99567   **May 1st—Sept 30th**
(907) 688-3150   **MP 26.0 Glenn Highway**

Exit the Glenn Highway at the Eklutna overpass and turn left at the "T". Follow the blacktop road which parallels the Glenn Highway north for 0.6 mile: 20 spaces; 15 full hookups; 5 w/o hookups; **sewage dump station**; flush toilets; drinking water; hot showers; laundry facilities; tables; grills; no time limit.

Eklutna Lodge and Restaurant operates a small motel, liquor store and bar as well as the RV camping area. Spaces are level and set back from the road. Tent camping is available.

EKLUTNA LAKE CAMPGROUND May 1st—Sept 30th
Alaska State Park System MP 26.5 Glenn Highway

Exit the Glenn Highway at the Eklutna overpass then turn right at the "T" for 0.4 mile. Turn onto the paved road (which becomes gravel in two miles) and continue for a total of ten miles: 50 spaces w/o hookups; 1 pull-through; pit toilets; 32 picnic sites; tables; fire rings; boat launch; fishing; trails; public phone; separate tenting area; 15 day limit.

Eklutna Lake Campground is set on the lake against a backdrop of rugged mountains. Spaces are wide, level and set on gravel bases. Space lengths vary but the largest RVs can be accommodated. An overflow area is also available. Pit toilets are accessible to the disabled. An unusual feature is the use of all terrain vehicles (ATVs) which is allowed. A fulltime host is on site. Birch, cottonwood and aspen trees abound as do grizzly bears, Dall sheep and moose. The beauty of the area compensates for the long, difficult drive into the campground.

GLENN HIGHWAY OPTION

THE GEORGE PARKS HIGHWAY: NORTH TO FAIRBANKS
Fairbanks is 323 miles north of the junction of the George Parks Highway and the Glenn Highway. Camping opportunities include Big Lake, the Nancy Lake Recreation Area, and Denali National Park and Preserve. The Denali Highway junction east to Paxson and the Richardson Highway is at Cantwell.

Note: The junction of the George Parks Highway with the Glenn Highway is at MP 34.3.

THE HOMESTEAD RV PARK privately operated
PO Box 354, Palmer, AK 99645 May 15th—Sept 15th
(907) 745-6005 MP 36 Glenn Highway

Located 0.5 mile northeast of the junction of the George Parks Highway with the Glenn Highway: 64 power and water hookups; 53 pull-throughs; **sewage dump station**; flush toilets; drinking water; hot showers; laundry facilities; tables; grills; public phone; no time limit.

The Homestead RV Park overlooks the Matanuska River valley and the Chugach mountain range. Pull-throughs can accommodate rigs up to 70 feet in length. Individual sites are separated by birch and cottonwood trees. An enclosed recreation center and picnic sites with grills and fire rings are available. Restrooms, built on concrete floors covered with dry deck, have ceramic tile in the showers, ivy plants as decor, hooks for clothing, and classical background music. Showers are clean and there is no charge for their use. Mobile dump services are available for longterm campers. Discounts are offered to Good Sam members.

KEPLER PARK CAMPGROUND   privately operated
Star Route B, Box 7810, Palmer, AK 99645   May 1st—Sept 15th
(907) 745-3053   **MP 37.3 Glenn Highway**

Located at MP 37.3 of the Glenn Highway, 1.8 miles northeast of the junction of the George Parks Highway and the Glenn Highway. Kepler Drive, the gravel road into the campground, doubles back to parallel the Glenn Highway which makes access difficult when driving east: 15 spaces w/o hookups; pit toilets; drinking water; tables; fire rings; fishing; swimming; trails; public phone; separate tenting area; no time limit.

Kepler Park Campground is located on Kepler Lake with access to Harriet and Bradley Lakes. A small wooden bridge, with weight restrictions, must be crossed to the designated camping area. Drivers with RVs longer than 22-25 feet should not consider camping here, not only because spaces are short, but also because little room for turning around is available. Lakes are stocked with trout by the State; boat rentals available.

RV SERVICES IN THE PALMER AREA

PALMER CHEVRON   **(907) 746-6363**
Located at the signal light at the intersection of the Glenn Highway and Evergreen Avenue: alignment; tires; general repairs; towing; **sewage dump station; propane**.

DEE'S TRUCK & EQUIPMENT PARTS   **(907) 745-1900**
Turn onto West Evergreen Avenue from the signal light at the intersection with the Glenn Highway. Cross the railroad tracks and turn right. Turn left on East Elmwood Avenue to 1226 South Chugach. A full selection of RV and trailer parts is available.

THE GLENN HIGHWAY (continued)

MOOSE CREEK STATE RECREATION SITE   open all year
Alaska State Park System   **MP 54.4 Glenn Highway**

Located at MP 54.4 of the Glenn Highway by the bridge at the bottom of the hill: 12 spaces w/o hookups; pit toilets; drinking water; 4 picnic shelters; fishing; trails; 7 day limit.

Moose Creek SRS has spaces which vary in length: two long spaces are specifically dedicated for use by the disabled. One space has such a steep slope blocking might not be possible. Covered picnic areas are on concrete slabs. Pit toilets are accessible to the disabled.

SUTTON

The heritage of Sutton is the development of its coal mines which first fueled the Alaska Railroad and later the army base at Fort Richardson. Hiking trails and fossils can be found in and around its abandoned coal mines. Follow Jonesville Road to Coyote Lake and the mining area. An unparalleled view of the Matanuska River valley and recreational opportunities will be your reward.

ALPINE HERITAGE AND CULTURAL CENTER

Located in Sutton on the grounds of the Matanuska-Susitna Historical Park at MP 61.5 of the Glenn Highway. The remnants of the Eska coal-washing plant built by the U.S. Navy in 1921-22, Chickaloon bunkhouse, Sutton Post Office and other historic buildings are displayed. Historical information on the area as well as the geology of the region is provided.

THE GLENN HIGHWAY (continued)

RIVERS EDGE RECREATIONAL PARK **privately operated**
PO Box 364, Sutton, AK 99674 **May 15th—Sept 7th**
(907) 746-CAMP **MP 62.4 Glenn Highway**

Located at MP 62.4 Glenn Highway on the east side of Granite Creek: 16 spaces; 4 power hookups; 12 w/o hookups; pit toilets; drinking water; covered picnic site; tables; fire rings; separate tenting area; no time limit.

Rivers Edge Recreational Park is a quiet campground bordering Granite Creek. Spaces, which are short and at right angles to the road, are separated by trees except for the power hookups which are side-by-side back-ins. A second loop is for tent campers. The covered pavilion has a gas grill. Look for a pair of bald eagles which nest in the area.

PINNACLE MOUNTAIN RV PARK **privately operated**
PO Box 1203, Chickaloon, AK 99674 **open all year**
(907) 745-0296 **MP 69.5 Glenn Highway**

Located at MP 69.5 of the Glenn Highway: 42 spaces; 18 pull-throughs; 14 full hookups; 16 power hookups; 12 w/o hookups; **sewage dump station**; flush toilets; drinking water; hot showers; laundry facilities; tables; fire rings; recreation room; trails; **propane**; public phone; separate tenting area; no time limit.

Pinnacle Mountain RV Park is set in a heavily wooded area with gravel roads leading to spaces which are gravel-based and level. A vegetable garden is free for campers' use. A recreation room, which is accessible to the disabled, is available twenty-four hours a day. A mail-forwarding service is available. Discounts are offered to Good Sam members.

KING MOUNTAIN STATE RECREATION SITE **open all year**
Alaska State Park System **MP 76 Glenn Highway**

Located on a narrow, dirt road at MP 76 of the Glenn Highway: 22 spaces w/o hookups; pit toilets; drinking water; 2 picnic sites; tables; fire rings; boat launch; 15 day limit.

King Mountain SRS is on the bank of the Matanuska River. The road inside the campground is narrow and directionally incorrect for parking because of the angle of the spaces. Furthermore, spaces are narrow and short which negates larger RVs from using the campground. A covered picnic site with a brick grill and tables is available. The Matanuska River flows swiftly at the point of the boat launch.

CHICKALOON STORE AND SERVICE STATION   (907) 745-4520
Located at MP 76.3 of the Glenn Highway: towing; **sewage dump station**; **propane**. Twenty-four hour towing service is available.

BONNIE LAKE STATE RECREATION SITE
Alaska State Park System
open all year
MP 83.3 Glenn Highway

Accessed by way of a graveled road at MP 83.3 of the Glenn Highway. No state highway signs identify the road's location which is diagonal to the highway: 10 spaces w/o hookups; pit toilets; no drinking water; tables; fire rings; trails; boat launch; fishing; 15 day limit.

It is apparent that the state does not want overnighters to use the Bonnie Lake SRS because of the danger presented by the steep, winding, two-mile road to the actual site. *Large RVs or rigs with trailers or towed vehicles should not attempt to drive this road* because of the extremely sharp turns presented. If you choose to visit this campground, take the right-hand fork at the first "Y." The campground is circular with back-in parking but has no designated sites. Water must be boiled or treated chemically. Upper and Lower Bonnie Lakes are connected by a stream. This campground is best suited for pickup trucks with campers, mini-motor homes or vans without boat trailers.

LONG LAKE STATE RECREATION SITE
Alaska State Park System
open all year
MP 85.3 Glenn Highway

Located at MP 85.3 of the Glenn Highway at the west end of Long Lake: 9 spaces w/o hookups; pit toilets; drinking water; picnic sites; tables; boat launch; fishing; 15 day limit.

Long Lake SRS is a circular area easily accessed from the highway. Spaces are not designated. A small bridge by the lake leads to the pit toilets. Because of its accessibility, this is an ideal lake for small boat users.

MATANUSKA GLACIER STATE RECREATION SITE open all year
Alaska State Park System
MP 101 Glenn Highway

Located at MP 101 of the Glenn Highway: 12 spaces w/o hookups; pit toilets; picnic sites; tables; trails; 15 day limit.

Matanuska Glacier SRS is set in a wooded area overlooking the river valley and glacier. Two separate parking areas are available with gravel-based spaces. Two sites can accommodate longer RVs. No individual grills or fire rings are provided at individual sites; a fire pit with tables is separately located. Pit toilets are accessible to the disabled. A wooden observation deck presents an excellent location for photographers. Maintained trails lead from the campground to the Matanuska Glacier.

GLACIER PARK RESORT
HC 03, Box 8449, Palmer, AK 99645
(907) 745-2534
privately operated
May 1st—Sept 30th
MP 102 Glenn Highway

Located one mile from MP 102: 36 spaces; 12 power and water hookups; 24 w/o hookups; **sewage dump station**; pit toilets; drinking water; tables; grills; **propane**; no time limit.

Glacier Park Resort is literally located at the base of the Matanuska Glacier. A steep, narrow road with some pull-outs descends from the Glenn Highway to the campground. Campers who wish to do so can park a few yards from the face of the glacier although the owner does not advocate this practice. A fee is charged for entrance at a toll booth.

SHEEP MOUNTAIN LODGE   privately operated
HC 03, Box 8490, Palmer, AK 99645   May 1st—Sept 30th
(907) 745-5121   FAX (907) 745-5121   **MP 113.5 Glenn Highway**

Located at MP 113.5 of the Glenn Highway: 22 spaces; 8 power and water hookups; 14 w/o hookups; flush toilets; drinking water; hot showers; trails; public phone; no time limit.

Sheep Mountain Lodge's major business is its restaurant, bar, gift shop and cabins. Spaces are located in the open parking area in front of the restaurant and cabins.

LITTLE NELCHINA SRS   open all year
Alaska State Park System   **MP 137.4 Glenn Highway**

Located 0.3 mile from the highway at MP 137.4. Entry is made by a gravel access road on the northeast side of the bridge: 12 spaces w/o hookups; no drinking water; tables; fire rings; boat launch; fishing; trails; dumpster; 15 day limit.

Little Nelchina SRS has spaces which are not level and butt up against trees restricting rig size. RVs up to about 25-27 feet can be accommodated. Water must be either boiled or treated chemically.

K.R.O.A. RV RESORT   privately operated
HC 03, Box 8795, Palmer, AK 99645   May 15th—Sept 30th
(907) 822-3346   **MP 153 Glenn Highway**

Located at MP 153 of the Glenn Highway: 100 spaces; 66 full hookups; 34 power and water hookups; 95 pull-throughs; **sewage dump station**; flush toilets; drinking water; hot showers; laundry facilities; picnic sites; tables; grills; boat launch; fishing; trails; no time limit.

KROA (Kampground Resorts of Alaska), not to be confused with the national KOA network, has a large camping area with trees throughout. Spaces are gravel-based and level. Cabins, a restaurant, and a gift shop are featured as is a small "drunken forest" tourist attraction. Good Sam discounts are offered.

LAKE LOUISE ROAD

LAKE LOUISE STATE RECREATION AREA   open all year
Alaska State Park System   **MP 160 Glenn Highway**

Located 16.8 miles north of the Glenn Highway at MP 160. Turn left for 0.5 mile at the "Y": 46 spaces w/o hookups; pit toilets; drinking water; covered picnic shelters; tables; fire rings; boat launch; fishing; swimming; trails; 15 day limit.

Lake Louise SRA is set on different levels with black spruce trees and undergrowth throughout. Spaces are back-in, gravel-based, level, and paired side-by-side with guard-rail style barriers. Spaces are long and can accommodate larger RVs. Covered picnic shelters and pit toilets are accessible to the disabled. Lake Louise SRA is one of the better state campgrounds and is popular with local campers. It is best to reach this campground early in the day in order to assure that it is not full.

LAKE LOUISE LODGE   **privately operated**
HC 01, Box 1716   **open all year**
(907) 822-3311   **MP 160 Glenn Highway**

Located 16.8 miles north of the Glenn Highway at MP 160. Turn right one mile at the sign: 10 spaces; 4 power hookups; 6 w/o hookups; flush toilets; drinking water; hot showers; tables; boat launch; fishing; swimming; trails; **propane**; public phone; separate tenting area; no time limit.

Lake Louise Lodge has limited RV parking. Fishing is good, especially for lake trout, grayling, and white fish. The lodge provides cabins, a restaurant and a lounge. Part of the original building and its roof has been retained and is incorporated as decor in the lounge area.

THE GLENN HIGHWAY (continued)

TOLSONA LAKE RESORT   **privately operated**
HC01, Box 1960, Glennallen, AK 99588   **open all year**
(907) 822-3433   1-800- 245-3342 **MP 170.2 Glenn Highway**

Located 0.7 mile from the Glenn Highway at MP 170.2 on a blacktopped road: 30 spaces w/o hookups; flush toilets; drinking water; hot showers, laundry facilities; boat launch; fishing; separate tenting area; public phone; no time limit.

Tolsona Lake Resort is located directly on Tolsona Lake. Not an RV campground as such, spaces are in an open area by the lodge. There is no charge for dry camping. A restaurant and bar are part of the lodge. The lake offers wind-surfing and tie-downs for float planes. This is a very attractive area. Rainbow trout, grayling and burbot are in the lake.

TOLSONA WILDERNESS CAMPGROUND **privately operated**
PO Box 23, Glennallen, AK 99588   **May 20th—Sept 10th**
(907) 822-3865   **MP 173 Glenn Highway**

Located on a packed dirt and gravel road one mile from MP 173 of the Glenn Highway: 57 spaces; 23 power and water hookups; 34 w/o hookups; 10 pull-throughs; **sewage dump station**; flush toilets; drinking water; hot showers; laundry facilities; tables; grills; fishing; no time limit.

Tolsona Wilderness Campground is divided into several separate sections set in a heavily wooded area. Most of the spaces are back-ins located directly on the creek bank. Spaces are widely separated from one another. The term "wilderness" is apt but does not describe how picturesque this campground is. Photos on the office walls attest to the fact that fish are being caught in the creek. Good Sam and AAA discounts offered.

BISHOP AND SONS RV CAMPER PARK privately operated
PO Box 367, Glennallen, AK 99588 open all year
(907) 822-3310 MP 187.5 Glenn Highway
Located at MP 187.5 of the Glenn Highway at the car wash: 12 full hookups; 7 pull-throughs; **sewage dump station**; no time limit.

Bishop and Sons RV Camper Park has level, gravel-based back-in spaces with full hookups. Recently reconstructed. A car wash is on the grounds.

NORTHERN LIGHTS privately operated
PO Box 206, Copper Center, AK 99573 May 15th—Sept 1st
(907) 822-3199 MP 188.7 Glenn Highway

Located at MP 188.7 of the Glenn Highway: 17 spaces; 12 power only hookups; 5 w/o hookups; 1 pull-through; porta-potties; tables; fire rings; separate tenting area; public phone; no time limit.

Northern Lights offers "no frills" camping. The spaces are level, gravel-based back-ins in a wooded setting.

GRUBSTAKE RV PARK privately operated
Located at MP 187.2 Glenn Highway: 17 spaces; 15 power and water hookups; 2 w/o hookups; porta-potty. Located behind the Last Frontier Pizza Parlor, it has level, gravel-based back-in spaces.

RV SERVICES ON THE GLENN HIGHWAY

THE HUB OF ALASKA, INC. (907) 822-3555
Located at the junction of the Glenn Highway with the Richardson Highway: alignment; brakes; mufflers; general repairs; emergency road service; towing; **propane**. The station is located next to the Copper River Visitor Center. It has two large bays for RVs. Two wreckers offer 24 hour emergency road service. Discounts are offered to senior citizens.

Note: Glennallen options on the Glenn Highway and the Richardson Highway are presented in the following chapter, "The Copper River Region."

Chapter 11

THE COPPER RIVER REGION

This chapter describes campgrounds and services from Glennallen to Tok, Delta Junction, and Valdez. Options include the Glenn Highway west to Anchorage; the Glenn Highway (Tok Cutoff) northeast to Tok; the Richardson Highway north to Delta Junction (including the Denali Highway); and the Richardson Highway south to Valdez. Valdez options include the Alaska Marine Highway System to Cordova, Whittier and Seward.

GLENNALLEN, ALASKA

Glennallen is the hub of the Copper River basin. It borders on the 13.2 million acre Wrangell-St. Elias National Park and Preserve. The park includes 9.7 million acres designated as wilderness and nine of the sixteen highest mountain peaks in the United States. Two roads give access to the park: Nabesna Road from the Glenn Highway (Tok Cutoff), and the road to McCarthy from the Edgerton Highway.

Four mountain ranges encompass the Copper River region: the Talkeetna, Chugach, Alaska, and Wrangell ranges. Two National Wild, Scenic and Recreational Rivers, the Gulkana and the Delta, are accessible from Glennallen. The junction with the Glenn and Richardson Highways in Glennallen offers travelers options to Tok, Delta Junction, Valdez and Anchorage.

WRANGELL–ST. ELIAS NATIONAL PARK
PO Box 29, Glennallen, AK 99588

COPPER RIVER VISITOR CENTER   MP 115 Richardson Highway
Junction of the Glenn Highway with the Richardson Highway

BUREAU OF LAND MANAGEMENT   Glennallen District Office
PO Box 147, Glennallen, AK 99588   (907) 822-3217

ALASKA STATE PARKS   Copper Basin District
PO Box 286, Glennallen, AK 99588   (907) 822-5536

HEALTH AND EMERGENCY SERVICES
Copper River EMS   (907) 822-3203 or 911
Glennallen Police   (907) 822-3263

GLENNALLEN OPTIONS

THE GLENN HIGHWAY: WEST TO ANCHORAGE
West on the Glenn Highway leads to Lake Louise, the Matanuska Glacier, Palmer and Anchorage. Anchorage, the largest city in Alaska, is the gateway to the Kenai Peninsula.

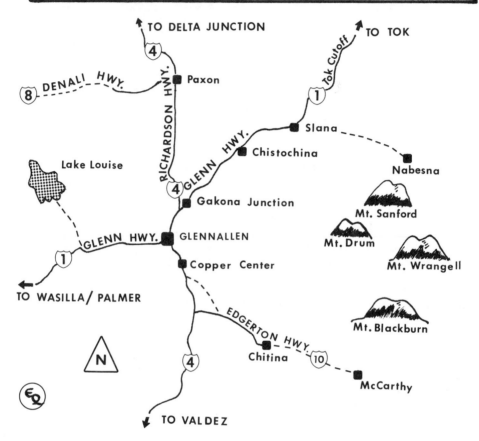

Glennallen and Copper River Region

TO DELTA JUNCTION

TO TOK

Tok Cutoff

④ RICHARDSON HWY.

⑧ DENALI HWY.

Paxon

①

Slana

GLENN HWY.

Chistochina

Nabesna

Lake Louise

④

Gakona Junction

Mt. Sanford

GLENN HWY.

GLENNALLEN

Mt. Drum

①

Copper Center

Mt. Wrangell

TO WASILLA / PALMER

EDGERTON HWY.

Mt. Blackburn

N

④

Chitina

⑩

TO VALDEZ

McCarthy

THE GLENN HIGHWAY: NORTHEAST TO TOK

This section of the Glenn Highway, also known as the Tok Cutoff, forms a junction with the Richardson Highway at Gakona fourteen miles north of Glennallen. This scenic highway offers the beauty of the Mentasta and Wrangell mountain ranges. It leads to the Alaska Highway and Tok.

RICHARDSON HIGHWAY: NORTH TO DELTA JUNCTION

North on the Richardson Highway leads to Paxson and the junction with the Denali Highway to Cantwell. There are excellent photo opportunities of the trans-Alaska oil pipeline. At Delta Junction the Richardson Highway leads west to Fairbanks. The Alaska Highway to Tok and the Canadian border is also an option at Delta Junction.

THE RICHARDSON HIGHWAY: SOUTH TO VALDEZ
South on the Richardson Highway leads to Copper Center with an option to the Edgerton Highway, Chitina and McCarthy. The highway continues to Thompson Pass, the Worthington Glacier and Valdez. The Alaska Marine Highway System terminal is located at the beginning of the Richardson Highway in Valdez.

Glennallen to Anchorage	189 miles
Glennallen to Delta Junction	151 miles
Glennallen to Tok	139 miles
Glennallen to Valdez	115 miles

THE GLENN HIGHWAY (TOK CUTOFF)

The Glenn Highway, which originates in Anchorage, is interrupted by the Richardson Highway for fourteen miles from Glennallen to its junction at Gakona. Also known as the Tok Cutoff, the continuation of the Glenn Highway begins at mile 128.6 of the Richardson Highway.

The one hundred twenty-five mile highway to Tok begins numeration as mile zero at Gakona. Caution must be exercised when driving north from Glennallen since the cutoff, which angles to the northeast, can be easily missed.

WRANGELL-ST. ELIAS—SLANA RANGER STATION
Mile 1, Nabesna Road, Slana, AK 99586　　　　　**(907) 822-5238**

The ranger station is located one mile east of the junction with the Glenn Highway (MP 59.8) and Nabesna Road.

MOUNTAIN VIEW LODGE　　　　　　　　　　　**(907) 822-3119**
SRA Box 1190, Slana, AK 99586　　　　　　**MP 6 Nabesna Road**

Mountain View Lodge is located six miles east of the junction with the Glenn Highway (MP 59.8) and the Nabesna Road. Dry camping only.

HEALTH AND EMERGENCY SERVICES

MP 0 to MP 63	Copper River EMS	(907) 822-3203 or 911
MP 63 to MP 125	Tok Ambulance Service	(907) 883-2300 or 911

RV CAMPGROUNDS ON THE TOK CUTOFF

DRY CREEK STATE RECREATION SITE　　　　　**open all year**
Alaska State Park System　　　　　**MP 118 Richardson Highway**

Located between Glennallen and the Glenn Highway (Tok cutoff) at Gakona at MP 118 of the Richardson Highway: 58 spaces w/o hookups; 10 pull-throughs; covered picnic sites; tables; fire rings; fishing; trails; separate tenting area; 15 day limit.

Dry Creek SRS has two cul-de-sacs which form star clusters and one long loop road. The back-in spaces vary in size and can handle some larger

The Wrangell Mountains north of Glennallen

RVs but are best suited to medium-sized rigs. The half-moon pullout near the camp entrance can accommodate two or three of the largest RVs. A campground host is on site.

GAKONA RV PARK privately operated
PO Box 160, Gakona, AK 99586 May 15th—Oct 1st
(907) 822-3550 MP 4.2 Glenn Highway Cutoff

Located at MP 4.2 of the Glenn Highway (Tok Cutoff): 24 spaces; 48 full hookups; 5 pull-throughs; 10 power and water hookups; 15 power only hookups; 9 w/o hookups; **sewage dump station**; flush toilets; drinking water; hot showers; laundry facilities; tables; grills; boat launch; fishing; no time limit.

Gakona RV Park is located on the Copper River with trees serving as a visual barrier to the highway. Spaces are level in a gravel-based, cleared section. Picnic tables are set up under the trees near a larger recreational area. This is a wilderness campground.

CHISTOCHINA LODGE AND TRADING POST privately operated
Mile 32 Tok Highway, Gakona, AK 99586 May 25th—Sept 15th
(907) 822-3366 MP 33 Glenn Highway Cutoff

Located at MP 33 of the Glenn Highway (Tok Cutoff): 6 full hookups; **sewage dump station**; flush toilets; drinking water; hot showers; **propane**; public phone; separate tenting area; no time limit.

Chistochina Lodge and Trading Post has gravel-based, level back-in spaces. The lodge borders an airstrip and is located about one mile south of the Chistochina River bridge which leads to the Chistochina gold mine.

SINONA CREEK RV CAMPGROUND privately operated
PO Box 224, Chistochina, AK 99586 May 15th—Sept 15th
(907) 822-3914 MP 34.4 Glenn Highway Cutoff

Located at MP 34.4 of the Glenn Highway (Tok Cutoff): 17 spaces with full hookups; 8 pull-throughs; **sewage dump station**; flush toilets; drinking water; hot showers; tables; no time limit.

Sinona Creek RV Campground is a rustic campground located in a wooded area. Spaces are gravel-based, level and separated from one another.

PORCUPINE CREEK STATE RECREATION SITE   open all year
Alaska State Park System   **MP 64.2 Glenn Highway Cutoff**

Located at MP 64.2 of the Glenn Highway (Tok Cutoff): 12 spaces w/o hookups; pit toilets; drinking water; tables; fire rings; fishing; trails; dumpster; 15 day limit.

Porcupine Creek SRS is a round, open campground set against spruce and willow trees and Porcupine Creek. Back-in spaces are level and can accommodate medium to large RVs.

EAGLE TRAIL STATE RECREATION SITE   open all year
Alaska State Park System   **MP 109.5 Glenn Highway Cutoff**

Located on the south side of the bridge at MP 109.5 of the Glenn Highway (Tok Cutoff): 40 spaces w/o hookups; 2 pull-throughs; pit toilets; drinking water; covered picnic sites; tables; trails; public phone; dumpster; 15 day limit.

Eagle Trail SRS has a unique campground design which features five cul-de-sacs with a picnic area in the center and back-in spaces on the outer rim of each loop. Three parallel parking sites will accommodate larger RVs. Roadways and spaces are gravel-based and level. Covered picnic tables, benches and charcoal grills with a campfire pit are in the center of the picnic areas. The campground is set on the bank of a fast-running creek. Several trails and an overlook trail are in the area.

SOURDOUGH CAMPGROUND   **privately operated**
PO Box 47, Tok, AK 9978   **May 15th—Sept 15th**
(907) 883-5543   **MP 122.8 Glenn Highway Cutoff**

Located at MP 122.8 of the Glenn Highway (Tok Cutoff), 1.7 miles south of the Alaska Highway junction: 75 spaces; 18 pull-throughs; 16 full hookups; 21 power and water hookups; 5 power only hookups; 33 w/o hookups; **sewage dump station**; flush toilets; drinking water; hot showers; laundry facilities; tables; no time limit.

Sourdough Campground provides a wooded setting with trees between camping spaces, gravel-based roads and level RV spaces. The owners take pride in offering "spacious private camp sites – not parking spaces." Each space has a lined garbage can. "Guaranteed" clean restrooms. An RV wash station with a high pressure hose is available. The restaurant could be considered an Alaskan museum since it is filled with authentic Alaskan memorabilia and many old photographs. Discounts are offered to senior citizens, Good Sam and AAA members.

GOLDEN BEAR CAMPER PARK   privately operated
PO Box 276, Tok, AK 99780   May 1st—Sept 30th
(907) 883-2561   MP 124.5 Glenn Highway Cutoff

Located at MP 124.5 of the Glenn Highway (Tok Cutoff) 0.3 mile south of
the Alaska Highway junction: 60 spaces; 33 pull-throughs; 15 full
hookups; 20 power and water hookups; 25 w/o hookups; **sewage dump
station**; flush toilets; hot showers; laundry facilities; tables; fire rings;
public phone; separate tenting area; no time limit.

Alaska State Park Ranger: Northern Region

Golden Bear Camper Park offers a wooded setting and level, gravel-based
spaces. Pull-throughs will accommodate the largest RVs. The shower
building is heated. Part of a motel-gift shop complex, the campground is
within walking distance to the center of Tok.

RV SERVICES ON THE GLENN HIGHWAY (TOK CUTOFF)

GAKONA TEXACO   (907) 822-5595
Located at MP 128.5 of the Richardson Highway at the junction with the
Tok Cutoff: suspension; electrical repairs; brakes; mufflers; general
repairs; welding. Emergency wrecker service is provided on a 24 hour
basis. Always the "cheapest gas" in the Copper River valley.

THE RICHARDSON HIGHWAY: NORTH TO DELTA JUNCTION

The Richardson Highway to Delta Junction is accessed by turning north
at the junction with the Glenn Highway. It joins the Denali Highway to
Cantwell at Paxson. Much of the trans-Alaska oil pipeline is visible with
numerous pullouts and walk-up photo opportunities. Glaciers, lakes and
streams are also visible from the highway.

ALYESKA PIPELINE PUMP STATION 9   **(907) 869-3270**

Alyeska Pipeline Service Company provides free daily tours of Pump Station 9 at MP 258 of the Richardson Highway. Stop at the pump station or telephone (907) 278-1611 for additional information.

HEALTH AND EMERGENCY SERVICES

MP 115 to MP 185	Copper River EMS	(907) 822-3203 or 911
MP 185 to MP 266	Delta Rescue Squad	(907) 895-4600 or 911
	Alaska State Troopers	(907) 895-4800

RV CAMPGROUNDS ON THE RICHARDSON HIGHWAY

DRY CREEK STATE RECREATION SITE   **open all year**
Alaska State Park System   **MP 118 Richardson Highway**

Located between Glennallen and Gakona Junction at MP 118 of the Richardson Highway: 58 spaces w/o hookups; 10 pull-throughs; covered picnic sites; tables; fire rings; fishing; trails; separate tenting area; dumpster; 15 day limit.

Dry Creek SRS has two cul-de-sacs which form star clusters and one long loop road. Back-in spaces vary in size and can handle some larger RVs but are best suited to medium-sized rigs. The half-moon pullout near the camp entrance can accommodate two or three of the largest RVs. A campground host is on site.

Visitors from Michigan wet a line at Sourdough Creek Campground

SOURDOUGH CREEK CAMPGROUND   **May 1st—Oct 1st**
Bureau of Land Management   **MP 147.5 Richardson Highway**

Turn onto a gravel access road at MP 147.5 of the Richardson Highway: 47 spaces w/o hookups; 12 pull-throughs; pit toilets; no drinking water; tables; fire rings; boat launch; fishing; 7 day limit.

Sourdough Creek Campground is a wooded area with individual spaces on gravel bases separated by trees or grass; side-by-side parking and pull-throughs are available. This campground can accommodate the largest RV. Wide trails made of finely crushed gravel, toilets on concrete vaults, and two dedicated spaces make the campground accessible to the disabled camper. Water must be boiled or treated chemically.

Canoeists, kayakers, and rafters have a short portage to a clearwater stream which accesses the Gulkana River (Class I, II, III waters). The boat launch is used for put-ins to the lower Gulkana River and take-outs from the upper Gulkana. Take out point for rafters who enter the river at Paxson.

PAXSON LAKE CAMPGROUND
Bureau of Land Management

June 1st—Oct 1st
MP 175 Richardson Highway

Located at MP 175 of the Richardson Highway, the campground is reached by a road which descends 1.6 miles: 40 spaces w/o hookups; 9 pull-throughs; **sewage dump station**; pit toilets; drinking water; tables; fire rings; boat launch; fishing; trails; separate tenting area; 10 day limit.

Paxson Lake Campground is quiet and scenic. Because there are so many spaces and pull-throughs, the largest RV should find a secure and level spot. Individual garbage cans are placed throughout the grounds. Pit toilets are set on concrete vaults and are accessible to the disabled. A BLM comment board had the following statement from an Austrian: "This is the place we have dreamed of when traveling to Alaska."

This boat launch is widely used as the put-in spot for Gulkana National Wild River trips and fishing.

FIELDING LAKE STATE RECREATION SITE
Alaska State Park System

open all year
MP 200.5 Richardson Highway

Located at MP 200.5 Richardson Highway on a poorly maintained gravel road 1.6 miles from the highway: 7 spaces w/o hookups; pit toilets; no drinking water; tables; fire rings; boat launch; fishing; 15 day limit.

Fielding Lake SRS is situated in an unprotected open area which allows for heavy winds. Spaces are large and level. The campground is well back from the highway and can accommodate RVs of any length; users with large rigs should drive the entrance road with caution. The lake is accessed by a stream. Water must be boiled or treated chemically.

DONNELLY CREEK STATE RECREATION SITE
Alaska State Park System

open all year
MP 238 Richardson Highway

Located on a gravel road at MP 238 of the Richardson Highway: 12 spaces w/o hookups; pit toilets; drinking water; tables; fire rings; trails; dumpster; 15 day limit.

Donnelly Creek SRS, which is circular in design and borders on the creek, is heavily wooded with Alaska spruce. Spaces are quite large and level.

Paxson Lake Campground

Six spaces face the wrong direction to the road for proper access. Flowers prominent in the area include mountain roses and buttercups.

RV SERVICES ON THE GLENN HIGHWAY (TOK CUTOFF)

GAKONA TEXACO   **(907) 822-5595**
Located at MP 128.5 of the Richardson Highway at the junction with the Tok Cutoff: suspension; electrical repairs; brakes; mufflers; general repairs; welding. Emergency wrecker service is provided on a 24 hour basis. Always the "cheapest gas" in the Copper River valley.

TEXACO SERVICE   **(907) 895-4625**
Located at MP 266 of the Richardson Highway south of the junction with the Alaska Highway: brakes; mufflers; general repairs; transmissions; towing; welding. Twenty-four hour towing is provided. Phone 895-4554 after station hours or the police dispatcher at 895-4800.

THE DENALI HIGHWAY

The Denali Highway forms a junction with the Richardson Highway at MP 188.5 at Paxson. The road was the only access to Denali National Park before the Parks Highway was completed. The one hundred thirty-four miles of gravel is narrow and rutted but offers unmatched views of this scenic wilderness. The Bureau of Land Management has an excellent brochure, *Denali Highway: Points of Interest*, which describes the terrain.

Archaeological studies of the area reveal four hundred sites in the Tangle Lakes Archaeological District. Ancient peoples occupied the area for a period of more than ten thousand years. These prehistoric sites lie between miles fifteen and forty-five.

Posted maximum speed is 35 MPH but prudent RVers will probably travel at much slower speeds. One couple who drove the road reported that they "took it easy all the way"; their only damage was two broken casserole dishes. Extra tires and a full tank of fuel are essential.

There are two lodges on the Denali Highway where dry RV parking is permitted. The first, Maclaren River Lodge, is located at mile 42 from the Paxson side. The second, Gracious House Lodge, is located at mile 82 from the Paxson side. Each lodge has a restaurant and bar. Gracious House Lodge also has gasoline available.

The Bureau of Land Management has five exhibits on the Denali Highway. Orientation panels are located at miles 13 and 115; an archaeology exhibit is located at Tangle Lakes, mile 22; a wildlife exhibit is located at mile 50; a geology exhibit is located at mile 94.

EMERGENCY SERVICES

MP 0 to MP 78	Copper River EMS	(907) 822-3203 or 911
MP 78 to MP 135	Cantwell Volunteer Ambulance	(907) 768-2982
	Alaska State Troopers	(907) 786-2202

RV CAMPGROUNDS ON THE DENALI HIGHWAY

TANGLE LAKES CAMPGROUND   **May 1st—Oct 1st**
Bureau of Land Management   **MP 21.5 Denali Highway**

Located at the eastern end of the Denali Highway or 21.5 miles before the junction of the Richardson Highway at Paxson (MP 188.5). Blacktop begins just past the campground entrance: 27 spaces w/o hookups; pit toilets; drinking water; tables; fire rings; boat launch; fishing; 7 day limit.

Tangle Lakes Campground is rough. Spaces are not level and require some blocking. The campground is surrounded by hills and mountains and is situated on a shallow, fast moving creek. Some scrub brush and small trees are in the area. Pit toilets are on concrete vaults and are accessible to the disabled. A handwritten comment on the bulletin board read "fishing good in creeks between lakes (grayling, trout)."

TANGLE RIVER CAMPGROUND   **May 1st—Oct 1st**
Bureau of Land Management   **MP 21.7 Denali Highway**

Located at the eastern end of the Denali Highway or 21.7 miles before the junction of the Richardson Highway at Paxson (MP 188.5). Blacktop begins just past the campground entrance: 7 spaces w/o hookups; pit toilets; drinking water; tables; boat launch; fishing; 7 day limit.

Tangle River Campground is near the Tangle Lakes Campground but on the opposite side of the road. The campground is narrow and parallels the river which allows road access at either end. This small campground will accommodate RVs of any size and should be considered before taking a larger RV into the Tangle Lakes Campground across the road.

This boat launch is widely used as a put-in location for Delta River float trips as well as fishing.

BRUSHKANA CREEK CAMPGROUND   **May 1st—Oct 1st**
Bureau of Land Management   **MP 104.3 Denali Highway**

The campground is located at MP 104.3 on the Denali Highway or 29.8 miles from the junction of the George Parks Highway (MP 209.9). At this point the Denali Highway is rough and sections are washboard-like: 17 spaces w/o hookups; pit toilets; drinking water; covered picnic site; tables; fire rings; fishing; 7 day limit.

Brushkana Creek Campground is bordered by low brush and spruce. It has back-in spaces which are not level. An overflow area can accommodate the largest RVs. Pit toilets are on concrete vaults and a group picnic shelter is provided. The campground is walking distance to the Brushkana River. It is a popular campsite for backpackers and bicyclists. Fish include dolly varden, lake trout, and grayling.

Young caribou on the Denali Highway west of Paxson

DENALI HIGHWAY OPTIONS AT CANTWELL

THE GEORGE PARKS HIGHWAY: NORTH TO FAIRBANKS
The entrance to Denali National Park and Preserve is 27 miles north from the junction with the Denali Highway at Cantwell. Fairbanks is 148 miles northeast. The Parks Highway follows a series of scenic ridges from Nenana to Fairbanks that overlook migratory bird breeding grounds.

THE GEORGE PARKS HIGHWAY: SOUTH TO ANCHORAGE
Anchorage is 210 miles south from the junction with the Denali Highway at Cantwell. This route offers a number of places to camp or visit including the town of Talkeetna, Nancy Lake Recreation Area, and Big Lake. The Parks Highway terminates at the Glenn Highway west of Anchorage.

THE RICHARDSON HIGHWAY: SOUTH TO VALDEZ

The Richardson Highway south from Glennallen leads to Valdez and Prince William Sound. Originally the road was used to reach Eagle, Alaska, and the Klondike gold fields and was known as the Valdez-Eagle Trail. Later 170 miles of the road was upgraded and it was renamed the Trans-Alaska Military Road. With the advent of World War II, a military need to reach Prince William Sound from the Alaska Highway was identified, and the road was extended by what is now known as the Tok Cutoff.

The highway first passes Copper Center. At mile 82.6 it forms a junction with the Edgerton Highway which leads to Chitina, McCarthy and the Kennicott copper mine. Thompson Pass and the Worthington Glacier are seen as the highway nears Valdez and Prince William Sound. Valdez is the terminus of the 800 mile trans-Alaska oil pipeline.

WRANGELL/ST. ELIAS NATIONAL PARK HEADQUARTERS
(907) 822-5234   **MP 105 Old Richardson Highway**
Park headquarters personnel can provide the RVer with pertinent information regarding the quality of roads from Chitina to McCarthy.

HEALTH AND EMERGENCY SERVICES

MP 60 to MP 115	Copper River EMS	(907) 822-3203 or 911
	Glennallen Police	(907) 822-3263
MP 0 to MP 60	Valdez Emergency Service	(907) 835-4560 or 911
	Alaska State Troopers	(907) 835-4359

RV CAMPGROUNDS SOUTH ON THE RICHARDSON HIGHWAY

TAZLINA RIVER RV PARK   privately operated
PO Box 322, Glennallen, AK 99588   June 15th—Sept 1st
(907) 822-3034   **MP 110.5 Richardson Highway**

Located at MP 110.5 of the Richardson Highway: 12 spaces with power and water hookups; 2 pull-throughs; **sewage dump station**; flush toilets; drinking water; hot showers; laundry facilities; covered picnic sites; no time limit.

Tazlina River RV Park has some permanent mobile homes set up adjacent to the campground. Circular in design, with back-in spaces on gravel bases, the largest RVs can be accommodated. The campground offers easy access and a quiet, secluded area away from the main highway. Several large grassed areas are provided for picnicking.

GROVE'S KLUTINA RIVER CHARTERS   privately operated
PO Box 236, Copper Center, AK 99573   June 15th—Sept 1st
(907) 822-5822   **MP 100.8 Old Richardson Highway**

Located at MP 100.8 Old Richardson Highway. Turn on the Copper Center cut-off (about MP 100 or MP 106) to the south side of the Klutina

River bridge: 22 power only hookups; drinking water; pit toilets; tables; no time limit.

Grove's Klutina River Charters campground offers power hookups as well as dry camping. Pit toilets are old and located in the woods. Salmon charters and scenic raft trips can be arranged.

KLUTINA SALMON CHARTERS... privately operated
PO Box 78, Copper Center, AK 99573 June 15th—Sept 1st
(907) 822-3991 MP 100.8 Old Richardson Highway

Located at MP 100.8 Old Richardson Highway. Turn on the Copper Center cut-off (about MP 100 or MP 106) to the north side of the Klutina River bridge: 35 spaces; 4 pull-throughs; 5 power hookups; 30 w/o hookups; **sewage dump station**; pit toilets; drinking water; tables; grills; fishing; no time limit.

Klutina Salmon Charters and Campground is open to the public, but its primary function is to provide space for a charter salmon fishing service.

SQUIRREL CREEK STATE RECREATION SITE open all year
Alaska State Park System MP 79.5 Richardson Highway

Located at MP 79.5 of the Richardson Highway on the south side of the Squirrel Creek bridge: 21 spaces w/o hookups; 11 pull-throughs; pit toilets; drinking water; tables; fire rings; fishing; 15 day limit.

Squirrel Creek SRS is set in heavy stands of birch trees where the creek enters the Tonsina River. The back-in spaces are level and can accommodate RVs of any size. The road through the camp is rough and caution is advised. An overflow area is also provided.

RV SERVICE ON THE RICHARDSON HIGHWAY

COPPER RIVER SAFE WATER CORPORATION
Located at MP 104.5 of the Old Richardson Highway: **sewage dump station**; flush toilets; hot showers; laundry facilities; drinking water; public phone. This laundromat is set back from the highway and hard to see.

THE EDGERTON HIGHWAY

WRANGELL/ST. ELIAS NATIONAL PARK AND PRESERVE
Chitina Ranger Station, Chitina, AK 99566 **(907) 823-2205**

The Edgerton Highway leads to Chitina and McCarthy. Chitina, with its abandoned buildings and railroad cars, has the feel of another period of time. McCarthy and the Kennecott Copper Mine are National Historic Landmarks and are part of the Wrangell/St. Elias National Park and Preserve. Many of the original buildings and structures remain as they were when the mine shut down in 1938.

The road from Chitina to McCarthy is laid on the original right-of-way for the Copper River and Northwestern Railway. Each time that the road is graded, new railroad spikes and sharp rocks are turned up which pose major tire problems for RVs. The bone-crushing sixty miles to McCarthy takes the prudent RVer about three hours. In addition the road can be quite slippery when wet. However, sweeping vistas of the Chugach Range and Wrangell Mountains make the drive worthwhile.

Dry parking is permitted in two lots at the end of McCarthy Road (MP 58.2). It is better to use the upper lot since flooding can occur at the lower lot. The only way to cross the Kennicott River is by means of hand-pulled cable platforms or trams. This is very difficult to accomplish and heavy gloves are a necessity to prevent chaffing.

The town of McCarthy and the ghost town of Kennicott are part of the Wrangell–St. Elias National Park and Preserve. All that remains of the historic Kennecott Copper empire is a sprawling complex of wooden buildings. (The town's name is a misspelling of the company name).

There are two campgrounds on the McCarthy Road where dry camping is permitted: Silver Lake Campground, mile eleven; Nelson's Lakeside Campground, mile twelve. Boat rentals are available at both places.

LIBERTY FALLS STATE RECREATION SITE   open all year
Alaska State Park System   MP 23.5 Edgerton Highway

Located at MP 23.5 of the Edgerton Highway. The highway junction is at MP 82.6 of the Richardson Highway: 8 spaces w/o hookups; pit toilets; no drinking water; tables; fire rings; trails; 4 day limit.

Liberty Falls SRS is set next to the waterfalls and offers an excellent view of the Wrangell mountains. Back-in spaces are not level and cannot accommodate larger RVs. Pit toilets are built on concrete vaults. Water must be boiled or treated chemically

Liberty Falls State Recreation Site: Edgerton Highway

DOT GAME MANAGEMENT CAMPGROUND
Department of Transportation

open all year
MP 35 Edgerton Highway

Located at MP 35 of the Edgerton Highway by the Copper River bridge: 12 spaces w/o hookups; pit toilets; no drinking water; tables; fire rings; time limit unknown.

The DOT campground has back-in spaces which are not level. Use this campground at your discretion but be prepared to relocate if asked to do so. No signs indicate that the campground is intended for public use; however, the grounds are clean and maintained. Water must be either boiled or treated chemically.

THE RICHARDSON HIGHWAY (continued)

LITTLE TONSINA STATE RECREATION SITE
Alaska State Park System

open all year
MP 65 Richardson Highway

Located at MP 65 of the Richardson Highway: 8 spaces w/o hookups; 1 pull-through; pit toilets; drinking water; tables; fire rings; fishing; dumpster; 15 day limit.

Little Tonsina SRS has a gravel road forming a loop through the campground. Some spaces face the wrong direction to the road making parking difficult. The campground is walking distance to a pipeline pump station.

TIEKEL RIVER LODGE
SR Box 110, Valdez, AK 99686
(907) 822-3259

privately operated
May 1st—Oct 1st
MP 56 Richardson Highway

Located at MP 56 of the Richardson Highway: 10 spaces; 5 full hookups; 5 w/o hookups; flush toilet; drinking water; hot shower; tables; grills; fishing; public phone; no time limit.

Tiekel River Lodge offers gravel-based spaces in a wooded area on the Tiekel River. Campers have use of one shared shower and toilet in the restaurant and lodge area. *Tiekel* is an Indian word which roughly translated means "no fish."

BLUEBERRY LAKE STATE RECREATION SITE
Alaska State Park System

open all year
MP 24 Richardson Highway

Located 0.8 mile from MP 24 of the Richardson Highway: 15 spaces w/o hookups; pit toilets; no drinking water; 4 covered picnic sites; tables; fire rings; fishing; trails; 15 day limit.

Blueberry Lake SRS has a gravel road which loops through the campground. Parking is back-in, side-by-side with a few individual spaces. Pit toilets are accessible to the disabled. Water must be either boiled or treated chemically. This is certainly one of the more scenic state campgrounds. Comments on the reader board included these: "We stayed last night when it was cold and rainy; came back today after it had cleared. Nice both ways!" as well as "Beautiful, intense, and free."

VALDEZ, ALASKA

VALDEZ CONVENTION & VISITORS BUREAU   **(907) 835-2984**
PO Box 1603-B, Valdez, AK 99686   **1-800-874-2748**

The original townsite was destroyed in 1964 by the Good Friday earthquake and tidal waves which followed. Seismologists have revised earlier estimates and now believe that the quake registered 9.2 on the Richter scale, the continent's strongest quake. It was centered forty miles west of Valdez and altered 100,000 square miles of land mass.

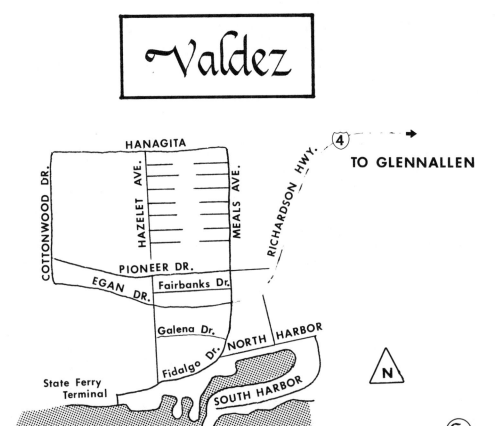

Valdez was relocated to its present location and has since become the terminus for the trans-Alaska oil pipeline; Prince William Sound offers year round ice-free conditions. Since currents flow toward the Pacific Ocean from Bligh Reef where the Exxon Valdez went aground, Valdez experienced no direct environmental damage to its shoreline.

The Chugach mountain range, Thompson Pass and Keystone Canyon, Bridal Veil and Horsetail Falls, Worthington Glacier, and Valdez Glacier are unspoiled and easily accessed by RVs. The Alaska Marine Highway System connects Valdez to Cordova, Whittier and Seward. The ferry system opens the Columbia Glacier and Prince William Sound to the RVer.

ALYESKA PIPELINE SERVICE COMPANY (907) 835-2686

The trans-Alaska oil pipeline reaches the Marine Terminal in Valdez. Free daily tours of the terminal can be arranged through the Visitor Center or by calling (907) 835-2686. It is best to make arrangements one or two days in advance.

HEALTH AND EMERGENCY SERVICES

Alaska State Troopers (907) 835-4359

Valdez Community Hospital (907) 835-2249

Valdez Department of Emergency Services (907) 835-4560 or 911

RV CAMPGROUNDS AT VALDEZ

VALDEZ GLACIER CAMPGROUND May 1st—Oct 1st
City of Valdez MP 2.3 Valdez Glacier Road

Turn on Valdez Glacier Road which is 3.6 miles north of Valdez. Follow the signs for 2.3 miles: 101 spaces w/o hookups; 14 pull-throughs; 2 picnic sites; tables; fire rings; 14 day limit.

Valdez Glacier Campground is located in a heavily wooded area against a mountain. Several rough gravel-based roads lead through the campground which features long, back-in spaces. Ample room separates the sites. A waterfall is adjacent to one of the sheltered picnic areas. Although the Valdez Glacier is within one-half mile, RVers should exercise caution if driving to the glacier because of the rough road surface.

ALLISON POINT (907) 835-4874
City of Valdez MP 3.0 Dayville Road

Located 4.5 miles from the Richardson Highway on Dayville Road: 96 spaces w/o hookups; porta-potties; fishing; public phone; no time limit.

Allison Point is operated by the City of Valdez in conjunction with the Valdez Fisheries Development Association. Spaces, which are on the roadway leading to the Alyeska Pipeline Terminal (follow signs), are marked and a fee is charged. It has graded graveled surfaces. Dedicated parking for the disabled is available. Nicknamed "Winnebago Heaven," fishing is permitted from the bank by the roadside.

EAGLE'S REST RV PARK privately operated
PO Box 610, Valdez, AK 99686 May 1st—Sept 30th
(907) 835-5267 1-800-553-7275 630 East Pioneer Drive

Located on the west side of the Richardson Highway at Pioneer Drive: 172 spaces; 36 pull-throughs; 83 full hookups; 40 power and water hookups; 49 w/o hookups; **sewage dump station**; flush toilets; drinking water; hot showers; laundry facilities; tables; public phone; separate tenting area; **propane**; no time limit.

Eagle's Rest RV Park has level, side-by-side, gravel-based spaces. The campground is walking distance to shopping centers. Fishing licenses can be purchased. Fish cleaning tables and a fish freezer are available. Good Sam discounts are offered.

GLACIER CHARTER SERVICE	privately operated
PO Box 1832, Valdez, AK 99686	May 30th—Sept 10th
(907) 835-5141	Kobuk Drive

Located one block south of the Richardson Highway on Chitina Drive. Turn right on Kobuk Drive: 9 spaces with full hookups; **sewage dump station**; fishing; no time limit.

The Glacier Charter Service can be identified by a large **LU-LU BELLE** sign above its office. The primary function of the organization is to provide small group fishing charters and not to serve as an RV campground. However, it is a small, attractive RV park. The raked gravel campground has been described as "an oasis in the desert." Since some campers stay for the entire summer, spaces may not be available.

BEAR PAW CAMPER PARK	privately operated
PO Box 93, Valdez, AK 99686	May 15th—Sept 15th
(907) 835-2530	100 North Harbor Drive

Turn south on Meals Avenue from the Richardson Highway. Drive two blocks to the corner of North Harbor Drive: 120 spaces; 10 pull-throughs; 80 full hookups; 20 power hookups; 20 w/o hookups; **sewage dump station**; flush toilets; drinking water; hot showers; laundry facilities; tables; fishing; public phone; no time limit.

Bear Paw Camper Park features a large, open design with raked gravel throughout. The level spaces are back-in, side-by-side, with pull-throughs for larger rigs. Lined garbage cans and fish cleaning tables are spaced throughout the campground. The toilets, non-metered showers, and laundry areas are exceptionally clean as is the entire campground. Quality service is stressed by the owner who claims, "We think we have the sweetest bathrooms this side of heaven." Shops, restaurants and museum are within walking distance. RV storage is available.

KAVIK RV PARK	privately operated
(907) 835-2205	South Harbor Drive

Turn south on Chitina Drive from the Richardson Highway. Drive one block then turn left on Kobuk Drive which becomes South Harbor Drive: 8 spaces with power hookups; drinking water; public phone; no time limit.

Kavik RV Park is an open lot with level back-in spaces. It offers parking and access to the boat harbor but no amenities.

SEA OTTER RV PARK	privately operated
PO Box 947, Valdez, AK 99686	April 15th—Oct 1st
(907) 835-2787	South Harbor Drive

Turn south on Chitina Drive from the Richardson Highway. Drive one block then turn left on Kobuk Drive which becomes South Harbor Drive: 150 spaces; 10 pull-throughs; 18 full hookups; 100 power and water hookups; 32 w/o hookups; **sewage dump station**; flush toilets; drinking water; hot showers; laundry facilities; fishing; public phone; no time limit.

Sea Otter RV Park is a large open gravel area with back-in, side-by-side level spaces. RVs are parked in rows with enough space between rigs for awning use. Located directly on Valdez Harbor, it offers a view of marine wildlife, several glaciers and the Alyeska tanker docks on the opposite side of the harbor.

RV SERVICES AT VALDEZ

Flightseeing services are available in Valdez. Charter air taxies offer outstanding views of Prince William Sound, Shoup and Columbia Glaciers, and Wrangell–St. Elias National Park and Preserve.

ERA HELICOPTER FLIGHTSEEING TOURS   **(907) 835-2595**

KETCHUM AIR SERVICE, INC.   **(907) 835-3789**

BIG WHEEL TEXACO SERVICE   **(907) 835-5230**
Located at MP 1 of the Richardson Highway: alignment; brakes; mufflers; general repairs; spring replacement; welding. The station stocks Firestone tires in camper and RV sizes.

ROOSEVELT LAKE TOURING AND RECOVERY   **(907) 835-2030**
A wheel lift wrecker for RV towing is available on a 24 hour basis.

VALDEZ TESORO   **(907) 835-4803**
Located at Meals Avenue and the Richardson Highway: **propane**.

NEW TOWN CHEVRON   **(907) 835-5300**
Located at Meals Avenue and the Richardson Highway: brakes; general repairs; tune ups; RV wash facility; **sewage dump station**; **propane**.

OSCAR'S
Turn south on Meals Avenue from the Richardson Highway. Drive two blocks to the corner of North Harbor Drive. Turn left: hot showers and a coin-operated RV wash station are located behind the building.

VALDEZ OPTIONS

THE RICHARDSON HIGHWAY: NORTH TO GLENNALLEN
The Richardson Highway from Valdez leads north through the heart of the Copper River basin country. The highway passes through scenic Keystone Canyon, over the crest of Thompson Pass, past the junction with the Edgerton Highway to Chitina, McCarthy and the Wrangell/St. Elias National Park and Preserve, by the cutoff to Copper Center and finally into Glennallen. From Glennallen there are three options: west to Anchorage, north to Delta Junction, and northeast to Tok.

THE ALASKA MARINE HIGHWAY SYSTEM (1-800-642-0066)
The Alaska Marine Highway System has three options from
Valdez: Cordova, Whittier and Seward. In Valdez call locally (835-
4436). Space is limited; reservations should be made as far in
advance of the date of travel as possible. Refer to the section on the
Alaska Marine Highway System for specific information.

 CORDOVA
Cordova (one of Alaska's best kept secrets) has less commercialism
and more charm. It can be reached only by water or by air. Since
the ferry does not operate daily, a visit will take several days
unless a flight is included in the itinerary. Things to do include
fishing, rafting, touring and birdwatching as well as the opportunity to
view the infamous "million dollar bridge" and Child's Glacier.

Odiak Camper Park, City of Cordova, PO Box 1210, Cordova 99574 (907)
424-6200 has RV spaces, showers and a **sewage dump station** for
campers who prefer to take their RVs. There are also several forest service campgrounds in the area, but they are not maintained for RVers.
Phone the Cordova Ranger District (907) 424-7661 for information.

 WHITTIER
Whittier is easily the most popular ferry destination since the four
mile face of the Columbia Glacier is included as part of the trip.
From Whittier, vehicles are driven onto railroad cars; the railroad
spur from Whittier passes through two major tunnels on its way to
Portage and the Seward Highway. It is possible to travel from Whittier to
Valdez as well.

 SEWARD
Seward is chosen less frequently as a Prince William Sound desti-
nation by RVers but is equally rewarding in terms of scenery.
Naturalists from the U.S. Fish and Wildlife Service are on board
the ferry M/V Tustumena during summer months. The Seward
Highway, designated as a National Scenic Byway by the U.S. Forest
Service, leads to Anchorage or Soldotna, Kenai and Homer.

RVing in Alaska:

Campgrounds and Services

Section III

Kenai Peninsula
REGION

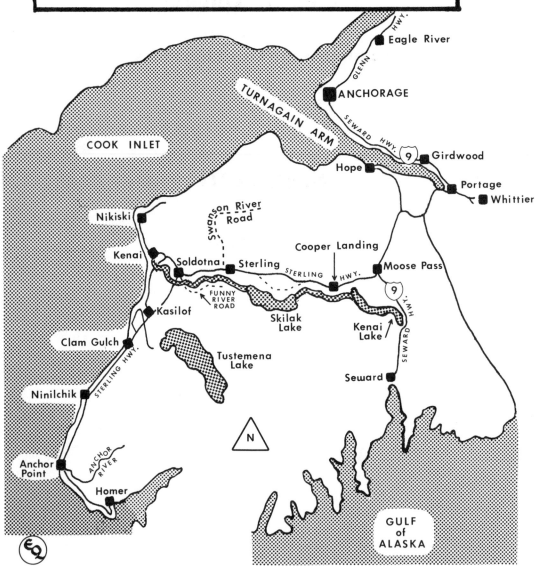

Chapter 12

THE HIGHWAY TO SEWARD

This chapter describes campgrounds and services on the Seward Highway from Anchorage to the city of Seward. Options include the cutoff to Hope; the Sterling Highway to Soldotna, Kenai and Homer; and the Alaska Marine Highway System to Valdez and Cordova to the east as well as to Kodiak, Homer and Seldovia to the west.

THE SEWARD HIGHWAY

Turnagain Arm south of Anchorage periodically displays an interesting phenomenon in the form of bore tides. These tides are especially likely to occur when rising tidewater is compressed by the narrowing Turnagain Arm during periods of strong winds. The churning waves from these tides can reach nearly six feet in height. The best chance for seeing a bore tide comes about two hours following low tide in Anchorage.

Caution: it is extremely dangerous to walk or drive on the mud flats and beaches of Cook Inlet because of its quicksand-like texture and glacial-silt composition.

The Kenai Peninsula was linked to Anchorage through Turnagain Pass in 1951. The fifty mile section north from Seward was the last section to be completed. The highway, which originates in Seward by Resurrection Bay, terminates one hundred twenty-seven miles later in Anchorage.

The Seward Highway is designated as a National Scenic Byway by the U.S. Forest Service. Scenic byway status is given to highways which draw attention to "areas that contain outstanding scenery and provide an opportunity to view well managed and changing forest landscapes."

SEWARD HIGHWAY SCENIC BYWAY VIEWPOINTS

MP 117.4	Potter Marsh	wildlife refuge, migratory birds
MP 110.3	Beluga Point	migratory whales, Turnagain Arm
MP 103.0	Indian Creek	glacier-carved valley, rugged peaks
MP 90.0	Mount Alyeska	resort and recreation area
MP 78.9	Portage Glacier	early route to Prince William Sound
MP 68.5	Turnagain Pass	showcase for the Kenai Mountains
MP 22.9	Kenai Lake	viewpoint, glacial-fed lake
MP 3.7	Exit Glacier	Harding Icefield, nature walk

CHUGACH STATE PARK VISITOR CENTER
(907) 345-5014

open all year
MP 115 Seward Highway

Located at MP 115 of the Seward Highway, just south of Potter Marsh Wildlife Refuge. The railroad museum is open during summer months only. Information about the state park, hiking trails, and other points of interest is available from Chugach State Park Headquarter's staff housed in the restored railroad section house. The building (circa 1929) is on the National Register of Historic Buildings.

CHUGACH NATIONAL FOREST VISITOR CENTER
(907) 783-3242

Glacier Ranger District

Located on Forest Station Way, one block east of the Seward Highway at MP 90, at the junction with Alyeska Highway at Girdwood. Information on hiking trails and points of interest in the area. Great view of the inlet.

BEGICH/ BOGGS VISITOR CENTER
(907) 271-2500

May—September
MP 5.5 Portage Glacier Road

The Begich/Boggs Visitor Center, located on Portage Lake, is the most popular tourist destination in Alaska. It offers an excellent view of icebergs and the Portage Glacier. Exhibits include displays of glacial ice and descriptions of the effects of the glaciers upon the valley. A special film depicting glacial activity in Alaska is shown throughout the day. Forest Service personnel conduct special nature walks in the Portage area. The parking area can accommodate the largest RVs. Three glaciers can be seen from Portage Glacier Road.

PORTAGE REMNANTS
MP 90.4 Seward Highway
Located south of the railroad crossing at MP 90.4 of the Seward Highway, the next several miles give evidence of the force of the 1964 earthquake. Plainly visible are destroyed trees and the abandoned buildings of Portage. As a result of the quake, ground in the area dropped and sea level in Turnagain Arm raised. The buildings are on private property but are easily photographed from the highway.

WHITTIER FERRY TRAIN STOP
MP 80.5 Seward Highway
Located on the east side of the Seward Highway at MP 80.5. This is the

onloading site for vehicles which will be transported to Whittier on flatbed railroad cars in order to connect with the ferry to Valdez. Vehicles from Valdez and Whittier are offloaded at this site.

HEALTH AND EMERGENCY SERVICES

MP 100 to MP 75	Girdwood Fire Department	911
MP 75 to MP 52	Hope/Sunrise EMS	(907) 782-3601
MP 55 to MP 30	Cooper Landing Rescue Squad	(907) 595-1111
MP 30 to MP 0	Seward Volunteer Ambulance	(907) 224-3338
		or 911

Alaska State Troopers   CB Channel 9 or (907) 262-4435

Emergency Call Boxes   (summer only)

MP 68.3	Turnagain Pass	MP 56	Hope Road Junction
MP 45.5	Summit Lake Lodge	MP 30	Sterling Highway

ALASKA TOWING & REPAIR   **(907) 783-3100**
Located at MP 90 of the Seward Highway, 24-hour towing is available; tire repairs and minor auto repair are offered.

RV CAMPGROUNDS ON THE SEWARD HIGHWAY

BIRD CREEK CAMPGROUND   **Memorial Day to Labor Day**
Alaska State Park System   **MP 101.5 Seward Highway**

Located at MP 101.5 of the Seward Highway: 25 spaces w/o hookups; pit toilets; drinking water; covered picnic sites; tables; fire rings; fishing; trails; 7 day limit.

Bird Creek Campground has several rough roads through stands of Sitka spruce. Spaces are not level back-ins with trees between spaces. Most large RVs can be accommodated. An overflow area is located directly across the highway. Pit toilets are set on concrete vaults and are accessible to the disabled. Nearby Bird Creek offers fishing. A fulltime campground host is on site.

RV CAMPGROUNDS ON PORTAGE GLACIER ROAD

BLACK BEAR CAMPGROUND   **Memorial Day to Labor Day**
U.S. Forest Service   **MP 3.9 Portage Glacier Road**

Turn east 3.9 miles from the junction of the Seward Highway with Portage Glacier Road: 12 spaces w/o hookups; 2 pull-throughs; pit toilets; drinking water; tables; fire rings; 14 day limit.

Black Bear Campground is located in a heavily wooded area adjacent to a small creek. The road and spaces are gravel-based. Spaces are back-in, short in length and level but best suited to campers and mini-motorhomes. The two pull-throughs will not accommodate larger RVs.

WILLIWAW CAMPGROUND
U.S. Forest Service

Memorial Day to Labor Day
MP 4.0 Portage Glacier Road

Turn east 4.0 miles from the junction of the Seward Highway with Portage Glacier Road: 38 spaces w/o hookups; pit toilets; drinking water; tables; fire rings; 14 day limit.

Williwaw Campground has two separate sections set in a wooded area. Spaces are back-ins and vary in length, but some spaces can accommodate larger RVs. An open area has room for seven RVs side-by-side. The campground is adjacent to Williwaw Creek and is walking distance to a salmon spawning viewing area. There are excellent photo opportunities of the Middle Glacier from this point.

THE SEWARD HIGHWAY (continued)

BERTHA LAKE CAMPGROUND
U.S. Forest Service

Memorial Day to Labor Day
MP 65.5 Seward Highway

Located at MP 65.5 of the Seward Highway: 12 spaces w/o hookups; pit toilets; drinking water; tables; grills; 14 day limit.

Bertha Creek Campground is located in a wooded area with thick underbrush. Spaces are back-in, level and separated by foliage. The campground is adjacent to the creek and walking distance to a state fish weir.

GRANITE CREEK CAMPGROUND
U.S. Forest Service

Memorial Day to Labor Day
MP 63 Seward Highway

Located at MP 63 of the Seward Highway: 19 spaces w/o hookups; pit toilets; drinking water; tables; grills; fishing; trails; 14 day limit.

Granite Creek Campground is set in heavy stands of spruce trees on the creek. Spaces are back-in, level and can accommodate longer RVs. The entry road is narrow and bordered by trees which could cause some difficulty for larger RVs. The campground has an undeveloped quality and is away from highway traffic noise.

RV CAMPGROUNDS ON THE HOPE (CUTOFF) HIGHWAY

Hope was the first gold rush town in Alaska. Resurrection Creek and Sixmile Creek quickly yielded enough gold to swell the population to 3,000 people. When the boom collapsed, the population dropped just as quickly. Gold rush period buildings still exist in Hope.

HENRY'S ONE STOP
PO Box 50, Hope, AK 99605
(907) 782-3222

privately operated
May 1st—Oct 30th
MP 15.8 Hope Highway

Drive 15.8 miles from the junction of the Seward Highway at MP 56.5 with the Hope Highway: 9 spaces; 4 pull-throughs; 4 full hookups; 5 power and water hookups; **sewage dump station**; flush toilets; drinking water; hot showers; laundry facilities; picnic sites; tables; trails; public phone; separate tenting area; no time limit.

Dall sheep as viewed from the Seward Highway south of Anchorage

Henry's One Stop has spaces which branch from a circular drive. Spaces are level and RVs of any length can be accommodated. A laundry, grocery store and motel are on site.

COEUR D'ALENE CAMPGROUND   **Memorial Day to Labor Day**
U.S. Forest Service   **MP 6.0 Palmer Creek Road**

Palmer Creek Road is not recommended for 5th wheels, trailers or motorhomes of any great length. Once committed to the road (6.4 miles), there is no place to turn around.

Palmer Creek Road which leads to the Coeur d'Alene Campground is a narrow, one-way road with numerous pull-outs and equally numerous switch-backs. The road is almost to the tree line before the campground is reached. This road is not for the timid RVer.

Drive 16.2 miles from the junction of the Seward Highway at MP 56.5 with the Hope Highway. Although the highway forks to the right, continue directly ahead on Resurrection Creek Road for 0.5 mile. Turn left for 6.4 miles on Palmer Creek Road: 6 spaces w/o hookups; 1 pull-through; pit toilets; no drinking water; picnic site; tables; trails; 14 day limit.

Coeur d'Alene Campground is scenic, isolated and adjacent to a small creek. Back-in parking is provided for RVs. Water must be either boiled or treated chemically. For the camper who wishes to "experience the real Alaska" and still be on the road system, this is a good place to start.

PORCUPINE CAMPGROUND   **Memorial Day to Labor Day**
U.S. Forest Service   **MP 17.8 Hope Highway**

Drive 17.8 miles from the junction of the Seward Highway (MP 56.5) with the Hope Highway: 24 spaces w/o hookups; 11 pull-throughs; pit toilets; drinking water; tables; fire rings; fishing; 14 day limit.

Porcupine Campground is located at the terminus of the Hope Highway in a heavily wooded area with birch, aspen, alder and spruce trees. The road through the campground and each individual space is blacktopped. Campsites are widely separated from one another. Spaces are level and vary in length, but the largest RV can be accommodated. Pit toilets are set on concrete vaults and are accessible to the disabled. There is a campground host on site and the small town of Hope is nearby.

THE SEWARD HIGHWAY (continued)

TENDERFOOT CREEK CAMPGROUND Memorial Day-Labor Day
U.S. Forest Service   **MP 46 Seward Highway**

Located 0.5 mile from the Seward Highway at MP 46; ignore all roads which branch to the right until the campground is reached: 27 spaces w/o hookups; 6 pull-throughs; pit toilets; drinking water; tables; grills; boat launch; fishing; trails; 14 day limit.

Tenderfoot Creek Campground borders the north end of Summit Lake and is heavily wooded. Spaces are level and vary in length. Pit toilets are accessible to the disabled. The lake is long and excellent for boating. Summit Lake Restaurant is located on the corner of the road leading to the campground.

The Sterling Highway forms a junction with the Seward Highway at MP 37.7. Tern Lake Campground is accessed at this point.

TERN LAKE CAMPGROUND   Memorial Day to Labor Day
U.S. Forest Service   **MP 37.7 Seward/Sterling Junction**

Turn west 0.5 mile from the junction with the Sterling Highway and the Seward Highway at MP 37. This is the second road cut-off when traveling south: 25 spaces w/o hookups; 1 pull-through; pit toilets; drinking water; tables; grills; boat launch; fishing; trails; 14 day limit.

Tern Lake Campground is partially wooded with spruce and birch trees. Spaces vary in length; some are quite short and blocking may be required. Pit toilets are accessible to the disabled. A large parking lot provides visitors access to the viewing area by the nearby salmon spawning creek. A small creek is at one part of the campground.

TRAIL RIVER CAMPGROUND   Memorial Day to Labor Day
U.S. Forest Service   **MP 24.2 Seward Highway**

Turn east from the junction with the Seward Highway at MP 24.2 for 1.2 miles onto a narrow, descending gravel-based road: 64 spaces w/o hookups; 4 pull-throughs; pit toilets; drinking water; day use picnic sites; tables; grills; fishing; trails; 14 day limit.

Trail River Campground is constructed around four loops on the Lower Trail River at Kenai Lake. Three of the loops are best suited to mini-motorhomes and smaller travel trailers but can park some rigs up to 28 feet in length. Individual spaces are well separated from one another. The four pull-throughs can accommodate the largest RVs. A campground host is on site. Pit toilets are on concrete vaults and are accessible to the disabled. This scenic, heavily wooded campground has access to both the river and Kenai Lake. Volleyball and horseshoe sites are available.

PTARMIGAN CREEK CAMPGROUND Memorial Day to Labor Day
U.S. Forest Service   **MP 23.1 Seward Highway**

Located at MP 23.1 of the Seward Highway: 16 spaces w/o hookups; pit toilets; drinking water; tables; grills; fishing; 14 day limit.

Ptarmigan Creek Campground is set in a wooded area with trails which lead to Ptarmigan Lake. Spaces are short in length and not level. Spaces are separated from one another and screened by trees. Pit toilets are set on concrete vaults and are accessible to the disabled.

PRIMROSE LANDING CAMPGROUND   Memorial Day-Labor Day
U.S. Forest Service   **MP 17 Seward Highway**

Turn west from the Seward Highway at MP 17 for 1.1 miles on the black-topped road (later turns to gravel) which parallels the highway: 10 spaces w/o hookups; pit toilets; drinking water; tables; grills; boat launch; fishing; trails; 14 day limit.

Primrose Landing Campground borders the south end of Kenai Lake and is the trailhead for the Primrose Trail. Spaces tend to be short and at least three of them are angled at the wrong direction to the campground road. Spaces are best suited to RVs up to 28 feet in length. Pit toilets are set on concrete vaults and are accessible to the disabled.

SEWARD, ALASKA

Resurrection Bay, which offers a year round ice-free port, was selected in 1903 to be the terminus for the Alaska Railroad. The town came into being as a result of the railroad and was named for William H. Seward who negotiated the purchase of Alaska from Russia in 1867. The drive from Anchorage to Seward takes between three and four hours. Tour buses and the Alaska Railroad also serve the community daily.

Special events in Seward include the annual Silver Salmon Derby, the Halibut Jackpot Tournament, the Mount Marathon Race and, for the hardy, the Polar Bear Jumpoff Festival into Resurrection Bay which is held in January. First run in 1909, the popular race to the top of Mount Marathon (3,022 feet) and back is run each Fourth of July. There are three classes: men, women, and juniors.

KENAI FJORDS NATIONAL PARK
The 670,000 acre Kenai Fjords National Park was established by Congress in 1980 as part of the Alaska National Interest Lands Conservation Act. In addition to its icefields, glaciers, and fjords, the park is home to mountain goats, bears, wolverines, marmots and other land

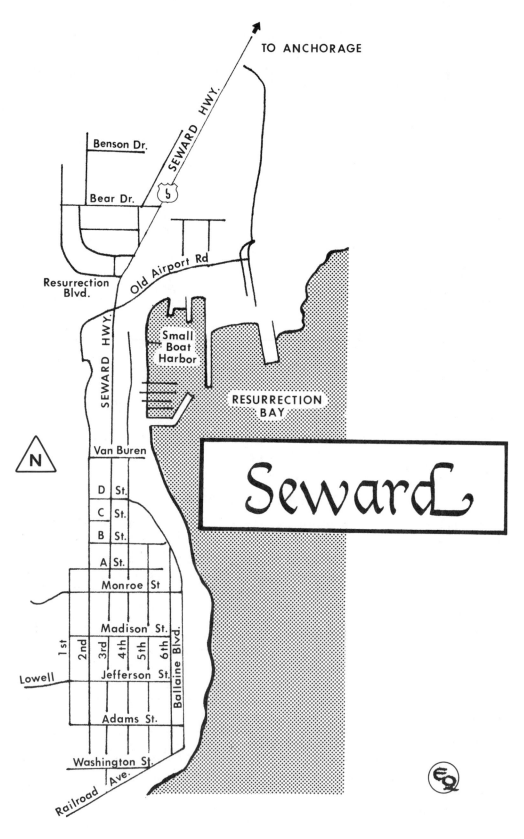

TO ANCHORAGE

SEWARD HWY.

Benson Dr.

Bear Dr.

Resurrection Blvd.

Old Airport Rd

SEWARD HWY.

Small Boat Harbor

RESURRECTION BAY

N

Van Buren

D St.

C St.

B St.

A St.

Monroe St

Madison St.

1st

2nd

3rd

4th

5th

6th

Ballaine Blvd.

Lowell

Jefferson St.

Adams St.

Washington St.

Railroad Ave.

Seward

mammals as well as porpoises, seals, otters, whales, eagles and puffins. Its most popular tourist attraction is the Exit Glacier which flows from the Harding Icefield.

The Harding Icefield, a fifteen hundred square mile area west of Seward, forms the major portion of the Kenai Fjords National Park. During the last glacial period, thirty thousand years ago, approximately fifty percent of Alaska was covered by ice. Today ice coverage is closer to five percent. By definition, a fjord is "a steep-sided valley carved by a glacier and partially filled with ocean water." Resurrection Bay is an excellent example of one of the many fjords in the immediate Seward area.

EXIT GLACIER   Memorial Day to Labor Day
Turn from the Seward Highway at MP 3.7. The Exit Glacier road is gravel-based and rough although large RVs can pass one another. Drive nine miles (approximately thirty minutes) to reach the Ranger Station parking area: no amenities. No overnight RV parking is provided with an exception made for persons registered to hike the Harding Icefield. A 0.5 mile trail with wayside exhibits leads to within 0.3 mile of the glacier. A three-mile loop nature trail across moraines and bedrock flanks the glacier.

CAINES HEAD STATE RECREATION AREA
Caines Head, six miles south of Seward, is filled with World War II relics, bunkers, six-inch guns, and other reminders of Fort McGilvray. Overlooking Resurrection Bay, the abandoned fort commanded a strategic area and was intended to defend the Port of Seward in case of attack.

The face of Exit Glacier: MP 3.7 Seward Highway

HEALTH AND EMERGENCY SERVICES

Seward Police	**(907) 224-3339**
Seward General Hospital	**(907) 224-5205**
Seward Volunteer Ambulance Corp	**(907) 224-3338 or 911**
Alaska State Troopers	**(907) 224-3346**

KENAI FJORDS PARK INFORMATION CENTER   **(907) 224-3874**
PO Box 390, Seward, AK 99664   **1212 Fourth Avenue**

The Kenai Fjords National Park Information Center has photographs, maps, natural history publications and displays reflecting the impact of glacier ice on the region. Evening programs include boardwalk talks and nature walks. Harding Icefield hikes are also conducted but these require prior registration and take an entire day.

CHAMBER OF COMMERCE RAILCAR   **(907) 224-3094**
PO Box 749, Seward, AK 99664   **Third Street at Jefferson**

The visitor center features photographs, literature and up-to-date information on activities in the Seward area.

RV CAMPGROUNDS AT SEWARD

A CREEKSIDE PARK   **privately operated**
HCR 64, Box 375, Seward, AK 99664   **May 1st—Sept 15th**
(907) 224-3647   **MP 6.6 Seward Highway**

Located at the junction of the Seward Highway at MP 6.6 with Bear Creek Road: 35 spaces; 1 pull-through; 35 power and water hookups; **sewage dump station**; flush toilets; drinking water; hot showers; public phone; **propane**; no time limit.

A Creekside Park is an open, gravel-based area. Spaces are back-ins with some spaces on the bank of the creek. Permanent mobile homes are set up at the edge of the campground. A senior discount is offered.

BEAR CREEK RV . . . PARK   **privately operated**
HCR 64, Box 386, Seward, AK 99664   **open all year**
(907) 224-5725   **MP 6.6 Seward Highway**

Turn east 0.5 mile at the junction of the Seward Highway at MP 6.6 with Bear Creek Road: 60 spaces; 8 pull-throughs; 20 full hookups; 30 power and water hookups; 10 w/o hookups; **sewage dump station**; flush toilets; drinking water; hot showers; laundry facilities; tables; recreation room; trails; **propane**; public phone; no time limit.

Bear Creek RV and Mobile Home Park has most of its spaces filled with permanent residents although limited overnight parking is available. Spaces are graveled and level. The road to the campsite is good and traffic noise is not a problem. Good Sam discounts are available. A small grocery store is on site with cable TV in the lounge.

FOREST ACRES PARK
City Parks and Recreation

May 15th—Sept 30th
Hemlock Street at Dimond Street

Turn east at the junction of Hemlock with the Seward Highway at MP 2.8. Drive to the "T" at Dimond Street, turn left 0.3 mile to entrance: 50 spaces w/o hookups; flush toilets; covered picnic sites; tables; separate tenting area; 14 day limit.

Forest Acres Park is located in a large open area with trees throughout. Roads throughout are narrow and uneven. Spaces are not level, vary in length, but tend to be small. An undetermined number of pull-throughs can accommodate larger RVs. Some blocking may be necessary.

SEWARD ARMY RECREATION CAMP Memorial Day to Labor Day
Fort Richardson, Bldg 600   Hemlock Street and Dimond Street

Turn east at the junction of Hemlock with the Seward Highway at MP 2.8. Drive to the "T" at Dimond Street, turn left 0.3 mile to entrance: 40 spaces with power and water hookups; **sewage dump station**; flush toilets; drinking water; hot showers; laundry facilities; tables; grills; recreation room; public phone; separate tenting area; 14 day limit.

The order for priority for RV camping at the Seward Recreation Camp is as follows: active duty military personnel and their families including National Guard and Army Reserve; retired military personnel and their families; and Department of Defense personnel. Reservations cannot be made at the camp itself and must be made through the I.T.R. (International Travel Reservations) office at Fort Richardson either in person or by phone (907/ 384-1649). Reservations must be made at least two weeks in advance of the time of stay.

SEWARD MILITARY RECREATION CAMP   May 18th—Sept 16th
Elmendorf Air Force Base   Dimond Street and Seward Highway

Turn northeast at the junction of the Seward Highway at MP 2.5 with Dimond Street: 63 spaces; 30 power only hookups; 33 w/o hookups; **sewage dump station**; flush toilets; drinking water; hot showers; laundry facilities; tables; grills; fishing; separate tenting area; 7 day limit.

Dimond Street is diagonal to the Seward Highway and may present a difficult turn for large RVs traveling south. Priority is given to active duty Air Force personnel and their families with secondary consideration given to retiree's, reservists and members of the National Guard. Only telephone reservations are accepted (907/ 224-5559). Mail reservations will not be honored. Phone reservations can also be made from Elmendorf AFB (907/ 552-5191 or 552-2674). Fishing reservations can be made aboard Air Force boats maintained at Seward.

KENAI FJORDS RV PARK
PO Box 2772, Seward, AK 99664
(907) 224-8779 (1-800-478-8007)

privately operated
May 1st—Oct 1st
Small Boat Harbor

Located between Third and Fourth Avenues on Van Buren adjacent to the Small Boat Harbor: 37 spaces with power and water hookups; chemical toilets; tables; grills; no time limit.

Kenai Fjords RV Park has back-in, level spaces on hard-packed gravel. Amenities are scarce and campers are limited to using on-site chemical porta-potties. Showers and laundry facilities are within walking distance. The small boat harbor offers a sewage dump station two blocks away.

LOWELL POINT CAMPGROUND   Memorial Day—Sept 15th
(907) 224-5827   **Lowell Point Road at Spruce Creek**

Follow the shoreline on Lowell Point Road from Railroad Avenue and the ferry dock. Turn left after Spruce Creek bridge is crossed. This campground is under construction and offers dry camping only. It will be open after Memorial Day through September 15th.

MILLER'S LANDING   privately operated
PO Box 81, Seward, AK 99664   May 15th—Sept 30th
(907) 224-5739   end of Lowell Road

Follow the shoreline on Lowell Point Road for 2.5 miles from Railroad Avenue and the ferry dock: 52 spaces; 14 power hookups; 38 w/o hookups; drinking water; pit toilets; tables; grills; boat launch; fishing; trails; separate tenting area; no time limit.

Miller's Landing is reached by a road which is rough but passable. There are two sections: an open level area and a heavily wooded area. A gravel-based road runs through the wooded section which has back-in spaces separated by trees. Primarily used for fishing and marine charters, the campground also has a small grocery, bait and tackle shop.

WATERFRONT PARK   Mat 15th—Sept 30th
City of Seward Parks and Recreation   **along Ballaine Boulevard**

Located along Ballaine Boulevard between the ferry terminal and the Harbormaster building at the small boat harbor. Dry camping only. A tent camping area is located at Jefferson Street. A caravan area at Monroe Street is reserved for scheduled groups. The Parks and Recreation Department, located in City Hall, 5th and Adams, offers a brochure with a comprehensive list of facilities. City employees with appropriate identification will collect parking fees. Permits must be displayed on the windshield. 14 day limit.

RV SERVICES AT SEWARD

BEAR CREEK RV . . . PARK   **(907) 224-5725**
Turn east 0.5 mile at the junction of the Seward Highway at MP 6.6 with Bear Creek Road: mechanical repairs of a limited nature are offered.

PUBLIC RV SEWAGE DUMP STATION   **Small Boat Harbor**
Located at MP 1.4 of the Seward Highway at the north end of the small boat harbor across the street from the Benny Benson Memorial.

BAY CITY MOTORS   (907) 224-5498
Located at Third Avenue and D Street: Brakes; emergency road service; generator repair; muffler system repair; repairs of a general nature; towing; welding. A large-sized bay can handle RVs up to 50 feet in length.

SEWARD TESORO   (907) 224-8611
Petroleum products; **sewage dump station**; propane. Free dump station use with fill up. Eight short-term full hookups are available.

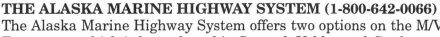

SEWARD OPTIONS

THE SEWARD HIGHWAY: NORTH TO ANCHORAGE
Anchorage is 127 miles north of Seward. The highway has excellent turnouts for viewing Kenai Lake, Turnagain Pass and Turnagain Arm. Options from the Seward Highway include the Sterling Highway at MP 38 to Soldotna, Kenai and Homer, and the Hope Cutoff at MP 56.5.

THE ALASKA MARINE HIGHWAY SYSTEM (1-800-642-0066)
The Alaska Marine Highway System offers two options on the M/V Tustumena which is home-based in Seward: Valdez and Cordova to the east, and Kodiak, Port Lions, Homer and Seldovia to the west. Naturalists from the U.S. Fish and Wildlife Service are on board the M/V Tustumena during summer months between the middle of June to the end of September.

In Seward call locally (224-5485). Space is limited; reservations should be made as far in advance of the date of travel as possible. Refer to the section on the Alaska Marine Highway System for specific information.

Trumpeter swan and mallard ducks

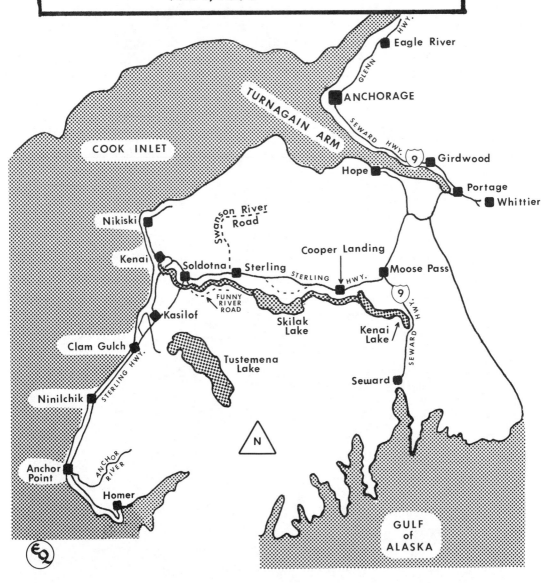

Kenai Peninsula
REGION

COOK INLET

TURNAGAIN ARM

GLENN HWY.

Eagle River

ANCHORAGE

SEWARD HWY.

Hope

Girdwood

9

Portage

Whittier

Nikiski

Swanson River Road

Cooper Landing

Kenai

Soldotna

Sterling

STERLING HWY.

Moose Pass

9

Kasilof

FUNNY RIVER ROAD

Skilak Lake

Kenai Lake

SEWARD HWY.

Clam Gulch

Tustemena Lake

Seward

STERLING HWY.

Ninilchik

ANCHOR RIVER

N

Anchor Point

Homer

GULF of ALASKA

Chapter 13

THE STERLING HIGHWAY TO SOLDOTNA

This chapter describes campgrounds and services on the Sterling Highway from its junction with the Seward Highway to the outskirts of Soldotna. Options include the Skilak Lake Road; the Swanson River Road; the Sterling Highway east to the Seward Highway; and the Sterling Highway south to Homer.

THE STERLING HIGHWAY

The Sterling Highway begins at MP 37.7 which is a one-way exit from the Seward Highway. Immediately beyond that exit is a second entry road at MP 37 which is a two-way junction with the highway. These roads converge and lead west to Cooper Landing, the Russian River, Skilak Lake, the Kenai River and the cities of Soldotna and Kenai. From Soldotna the highway turns south to Kasilof, Ninilchik, Anchor Point and Homer. Milepost numbers on the Sterling Highway continue without interruption the numeration of the Seward Highway.

Representatives of the Kenai Peninsula Borough estimate that the peninsula is host to 180,000 visitors during the summer months about half of whom are non-Anchorage people. RVers are attracted by the overall quality of the campgrounds as well as by the region's rivers and lakes, and views of glaciers and volcanos. Fishing from the banks of the Russian and Kenai Rivers for king salmon, clamming on the beaches of Clam Gulch, and charterboat ocean fishing for halibut from Homer contribute to the influx of summer visitors.

KENAI NATIONAL WILDLIFE REFUGE VISITOR CENTER
Skilak Wildlife Recreation Area   **MP 58 Sterling Highway**

Unlike most visitor information centers, this center is not located near a major community; it is, however, on the Sterling Highway near two large fishing/recreation campgrounds. Maps and general information on hiking, fishing and campgrounds in the Kenai Moose Range are provided.

HEALTH AND EMERGENCY SERVICES

MP 38 to 62	**Cooper Landing Volunteer Rescue**	**(907) 595-1111**
MP 62 to 121	**Central Peninsula EMS**	**911**
Alaska State Troopers		**(907) 262-4453**
Emergency Call Box	**(summer only)**	**MP 38 Sterling Highway**

RV CAMPGROUNDS ON THE STERLING HIGHWAY

TERN LAKE CAMPGROUND   Memorial Day-Labor Day
U.S. Forest Service   MP 37 Seward/Sterling Highway

Turn west 0.5 mile from the junction with the Sterling Highway and the Seward Highway at MP 37. This is the second road cut-off when traveling south: 25 spaces w/o hookups; 1 pull-through; pit toilets; drinking water; tables; grills; boat launch; fishing; trails; 14 day limit.

Tern Lake Campground is partially wooded with spruce and birch trees. Spaces vary in length; some are quite short and blocking may be required. Pit toilets are accessible to the disabled. A large parking lot provides visitors with access to the viewing area by the nearby salmon spawning creek.

SUNRISE INN RV PARK   **privately operated**
MP 45 Sterling Highway, Sterling, AK 99572   May 15th—Sept 30th
(907) 595-1222   **MP 45 Sterling Highway**

Located at MP 45 of the Sterling Highway by the Sunrise Inn Lodge: 15 spaces; 1 pull-through; 12 power hookups; 3 w/o hookups; flush toilets; drinking water; picnic sites; trails; public phone; no time limit.

Sunrise Inn RV Park is part of a larger restaurant, gift shop, motel, service station complex. Spaces vary in length but are wide and level on gravel bases. They are located in a wooded area away from highway road noise and separated from one another by trees. Toilets are in the motel.

QUARTZ CREEK CAMPGROUND   Memorial Day-Labor Day
U.S. Forest Service   MP 45 Sterling Highway

Located 0.3 mile south of the Sterling Highway at MP 45 on Quartz Creek Road west of Sunrise Inn Lodge: 32 spaces w/o hookups; 8 pull-throughs; pit toilets; flush toilets; drinking water; tables; grills; boat launch; fishing; trails; 14 day limit.

Quartz Creek Campground is heavily wooded and has two loops which form camping areas with a common blacktopped road throughout. All spaces are blacktopped and level. The largest RV can be accommodated. One space is dedicated to the disabled; both pit and flush toilets are accessible to the disabled. The campground has creek access to Kenai Lake with a large parking area provided for boat trailers. A fulltime campground host is available.

CRESCENT CREEK CAMPGROUND   Memorial Day-Labor Day
U.S. Forest Service   MP 3.0 Quartz Creek Road

Located 2.9 miles south of the Sterling Highway at MP 45 on Quartz Creek Road west of Sunrise Inn Lodge: 9 spaces w/o hookups; pit toilets; drinking water; tables; grills; fishing; trails; 14 day limit.

Crescent Creek Campground is heavily wooded and secluded. Spaces are on gravel bases and vary in length. Two spaces are incorrectly angled to the road. Pit toilets on a concrete vault are accessible to the disabled.

KENAI PRINCESS RV PARK　　　　　　**privately operated**
329 "F" Street, #207, Anchorage, AK 99501　　**May 15th—Sept 20th**
(907) 258-5993　1-800- 541-5174　　　　**MP 1.8 Bean Creek Road**

Located 1.8 miles north of the Sterling Highway on a gravel road at the junction with Bean Creek Road at MP 47.4 by the Kenai River bridge: 37 spaces with full hookups; **sewage dump station**; flush toilets; drinking water; hot showers; laundry facilities; tables; fire rings; fishing; public phone; no time limit.

Kenai Princess RV Park is part of a larger lodge/restaurant complex with 1,900 feet of Kenai River frontage. Spaces are blacktopped and approximately 55 feet by 20 feet. Spaces are blacktopped back-ins. Restroom/shower areas are designed for the disabled. Open fires are prohibited. The spa and weight room at the lodge are available to RVers at no extra charge. Good Sam discounts are offered.

HAMILTON'S PLACE　　　　　　**privately operated**
PO Box 505, Sterling, AK 99572　　　　**open all year**
(907) 595-1260　　　　**MP 48.5 Sterling Highway**

Located at MP 48.5 of the Sterling Highway by the Kenai River bridge: 24 spaces; 4 full hookups; 20 power hookups; flush toilets; drinking water; hot showers; laundry facilities; boat launch; fishing; **propane**; separate tenting area; no time limit.

Hamilton's Place's primary business is its restaurant/lounge, service station, boat rentals and tackle shop. The hard-packed, level back-in RV spaces are located in an open area near the highway with some fenced enclosures which serve as a visual barrier. Although this campground might normally be considered only as an overnight stop, the availability of boat rentals, tackle and Kenai River access for salmon fishing could encourage a longer stay.

MILLER'S HOMESTEAD　　　　　　**privately operated**
PO Box 693, Cooper Landing, AK 99572　　**May 1st—Oct 1st**
(907) 595-1406　　　　**MP 49.7 Sterling Highway**

Located at MP 49.7 of the Sterling Highway: 18 power only spaces; 18 pull-throughs; **sewage dump station**; flush toilets; drinking water; hot showers; fishing; public phones; no time limit.

Miller's Homestead is an open, graveled area surrounded by trees. Spaces are level. The campground is behind a bed and breakfast building. The Kenai River is accessed by a trail. Charter raft trips can be arranged.

COOPER CREEK CAMPGROUND　　**Memorial Day-Labor Day**
U.S. Forest Service　　　　**MP 50.7 Sterling Highway**

Located at MP 50.7 of the Sterling Highway, west of Cooper Creek; this campground is divided into two sections one on each side of the highway: 26 spaces w/o hookups; pit toilets; drinking water; tables; fire rings; boat launch; fishing; separate tenting area; 14 day limit.

Cooper Creek Campground is located in wooded areas with gravel roads through both sections. The south portion borders Cooper Creek and the north portion borders the Kenai River. Spaces vary in length but some can accommodate the largest RVs. A campground host is located on the north side of the Sterling Highway.

RUSSIAN RIVER CAMPGROUND
U.S. Forest Service

Memorial Day-Labor Day
MP 52.6 Sterling Highway

Located on a blacktopped road at MP 52.6 of the Sterling Highway: 98 spaces w/o hookups; 13 pull-throughs; **sewage dump station**; pit toilets; flush toilets; drinking water; tables; fire rings; fishing; trails; dumpsters; public phone.

Russian River Campground is located between the Kenai and Russian rivers, upstream from their confluence. Spaces are assigned by Forest Service personnel and a daily fee is charged. Campgrounds are set-off in a series of blacktopped, loop roads over 1.9 miles. Spaces are back-in, black-topped and level. Dedicated spaces for the disabled are provided, and both pit toilets and flush toilets are accessible to the disabled. Camping during the peak salmon runs (mid-June through mid-August) is restricted to three consecutive days although fourteen day camping is permitted at other times of the year.

KENAI-RUSSIAN RIVER FERRY RECREATION AREA
U.S. Fish and Wildlife Service   **MP 55 Sterling Highway**

Located at MP 55 of the Sterling Highway: 180 spaces w/o hookups; pit toilets; drinking water; picnic sites; boat launch; fishing; 2 day limit.

The Kenai-Russian River Ferry Recreation Area is a large, circular, gravel parking area. Parking is back-in, side-by-side with no dedicated spaces as such. There is also an overflow parking area and a boat ramp parking area. No grills or fire rings are available. Pit toilets are on concrete vaults and are accessible to the disabled. Fly fishing only is allowed; a current propelled, disabled accessible, ferry is used to cross the river.

SKILAK LAKE ROAD

Skilak Lake Road is a twenty mile long gravel road which intersects with the Sterling Highway at MP 58 to the east and MP 75.2 to the west.

Mile markers are not posted on this road. Seven U.S. Fish and Wildlife Service campgrounds are available. Camping is permitted for no more than fourteen days during any thirty day period. Glacially fed by the Kenai River, Skilak Lake is ten miles long and reaches depths to 1,200 feet. Records show that it has the state's highest per capita fatality rate from boating accidents; hypothermia as well as drowning contributes to the figures. The U.S. Fish and Wildlife Service patrols the lake and performs boat checks for life preservers and fishing licenses. Boaters should carry blankets, a change of warm clothing and the means to start an emergency fire.

Since clear skies and calm water surfaces can rapidly change, boaters should head for shore at the first indication of change in the winds or weather. Flat bottomed river boats are especially dangerous since wind-whipped waves can reach heights of five and six feet.

Combat fishing on the Russian River

JIM'S LANDING CAMPGROUND　　　**Memorial Day-Labor Day**
U.S. Fish and Wildlife Service　　　**Mile 0.2 Skilak Lake Road**

Located 0.2 mile from the *east junction* with the Sterling Highway and Skilak Lake Road: 5 spaces w/o hookups; pit toilets; drinking water; tables; fire rings; boat launch; fishing; trails; 7 day limit.

Jim's Landing Campground is located directly on the Kenai River and has short spaces which are not level. The campground is best suited for mini-motor homes and short travel trailers. Pit toilets are set on a concrete vault. An area is provided for boat trailer parking. This site offers drift access to the Kenai River.

HIDDEN LAKE CAMPGROUND　　　**Memorial Day-Labor Day**
U.S. Fish and Wildlife Service　　　**Mile 4 Skilak Lake Road**

Located 4 miles from the *east junction* with the Sterling Highway and Skilak Lake Road: 44 spaces w/o hookups; **sewage dump station**; pit toilets; drinking water; covered picnic areas; observation deck; tables; fire rings; boat launch; fishing; trails; 7 day limit.

Hidden Lake Campground has a number of separated loop roads. All roads and spaces are blacktopped. Overflow parking is available. Campers must have handicapped plates (HCP) or special permits on their vehicles in order to use dedicated spaces. Pit toilets on concrete vaults are accessible to the disabled. Wide trails, extended ends on picnic tables, and raised cooking grates make this campground disabled accessible. A campground host is on site. Park Rangers offer nature lectures and walks.

UPPER SKILAK LAKE CAMPGROUND Memorial Day-Labor Day
U.S. Fish and Wildlife Service Mile 8 Skilak Lake Road

Turn south for 1.9 miles onto a gravel road at mile 8 from Skilak Lake Road: 15 spaces w/o hookups; pit toilets; drinking water; tables; fire rings; boat launch; fishing; trails; 7 day limit.

Upper Skilak Lake Campground is located directly on the lake. There are two loop roads: one for automobiles and RVs, and the other for tent campers only. Roads and spaces are blacktopped.

LOWER OHMER LAKE RECREATION SITE Memorial–Labor Day
U.S. Fish and Wildlife Service Mile 8.5 Skilak Lake Road

Located at mile 8.5 Skilak Lake Road: 14 spaces w/o hookups; pit toilets; no drinking water; tables; fire rings; boat launch; fishing; 3 day limit.

Lower Ohmer Lake Recreation Site has spaces which are graveled but not level. Water must be either boiled or treated chemically.

ENGINEER LAKE RECREATION SITE Memorial Day-Labor Day
U.S. Fish and Wildlife Service Mile 9.5 Skilak Lake Road

Located at mile 9.5 Skilak Lake Road: 8 spaces w/o hookups; pit toilets; drinking water; tables; fire rings; boat launch; fishing; 14 day limit.

Engineer Lake Recreation Site has a gravel, circular turn-around design with back-in, side-by-side RV parking.

LOWER SKILAK LAKE CAMPGROUND Memorial Day-Labor Day
U.S. Fish and Wildlife Service Mile 15 Skilak Lake Road

Located 4.9 miles from the **west junction** with the Sterling Highway at mile 15 Skilak Lake Road. Turn 0.9 mile onto a gravel road: 14 spaces w/o hookups; pit toilets; drinking water; tables; fire rings; boat launch; fishing; 14 day limit.

Lower Skilak Lake Campground is set in a wooded area with a narrow road through the grounds. Spaces are short in length and are not level. Some spaces face the wrong angle to the road. This campground will not accommodate the largest RVs, but the trailer parking area can provide for longer rigs if Rangers will allow it. Pit toilets are set on a concrete vault.

BOTTINENTNIN LAKE CAMPGROUND Memorial Day-Labor Day
U.S. Fish and Wildlife Service Mile 19.4 Skilak Lake Road

Located 0.5 mile from the **_west junction_** with the Sterling Highway at mile 19.4 Skilak Lake Road: 3 spaces w/o hookups; fishing; 14 day limit.

Bottinentnin Lake Campground has some trees but offers no amenities such as pit toilets, tables and grills. The circular graveled turnaround area will not accommodate larger RVs. Water must be either boiled or treated chemically.

THE STERLING HIGHWAY (continued)

JEAN LAKE RECREATION SITE   Memorial Day-Labor Day
U.S. Fish and Wildlife Service   MP 59.8 Sterling Highway

Located at MP 59.8 Sterling Highway: 3 spaces w/o hookups; pit toilets; no drinking water; tables; fire rings; boat launch; fishing; 14 day limit.

Jean Lake Recreation Site has three spaces, one of which will accommodate the largest RV. Return to the highway may be a problem for larger RVs because of limited turnaround space and the narrow, steep road accessing the highway. Water must be either boiled or treated chemically.

KELLY LAKE CAMPGROUND   Memorial Day-Labor Day
U.S. Fish and Wildlife Service   MP 68.5 Sterling Highway

Located on a gravel road at MP 68.5 Sterling Highway. Drive 0.5 mile to the "Y" then turn left for 0.3 mile: 3 spaces w/o hookups; pit toilets; drinking water; tables; fire rings; boat launch; fishing; trails; 14 day limit.

Kelly Lake Recreation Site is a circular, gravel-based open area which can accommodate the largest RVs. It is part of the "Seven Lakes Trail."

PETERSON LAKE RECREATION SITE   Memorial Day-Labor Day
U.S. Fish and Wildlife Service   MP 68.5 Sterling Highway

Located on a gravel road at MP 68.5 Sterling Highway. Drive 0.5 mile to the "Y" then turn right for 0.3 mile: 3 spaces w/o hookups; pit toilets; drinking water; tables; fire rings; boat launch; fishing; 14 day limit.

Peterson Lake Recreation Site, a large, circular, gravel-based open area, can accommodate the largest RV. It is part of the "Seven Lakes Trail."

WATSON LAKE RECREATION SITE   Memorial Day-Labor Day
U.S. Fish and Wildlife Service   MP 70.8 Sterling Highway

Located on a gravel road at MP 70.8 of the Sterling Highway: 3 spaces w/o hookups; pit toilets; drinking water; picnic site; tables; fire rings; boat launch; fishing; 14 day limit.

Watson Lake Recreation Site is in an area with spruce and birch trees and low undergrowth. A large, circular turnaround with back-in spaces is provided. Any length of RV can be accommodated.

KNOWLTON'S KENAI RIVER RV CAMP   privately operated
HC 78, Box 1010, Chugiak, AK 99567   June 10th—Sept 30th
(907) 262-7765   MP 79.2 Sterling Highway

Located 2.4 miles south of the Sterling Highway at MP 79.2 and the junction with Kenai Keys Road: 21 spaces; 16 power and water hookups; 5 w/o hookups; **sewage dump station**; flush toilets; drinking water; hot showers; tables; boat launch; fishing; recreation room; no time limit.

Knowlton's Kenai River RV Camp is located in a wooded setting directly above the Kenai River. Parking is side-by-side on level, gravel spaces. Restrooms and showers are exceptionally clean. A gift shop, three rooms with private baths (which must be reserved in advance) and 18 foot rental boats and fishing tackle are also available.

BING'S LANDING STATE RECREATION SITE   open all year
Alaska State Park System   MP 80.2 Sterling Highway

Located on a gravel road at MP 80.2 Sterling Highway: 37 spaces w/o hookups; pit toilets; drinking water; 20 picnic sites; tables; fire rings; boat launch; fishing; 7 day limit.

Bing's Landing SRS is located directly on the Kenai River. Spaces are back-in, side-by-side located in a large, gravel parking area. Any length of RV can be accommodated. A designated space is provided for disabled parking; pit toilets, which are on a concrete vault, are accessible to the disabled. Parking is available for boat trailers. A camp host is on site.

BING BROWN'S SPORTSMAN'S RV PARK   privately operated
PO Box 235, Sterling, AK 99672   May 15th—Sept 30th
(907) 262-4780   MP 81 Sterling Highway

Located at MP 81, north of the Sterling Highway: 40 spaces; 10 full hookups; 10 power hookups; 20 w/o hookups; **sewage dump station**; flush toilets; drinking water; hot showers; laundry facilities; tables; fire rings; public phone; separate tenting area; no time limit.

Bing Brown's Sportsman's RV Park and Campground is part of a larger complex which includes a motel and grocery/liquor store. Parking is on back-in gravel spaces as well as in a large open area surrounded by trees. Wood-burning fireplaces are set aside for camper use.

IZAAK WALTON STATE RECREATION SITE   open all year
Alaska State Park System   MP 81 Sterling Highway

Turn onto a paved road at MP 81, on the east side of the Moose River bridge, which doubles back to parallel the highway: 38 spaces w/o hookups; pit toilets; drinking water; tables; fire rings; boat launch; fishing; trails; 7 day limit.

Izaak Walton SRS is located in a heavily wooded area at the confluence of the Moose and Kenai rivers. A blacktopped road leads through the campground. Many of the spaces are back-in, side-by-side on blacktop, while others, which vary in length, are separated spaces. At least one pull-through is available. Space is provided for a few larger RVs. Pit toilets, on a concrete vault, are accessible to the disabled. A day-use parking area is available for boat trailers. Fly fishing only on the Moose River.

HILER'S RV PARK
PO Box 372, Sterling, AK 99672
(907) 262-7970

privately operated
May 15th—Sept 30th
MP 83.1 Sterling Highway

Located at MP 83.1 Sterling Highway: 20 spaces with power hookups; **sewage dump station**; chemical toilets; drinking water; tables; fire rings; no time limit.

Hiler's RV Park is attached to a grocery store and full service tackle shop. The RV portion is located on an open area sloping to a nearby pond. Spaces are back-in on level, gravel bases. Large RVs can be accommodated. Showers and a laundromat are located one block away.

SCOUT LAKE STATE RECREATION SITE
Alaska State Park System

open all year
MP 84.8 Sterling Highway

Located at MP 84.8 of the Sterling Highway at the junction with Scout Lake Loop Road: 8 spaces w/o hookups; pit toilets; drinking water; covered picnic site; fishing; trails; 7 day limit.

Scout Lake SRS is a large, open, gravel area with both day use and overnight camping. Parking is back-in, side-by-side on undesignated spaces. Pit toilets on a concrete vault are accessible to the disabled.

MORGAN'S LANDING STATE RECREATION SITE
Alaska State Park System

open all year
Lou Morgan Road

Turn at the junction of Scout Lake Loop Road with the Sterling Highway (MP 84.8). The campground is 4.2 miles: follow Scout Lake Loop Road to the "T." Turn right on Lou Morgan Road: 40 spaces w/o hookups; 13 pull-throughs; pit toilets; drinking water; fishing; trails; 7 day limit.

Morgan Landing SRA is set on a bluff overlooking the Kenai River. Spaces are level, gravel-based back-ins, pull-throughs and four side-by-side in a large, grassed area. Others are individual spaces in a secluded wooded section. The largest RV can be accommodated. Pit toilets are on concrete vaults and are accessible to the disabled. Only campers who are disabled are allowed to drive to the river's edge. A campground host is on site. The District Headquarters for the Alaska State Division of Parks and Outdoor Recreation is located at this campground.

SWANSON RIVER ROAD

DOLLY VARDEN LAKE CAMPGROUND Memorial Day-Labor Day
U.S. Fish and Wildlife Service

MP 14.5 Swanson River Road

Turn onto Robinson Loop/Swanson River Road at the junction with the Sterling Highway at MP 83.8. Drive 14.5 miles: 12 spaces w/o hookups; pit toilets; drinking water; tables; fire rings; boat launch; fishing; dumpster; 14 day limit.

Dolly Varden Lake Campground is set in heavy stands of birch and spruce trees. A narrow, gravel road leads through the campground to the lake. Spaces vary in length but are level. This campground is not recommended for larger RVs.

RAINBOW LAKE CAMPGROUND   **Memorial Day to Labor Day**
U.S. Fish and Wildlife Service   **MP 16 Swanson River Road**

Turn onto Robinson Loop/Swanson River Road at the junction with the Sterling Highway at MP 83.8. Drive 16 miles: 4 spaces w/o hookups; pit toilets; drinking water; tables; fire rings; boat launch; fishing; dumpster; 14 day limit.

Rainbow Lake Campground is wooded and entered by way of a steep, narrow road. Spaces are gravel-based and level and set apart from one another. This campground is not recommended for larger RVs. Boats with motors are allowed on the lake but cannot generate wakes.

SWANSON RIVER CAMPGROUND   **Memorial Day to Labor Day**
U.S. Fish and Wildlife Service   **MP 18 Swanson River Road**

Turn onto Robinson Loop/Swanson River Road at the junction with the Sterling Highway at MP 83.8. Drive 18 miles: 8 spaces w/o hookups; pit toilets; drinking water; tables; fire rings; boat launch; fishing; dumpster; 14 day limit.

Swanson River Campground is a circular, gravel area. The final four miles of road to the campsite are quite narrow. The campground can accommodate larger RVs because spaces are not designated. Pit toilets are on a concrete vault. The campground is about 0.25 mile from the boat launch; the waterway is shallow at this point and best suited to canoes, rubber rafts or smaller boats.

RV SERVICES ON THE STERLING HIGHWAY

HAMILTON'S PLACE   **(907) 595-1260**
Located at MP 48.5 Sterling Highway: tires; general repairs; emergency road service; towing; **propane**.

MOOSE RIVER AUTO PARTS AND TOWING   **(907) 262-5333**
Located at MP 81 of the Sterling Highway: 24-hour towing; emergency road service; general repairs.

STERLING GARAGE AND AUTO PARTS   **(907) 262-9626**
Located in a business complex at MP 81.6 Sterling Highway: tires; brakes; mufflers; general repairs; emergency road service; towing.

STERLING TESORO   **(907) 262-5969**
Located at MP 81.7 of the Sterling Highway: **sewage dump station**; **propane**. Open 24 hours-a-day between June first and Labor Day. Free water and sewage dump station use with fuel fill-ups.

BIG JOHN'S TEXACO OF SOLDOTNA   (907) 262-3933
Located at MP 91.3 of the Sterling Highway: **sewage dump station**; **propane**. Free water and sewage dump station use with fuel fill-ups.

JACK'S TESORO SOURDOUGH SERVICE   (907) 262-4788
Located at MP 91.5 of the Sterling Highway: **sewage dump station**; **propane**. Free water and sewage dump station use with fuel fill-ups.

STERLING HIGHWAY OPTIONS

THE STERLING HIGHWAY: SOUTH TO HOMER
From Soldotna the Sterling Highway turns south for about seventy-five miles past Kasilof, Clam Gulch, Ninilchik, Deep Creek and Anchor Point to Homer and Kachemak Bay.

STERLING HIGHWAY: EAST TO THE SEWARD HIGHWAY
From Soldotna the Sterling Highway turns east past Sterling, Skilak Lake cut-off, and Cooper Landing to mile 37 where it terminates at the Seward Highway.

THE SEWARD HIGHWAY
The Seward Highway, Alaska's only National Scenic Byway, offers two options at its junction with the Sterling Highway: south 37 miles to the City of Seward or north 90 miles to Anchorage.

Enjoying the good life at Hidden Lake Campground

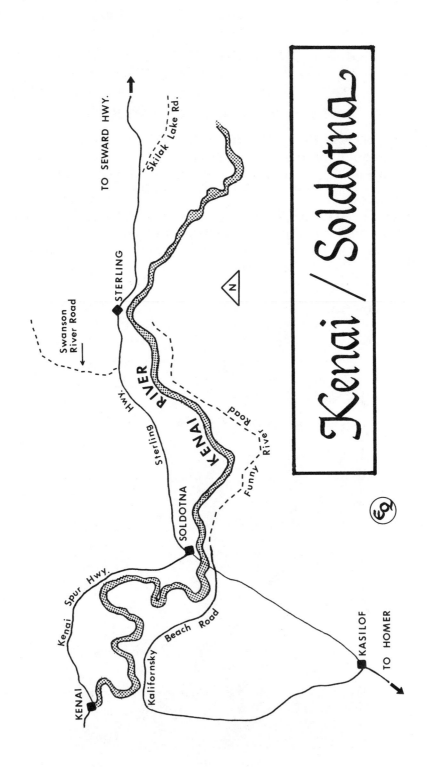

TO SEWARD HWY.

Skilak Lake Rd.

STERLING

Swanson River Road

KENAI RIVER

Sterling Hwy.

Funny River Road

N

SOLDOTNA

Kenai Spur Hwy.

Kalifornsky Beach Road

KENAI

KASILOF

TO HOMER

Kenai / Soldotna

Chapter 14

KENAI AND SOLDOTNA

This chapter describes campgrounds and services in the cities of Kenai and Soldotna. Options include the Sterling Highway east to its junction with the Seward Highway or south to Homer.

KENAI AND SOLDOTNA

Soldotna bursts into view and greets the visitor with an overwhelming array of signs, service stations, and motels along an art deco boulevard of commercial enterprises: Stop here! See this! Do that! Everything, it seems, centers around fishing. Commercial fishermen and women have setnets along the shores of Cook Inlet or fish directly from drift boats and seiners. From May until September, thousands of people cast their lines and hopes into the Kenai River for that world class king salmon which will make their vacations and photo albums complete. Soldotna radiates excitement.

By contrast the city of Kenai seems subdued. Referred to as the "twin cities" because of their proximity, Kenai and Soldotna are noticeably different. Although fishing plays a part in Kenai's economy, as does the petroleum industry, much of its charm is based on its past. St. Nicholas (1791), now the city of Kenai, was the first Russian settlement on the Kenai Peninsula. A log replica of Fort Kenay's barracks (circa 1869); the rectory of the Russian Orthodox Church built in 1886, today a National Historic Landmark; and the site of an agricultural experimental station that closed in 1908, can still be seen. Historic sites plus panoramic views of the Cook Inlet, the mouth of the Kenai River, and the Alaska range with Mount Iliamna and Mount Redoubt add to the contrasts.

KENAI PENINSULA VISITOR CENTER (907) 262-1337 or 262-9814
PO Box 236, Soldotna, AK 99669

Located at 44790 Sterling Highway, the Greater Soldotna Chamber of Commerce center offers visitor information, photo displays, maps and brochures as well as pedestrian access to the Kenai River.

KENAI NATIONAL WILDLIFE REFUGE VISITOR CENTER
PO Box 2139, Soldotna, AK 99669   **(907) 262-7021**

Located at MP 1, Ski Hill Road (accessed by Funny River Road), the center offers information on wildlife viewing, films and videos about the wildlife refuge and the Kenai Peninsula, plus scheduled nature programs.

KENAI CHAMBER OF COMMERCE INFORMATION CENTER
PO Box 497, Kenai, AK 99611   **(907) 283-7989**

Located at 402 Overland near the intersection of Kenai Spur Road with Main Street. This small visitor center is not as elaborate as those mentioned above, but staff members are available to offer assistance and information about the Kenai area.

KENAI BICENTENNIAL VISITORS and CULTURAL CENTER
PO Box 1991, Kenai, AK 99611   **open all year**
(907) 283-1991   FAX (907) 283-2230   **11411 Kenai Spur Highway**

Located at 11411 Kenai Spur Road, one block from the intersection of Kenai Spur Road and Main Street, the center features historic displays, a cultural exhibition area, video viewing arena, and standing displays depicting the oil industry, commercial fishing industry and Native heritage. Staff members are available to provide information about the area.

KENAI RIVER FLATS VIEWING AREA   Bridge Access Road

Turn left from Kenai Spur Road at the light at Bridge Access Road. Drive to the bridge crossing the Kenai River. There is ample parking and a boardwalk which leads to the viewing area. Excellent view of the mountains and Cook Inlet and always a possibility that wildlife will be visible.

HEALTH AND EMERGENCY SERVICES

Central Peninsula General Hospital	**(907) 262-4404**
Kenai Medical Center	**(907) 283-4611**
Alaska State Troopers	**(907) 262-4453 or 911**
Kenai Police	**911**
Soldotna Police	**911**

RV CAMPGROUNDS AT KENAI

McCONNELL'S RV PARKING   **privately operated**
PO Box 871, Soldotna, AK 99669   **May 15th—Sept 15th**
(907) 262-9252   **MP 0.09 Big Eddy Road**

Turn northwest at the signal light junction of the Sterling Highway with Kenai Spur Road. Drive two miles and turn left onto Big Eddy Road. Drive 0.9 miles:10 water only hookups; porta-potty; drinking water; tables; grill; boat launch; fishing; no time limit.

McConnell's RV Parking is a small campground which primarily offers long-term space rentals. Spaces are back-ins, separated by trees, directly on the Kenai River. Boat trailer parking and boat tie-ups are offered.

KENAI RIVER FAMILY CAMPGROUND   **privately operated**
HC 1, Box 8616, Soldotna, AK 99669   **June 1st—Sept 30th**
(907) 262-2444   **end of Big Eddy Road**

Turn northwest at the signal light junction of the Sterling Highway with Kenai Spur Road. Drive two miles and turn left onto Big Eddy Road. Drive 2.2 miles to the end of the road: 50 spaces; 30 power and water hookups; 20 w/o hookups; porta-potties; drinking water; tables; boat launch; fishing; separate tenting area; no time limit.

Kenai River Family Campground has back-in spaces in an open area. Some parking is available by the trees which surround the campground. There are few amenities at this site and none in the vicinity. This campground is intended for the "industrial strength fisherman." The sole function is catching fish. It offers a sheltered boat launch and tent camping.

KENAI RV PARK — privately operated
PO Box 1913, Kenai, AK 99611 — May 15th—Sept 30th
(907) 283-2665 — 912 Highland Avenue

Turn northwest at the signal light junction of the Sterling Highway with Kenai Spur Road. Drive 11.3 miles to Main Street, then turn one block (past the log Chamber of Commerce building): 33 spaces; 28 full hookups; 5 w/o hookups; **sewage dump station**; flush toilets; drinking water; hot showers; laundry facilities; no time limit.

Kenai RV Park is set in a quiet area walking distance to a cliff overlooking the mouth of the Kenai River and the Cook Inlet. Spaces are gravel-based back-ins with a few pull-throughs. This RV park is located on city sewer and water. Long term parking is available.

OVERLAND RV PARK — privately operated
PO Box 326, Kenai, AK 99611 — May 15th—Sept 30th
(907) 283-4512   FAX (907) 283-4013 — MP 11.5 Kenai Spur Road

Turn northwest at the signal light junction of the Sterling Highway with Kenai Spur Road. Drive 11.5 miles to 410 Overland Avenue: 50 spaces with full hookups; 5 pull-throughs; **sewage dump station**; flush toilets; drinking water; hot showers; laundry facilities; no time limit.

Overland RV Park is a large, level, gravel-based campground. Spaces are back-in, side-by-side. The largest RV can be accommodated. It is located near shopping centers and is walking distance to the river bluff, Fort Kenay (circa 1869) and the historic Russian Orthodox Church.

BELUGA LOOKOUT RV PARK — privately operated
929 Mission Avenue, Kenai, AK 99611 — May 15th—Sept 30th
(907) 283-5999 — 929 Mission Avenue

Turn northwest at the signal light junction of the Sterling Highway with Kenai Spur Road. Drive 11.5 miles to the signal light at Main Street and turn left. Drive two blocks, then turn right on Cook Drive: 81 spaces with full hookups; flush toilets; drinking water; hot showers; laundry facilities; tables; grills; cable TV; public phone; no time limit.

Beluga Outlook RV Park is located on a bluff overlooking the Cook Inlet. Spaces are level and graveled. Each site has its own telephone jack and cable TV connection. Fish cleaning tables, smokers and freezers are available. Roads through the campground will be blacktopped in 1994. The campground is located near shopping centers and is walking distance to Fort Kenay (circa 1869) and the historic Russian Orthodox Church.

KENAI MUNICIPAL PARK
City of Kenai Parks and Recreation
open all year
South Forest Drive

Turn northwest at the signal light junction of the Sterling Highway with Kenai Spur Road. Drive 12.3 miles, turn on Forest Drive Avenue at the National Guard Armory: 30 spaces w/o hookups; pit toilets; drinking water; tables; fire rings; 3 day limit.

The Kenai Municipal Park is located in a lush, wooded area overlooking the Cook Inlet. Parking is back-in on level, gravel pads. The planners have maintained the integrity of the natural area by leaving the trees and ground cover such as low bush and high bush cranberries untouched.

BERNICE LAKE STATE RECREATION SITE
Alaska State Park System
open all year
MP 21.3 Kenai Spur Road

Turn northwest at the signal light junction of the Sterling Highway with Kenai Spur Road. Drive 21.3 miles, turn 0.8 mile on Miller Road across from the refinery to Bernice Lake Road, one mile: 11 spaces w/o hookups; pit toilets; drinking water; picnic site; tables; fire rings; boat launch; dumpster; 15 day limit.

Bernice Lake SRS is located in an isolated, wooded area with access to the lake. A narrow gravel road leads through the campground. Spaces are back-in, not level, and vary in length. Blocking may be required. Pit toilets are accessible to the disabled.

BISHOP CREEK CAMPGROUND
Alaska State Park System
open all year
MP 36 Kenai Spur Road

Turn northwest at the signal light junction of the Sterling Highway with Kenai Spur Road. Drive 36 miles to the entrance: 12 spaces w/o hookups; pit toilets; drinking water; tables; fire rings; fishing; trails; 15 day limit.

Bishop Creek Campground is part of the Captain Cook State Recreation Area. It has a small, gravel, circular turnaround area. Spaces are level, back-in, side-by-side and can accommodate the largest RV.

SWANSON RIVER LANDING CAMPGROUND
Alaska State Park System
open all year
MP 38.5 Kenai Spur Road

Turn northwest at the signal light junction of the Sterling Highway with Kenai Spur Road. Drive 38.5 miles to the entrance: 1 space w/o hookup; pit toilets; no drinking water; fishing; 15 day limit.

Swanson River Landing Campground is part of the Captain Cook State Recreation Area. It is intended for day use camping (12 hours only) with the exception of one RV space. Trails lead to the river but not to a direct boat launch. Pit toilets are on a concrete vault and are accessible to the disabled. Water must be either boiled or treated chemically.

DISCOVERY CAMPGROUND **MP 39 Kenai Spur Road**
Alaska State Park System **open all year**

Turn northwest at the signal light junction of the Sterling Highway with Kenai Spur Road. Drive 39 miles, turn 0.5 mile to the entrance: 57 spaces w/o hookups; pit toilets; drinking water; tables; fire rings; boat launch; fishing; 15 day limit.

Discovery Campground is part of the Captain Cook State Recreation Area and is located in a wooded area which overlooks the Cook Inlet. Spaces are gravel-based and vary in length. Many spaces are not level and blocking will be required. RVs of any size can be accommodated. Pit toilets are on concrete vaults and are accessible to the disabled. This campground is well worth the nearly forty mile drive. A campground host and a park ranger are located on the grounds.

RV CAMPGROUNDS AT SOLDOTNA

SWIFTWATER CAMPGROUND **May 1st—Sept 25th**
City of Soldotna Parks and Recreation **MP 34 Sterling Highway**

Turn east 0.5 mile from the Sterling Highway at MP 94 at the junction with East Redoubt Avenue: 32 spaces w/o hookups; 10 pull-throughs; **sewage dump station**; pit toilets; covered picnic site; tables; fire rings; boat launch; fishing; 7 day limit.

Swiftwater Campground is located directly on the Kenai River. Spaces are gravel-based back-ins. The largest RV can be accommodated. A separate area is provided for boat trailer parking.

MOOSE RANGE MEADOWS RV PARK **privately operated**
PO Box 2682, Kenai, AK 99611 **May 15th—Aug 30th**
(907) 283-7864 **MP 3.6 East Redoubt**

Turn east 3.6 miles from the Sterling Highway at MP 94 at the junction with East Redoubt Avenue: 49 spaces w/o hookups; **sewage dump station**; pit toilets; drinking water; tables; fire rings; boat launch; fishing; no time limit.

Moose Range Meadows RV Park is located in a heavily wooded area directly on the Kenai River. A gravel-based road leads through the campground. Spaces are short and are not level. Larger RVs cannot be accommodated. This campground is best suited to mini-motor homes, camper pickups, and shorter travel trailers or 5th wheels. A separate area is provided for boat trailer parking. Somewhat out-of-the-way, the campground may have spaces available during peak periods when other campgrounds are filled.

RIVER TERRACE RV CAMPGROUND **privately operated**
PO Box 322 Soldotna, AK 99669 **May 15th—Oct 1st**
(907) 262-5593 **44761 Sterling Highway**

Located at the southeast corner of the Sterling Highway at MP 95.7 at the Soldotna side of the Kenai River Bridge: 81 spaces; 20 full hookups; 61 power hookups; **sewage dump station**; flush toilet; 2 porta-potties; drinking water; hot showers; laundry facilities; tables; public phone; fishing; no time limit.

River Terrace RV Campground has three tiers on a slope to the bank of the Kenai River. Parking is back-in, side-by-side with level gravel spaces. Some RVs are permanently occupied during the summer months. Boat rentals and fishing charters can be arranged. Fish processing is available. Charter fishing can be arranged.

CENTENNIAL PARK CAMPGROUND   May 1st—Sept 15th
City of Soldotna Parks and Recreation   MP 96 Sterling Highway

Turn at the signal light at the Kenai River bridge on Kalifornski Beach Road from MP 96.1 of the Sterling Highway: 160 spaces w/o hookups; **sewage dump station**; pit toilets; drinking water; covered picnic sites; tables; fire rings; boat launch; fishing; separate tenting area; 7 day limit.

Centennial Park Campground is located directly on the Kenai River. Spaces are back-ins with no pull-throughs. The largest RV can be accommodated. Boat trailers must be parked in the designated trailer parking area or at the individual camp space. An overflow area provides spaces for about thirty RVs. A fulltime campground manager is on site. Advance reservations are not accepted

EDGEWATER RV CAMPGROUND   privately operated
PO Box 3456, Soldotna, AK 99669   May 1st—Oct 15th
(907) 262-7733   44780 Funny River Road

Turn on Funny River Road from the Sterling Highway at the signal light by the Kenai River bridge: 64 spaces; 42 pull-throughs; 42 full hookups; 12 power hookups; 10 w/o hookups; **sewage dump station**; flush toilets; drinking water; hot showers; laundry facilities; covered picnic sites; fishing; no time limit.

Edgewater RV Campground is a large, gravel-based campground with grass areas throughout. A fence shields the highway. Spaces are level, gravel-based pull-throughs with a few back-ins. The largest RVs can be accommodated.

FUNNY RIVER STATE RECREATION AREA   open all year
Alaska State Park System   MP 12 Funny River Road

Turn on Funny River Road 12 miles from the Sterling Highway at the signal light by the Kenai River bridge: 5 spaces w/o hookups; pit toilets; drinking water; tables; fire rings; fishing; 15 day limit.

Funny River SRA is a circular, gravel-based campsite, located directly on the Kenai River. Four spaces and one tent site are available. The pit toilet is on a concrete vault and is accessible to the disabled. The river flows swiftly at this point, but rubber rafts, canoes and small boats can be launched safely. A park ranger is based at this SRA.

KENAI RIVERBEND CAMPGROUND privately operated
PO Box 1270, Soldotna, AK 99669 May 15th—Oct 1st
(907) 283-9489   FAX (907) 283-8449 Porter Road

Turn on Kalifornski Beach Road from the Sterling Highway at the signal light by the Kenai River bridge. Drive 4.7 miles to Cienchanski Loop Road. Turn right for 2.5 miles, then left at the "T." Continue to Porter Road, turn right to the "Y" then turn left: 300 spaces; 150 full hookups; 50 power hookups; 100 w/o hookups; **sewage dump station**; flush toilets; drinking water; hot showers; laundry facilities; tables; boat launch; fishing; **propane**; public phone; separate tenting area; no time limit.

Kenai Riverbend Campground is located on the Kenai River with 1,600 feet of river frontage and is part of a larger complex which includes a motel, grocery store and tackle shop as well as guide and charter fishing services. Spaces are back-in, side-by-side on a large, gravel-based campground. Spaces are wide and separated from others. A separate boat trailer parking area is located on the grounds.

RIVER QUEST RV PARK privately operated
PO Box 3457, Soldotna, AK 99669 May 1st—Oct 1st
(907) 283-4991 45933 Porter Road

Turn on Kalifornski Beach Road from the Sterling Highway at the signal light by the Kenai River bridge. Drive 4.7 miles to Cienchanski Loop Road. Turn right for 2.5 miles, then left at the "T." Continue to Porter Road, turn right to the "Y" then turn right: 325 spaces; 7 pull-throughs; 200 power and water hookups; 25 water hookups; 100 w/o hookups; **sewage dump station**; chemical toilets; drinking water; hot showers; laundry facilities; tables; fire rings; boat launch; fishing; **propane**; public phone; no time limit.

River Quest RV Park is located on fifty-seven acres in a semi-wooded area with Kenai River frontage. Spaces are gravel, level, back-ins and nearly all are located on a creek or the Kenai River. The largest RV can be accommodated. Boat trailer parking space is provided. A cafe and tackle shop are on the grounds. Fishing guide services can be arranged.

RV SERVICES AT KENAI AND SOLDOTNA

RAPID CAR WASH
Located at MP 1.2 of Kenai Spur Road: two, large, self-service bays.

PETROLANE (907) 262-4683
Located at MP 1.2 of Kenai Spur Road; **propane**.

TWIN CITIES RV, INC. (907) 283-5115
Located at Edgewater RV Campground: brakes; RV parts and accessories; general repairs; chassis repair; tank repairs; furnace and heater repair.

G AND M CHEVRON   (907) 283-5010
Located at 11152 Kenai Spur Road: petroleum products; tires; **sewage dump station**; **propane**.

WILDWOOD CHEVRON   (907) 283-4146
Located at MP 13.5 Kenai Spur Road: brakes; mufflers; general repairs; emergency road service; towing; **sewage dump station**; **propane**. AAA "Emergency Service Contracts" are honored; towing on a 24 hour basis.

SOLDOTNA "Y" CHEVRON   (907) 262-4513
Located at 44024 Sterling Highway: alignment; brakes; mufflers; general repairs; emergency road service; towing; **sewage dump station**; **propane**. Soldotna "Y" Chevron has two large bays for RVs.

HUTCHINGS CHEVROLET PRO SHOP   (907) 262-5891
Located at 44055 Sterling Highway: alignment; brakes; ONAN generator set repair; electrical repairs; mufflers; general repairs; towing; welding. RV repairs a "specialty." Warranty work on Chevrolet models. Also phone 1-800- 478-5892.

THOMPSON'S CENTER GAS STATION   (907) 262-9071
Located at 44224 Sterling Highway: petroleum products; **sewage dump station**; **propane**.

KENAI AND SOLDOTNA OPTIONS

THE STERLING HIGHWAY: SOUTH TO HOMER
From Soldotna the Sterling Highway turns south for about seventy-five miles past Kasilof, Clam Gulch, Ninilchik, Deep Creek and Anchor Point to Homer and Kachemak Bay.

STERLING HIGHWAY: EAST TO THE SEWARD HIGHWAY
From Soldotna the Sterling Highway turns east past Sterling, Skilak Lake cut-off, and Cooper Landing to mile 37 where it terminates at the Seward Highway.

THE SEWARD HIGHWAY
The Seward Highway, Alaska's only National Scenic Byway, offers two options at its junction with the Sterling Highway: south 37 miles to the City of Seward or north 90 miles to Anchorage.

Chapter 15

SOLDOTNA TO HOMER

This chapter describes campgrounds and services on the Sterling Highway from Soldotna to Homer. Campgrounds and services in Homer are also described. Options include the Sterling Highway to its terminus at the Seward Highway; the Alaska Marine Highway System to Seldovia, Kodiak and Seward; and a six day round trip to Dutch Harbor in the Aleutian Islands.

THE STERLING HIGHWAY FROM SOLDOTNA TO HOMER

The Sterling Highway south of Soldotna traverses the Kenai National Wildlife Refuge. The highway offers excellent views of Cook Inlet and several volcanos including Redoubt and Augustine. Chances of seeing moose from the highway are good during the summer months. Other wildlife are less likely to be encountered although bears are occasionally seen near salmon spawning streams. Towns along the way include Kasilof, Ninilchik, Clam Gulch and Anchor Point. In Homer the Harding Icefield can be seen at a distance as it tumbles toward Kachemak Bay from the Kenai Mountains.

The Anchor River Recreation Area is the westernmost campground on the continuous highway system on the North American Continent which may be an incentive to camp there for at least one night. An area established for picture taking commemorates the most western point.

HEALTH AND EMERGENCY SERVICES

Ninilchik Community Clinic	(907) 567-3970 or 911
Anchor Point Volunteer Fire and Rescue	911
South Peninsula Hospital (Homer)	(907) 235-8101
Alaska State Troopers (Homer)	(907) 235-8239

RV CAMPGROUNDS ON THE STERLING HIGHWAY

DECANTER INN
PO Box 631, Kasilof, AK 99610
(907) 262-5917

privately operated
open all year
MP 107 Sterling Highway

Located at MP 107 of the Sterling Highway: 15 spaces w/o hookups; flush toilets; fishing.

Decanter Inn's primary business is its lodge and bar business. Spaces are not specifically designated and are dry camping only. Flush toilets are available at the lodge. The largest RV can be accommodated. The lake across the Sterling Highway is stocked with fish.

KASILOF RIVER STATE RECREATION SITE   open all year
Alaska State Park System   MP 109.5 Sterling Highway

Located on the south side of the Kasilof River bridge at MP 109.5 of the Sterling Highway: 36 spaces w/o hookups; pit toilets; drinking water; tables; fire rings; boat launch; fishing; trails; 15 day limit.

Kasilof SRS is divided into two loops, one of which is on the Kasilof River. Spaces are gravel-based and not level. Blocking may be required. Day use parking area is available. A campground host is on site.

JOHNSON LAKE STATE RECREATION AREA   open all year
Alaska State Park System   MP 0.1 Tustumena Road

Turn onto Johnson Creek Road from the Sterling Highway at MP 110 (across from Cohoe Loop Road). Turn at second right (0.3 mile) onto Tustumena Road: 50 spaces w/o hookups; 3 pull-throughs; pit toilets; drinking water; covered picnic site; tables; fire rings; boat launch; fishing; trails; separate tenting area; public phone; 15 day limit.

Johnson Lake SRA is a secluded campground with two loops through a wooded area. Spaces are level, gravel-based back-ins with some side-by-side back-ins. Some spaces face the wrong direction to the entry road. The largest RV can be accommodated. A campground host is on site. Johnson Lake is stocked with trout by the State.

TUSTUMENA LAKE CAMPGROUND   Memorial Day to Labor Day
U.S. Fish and Wildlife Service   MP 5.9 Tustumena Road

Turn onto Johnson Creek Road from the Sterling Highway at MP 110 (across from Cohoe Loop Road). Turn at second right (0.3 mile) onto Tustumena Road: 10 spaces w/o hookups; pit toilets; drinking water; tables; fire rings; boat launch; fishing; 14 day limit.

Tustumena Lake Campground is part of the Kenai National Wildlife Refuge and has been left in its natural state as much as possible. Spaces are separated by trees and ground cover. Spaces can accommodate large RVs but are not level. Blocking may be required. A separate area is provided for boat trailers.

CROOKED CREEK STATE RECREATION SITE   open all year
Alaska State Park System   MP 0.5 Crooked Creek Road

Turn onto Cohoe Loop Road from the Sterling Highway at MP 110 (across from Johnson Creek Road). Drive 1.6 miles to Crooked Creek Road (also known as Rilinda Road). Drive 0.5 mile, turn left at the "Y": 116 spaces w/o hookups; pit toilets; drinking water; 5 picnic sites; tables; fire rings; fishing; trails; 7 day limit.

Crooked Creek SRS is a joint venture between the Department of Fish and Game and the Division of Parks and Outdoor Recreation using Federal funds as part of a sports fish restoration program. Parking is back-in, side-by-side in a large open area. Thirty-six spaces are reserved for day use. The campground is located one hundred yards by trail from the confluence of Crooked Creek and the Kasilof River. A campground host is on site.

Fishing from the bank of the Kenai River

CROOKED CREEK RV PARK
PO Box 601, Kasilof, AK 99610
(907) 262-1299

privately operated
May 1st—Sept 30th
MP 0.5 Crooked Creek Road

Turn onto Cohoe Loop Road from the Sterling Highway at MP 110 (across from Johnson Creek Road). Drive 1.6 miles to Crooked Creek Road (also known as Rilinda Road). Drive 0.5 mile, turn left at the "Y." Next to Crooked Creek SRS: 62 spaces; 24 full hookups; 7 power hookups; **sewage dump station**; flush toilets; drinking water; hot showers; laundry facilities; tables; grills; fishing; public phone; separate tenting area; no time limit.

Crooked Creek RV Park has a series of short gravel roads at right angles to the main road which extends the length of the park. Spaces are 40 by 50 feet in length and level. At least fifteen of them are owner occupied. A dry camping overflow area is available. Boats are available for rent.

COHOE COVE ... CAMPER PARK
PO Box 3864, Kenai, AK 99611
(907) 283-3912

privately operated
May 1st—Sept 30th
MP 0.07 Webb-Ramsell Road

Turn onto Cohoe Loop Road from the Sterling Highway at MP 110 (across from Johnson Creek Road). Drive 3.2 miles to Webb-Ramsell Road for 0.7 mile; turn right at the"Y": 25 spaces w/o hookups; porta-potty; drinking water; tables; grills; boat launch; public phone; no time limit.

Cohoe Cove Recreation Camper Park is located in a heavily wooded, rustic setting, directly on the Kasilof River. Spaces are set in the trees, back-in and not level. Easy access to the river. Excellent fishing in the area.

CLAM GULCH STATE RECREATION AREA open all year
Alaska State Park System MP 117.5 Sterling Highway

Turn west from the junction of the Sterling Highway at MP 117.5 with Clam Gulch Road: 116 spaces w/o hookups; pit toilets; drinking water; tables; fire rings; fishing; trails; separate tenting area; 15 day limit.

Clam Gulch SRA is located on a bluff overlooking the Cook Inlet, approximately two hundred yards from the beaches. Parking is back-in, side-by-side wherever space is available. The parking area, which is not level, can accommodate any size RV. Tables and fire rings are randomly placed throughout the area. Clam Gulch SRA fills to capacity during periods of extremely low (clamming) tides. Four wheel drive and all terrain vehicles (ATVs) are allowed access to the beach. A campground host is on site.

SCENIC VIEW RV PARK privately operated
PO Box 202553, Anchorage, AK 99520 May 15th—Sept 1st
(907) 567-3909 MP 127 Sterling Highway

Located at MP 127 of the Sterling Highway by a turnout area: 27 spaces; 5 full hookups; 18 power hookups; **sewage dump station**; flush toilets; drinking water; hot showers; laundry facilities; fishing; no time limit.

Scenic View RV Park is situated on a bluff overlooking the Cook Inlet. Spaces are back-ins, tiered on a declining, circular area. The largest RV can be accommodated. Toilets and showers are accessible to the disabled and are well maintained. Dry camping and boat storage is available. Sightseeing, raft and fishing charters can be arranged.

NINILCHIK STATE RECREATION AREA open all year
Alaska State Park System MP 134 Sterling Highway

Located by the Ninilchik River bridge at MP 134 of the Sterling Highway: 43 spaces w/o hookups; pit toilets; drinking water; covered picnic site; tables; fire rings; trails; 15 day limit.

Ninilchik SRA is one of three campgrounds located within a mile of one another which comprise the larger state recreation area. Designed around two loops situated in heavy stands of spruce trees, spaces are side-by-side on level gravel bases with some tree separation. The largest RV can be accommodated. A campground host is on site.

NINILCHIK BEACH STATE RECREATION SITE open all year
Alaska State Park System MP 134.5 Sterling Highway

Located west of the junction of Beach Access Road with the Sterling Highway at MP 134.5 south of the Ninilchik River bridge: 100 spaces w/o hookups; pit toilets; no drinking water; boat launch; fishing; 15 day limit.

Ninilchik Beach SRS is a large open area located directly on the beach facing the Cook Inlet. Parking is gravel-based wherever space is available. The campground is adjacent to a day use camping area. The largest RV can be accommodated. A boat ramp accesses the Ninilchik River.

BEACHCOMBER RV PARK AND MOTEL
PO Box 367, Ninilchik, AK 99639
(907) 567-3417

privately operated
May 1st—Sept 30th
MP 135.1 Sterling Highway

Located west of the junction of Beach Access Road with the Sterling Highway at MP 135.1 south of the Ninilchik River bridge. Take the right fork from the road paralleling the river: 15 spaces with full hookups; drinking water; boat launch; fishing.

Beachcomber RV Park and Motel is located on the Cook Inlet by the Ninilchik River. Spaces are back-ins with full hookups. This campground is clean and orderly and strictly monitored. Housekeeping cabins are available. Fish and clam cleaning tables are provided. Excellent drinking water from an artesian well. Fishing charters can be arranged.

Riverbend Campground on the Kenai River

HYLEN'S CAMPER PARK
PO Box 39361, Ninilchik, AK 99639
(907) 567-3393

privately operated
May 1st—Sept 30th
MP 135.4 Sterling Highway

Turn east 0.2 mile at the junction of the Sterling Highway at MP 135.4 with Kingsley Road: 66 spaces; 52 full hookups; 14 power and water hookups; **sewage dump station**; flush toilets; drinking water; hot showers; laundry facilities; fishing; public phone; no time limit.

Hylen's Camper Park is a large open area with access to nearby clamming beaches. Spaces are level, gravel-based and wide. The largest RV can be accommodated. RV storage by the year can be arranged.

NINILCHIK CORNERS
PO Box 39076, Ninilchik, AK 99639
(907) 567-3929

privately operated
May 1st—Oct 1st
Oilwell and Kingsley Roads

Turn east at the junction of the Sterling Highway at MP 135.4 with Kingsley Road. Located at the top of the hill at the corner of Oilwell Road: 19 spaces w/o hookups; flush toilets; drinking water; hot showers; laundry facilities; tables; public phone; no time limit.

Ninilchik Corners is a laundry, shower, video, tackle and bait shop complex. Spaces are gravel-based, back-ins separated by low ground cover. RVs of any length can be accommodated. Dry camping only.

NINILCHIK VIEW (upper overflow area)   open all year
Alaska State Park System   MP 135.7 Sterling Highway

Located at MP 135.7 of the Sterling Highway between Kingsley and Oilwell roads: 13 w/o hookups; **(2) sewage dump stations**; pit toilets; public phone; 15 day limit.

This state overflow area is not a campground in the normal sense of the term. However, it provides sewage dump stations and a public telephone for the four state campgrounds within the immediate area.

NINILCHIK VIEW STATE RECREATION SITE   open all year
Alaska State Park System   MP 135.7 Sterling Highway

Located at MP 135.7 of the Sterling Highway between Kingsley and Oilwell Roads: 11 spaces w/o hookups; pit toilets; drinking water; covered picnic site; tables; fire rings; fishing; trails; 15 day limit.

Ninilchik View SRS is a heavily wooded, circular campground with branching roads situated on the bluff above Cook Inlet. Spaces are level, gravel-based and, in some cases, paired. Camping areas are separated by trees and ground cover. A stairway and trails lead to the beach. This campground is small but offers excellent views of Mount Iliamna, Mount Redoubt and Mount Spurr. A campground host is on site.

CREEKSIDE LODGE AND RV PARK   privately operated
PO Box 39326, Ninilchik, AK 99636   May 1st—Sept 1st
(907) 567-7333   MP 136.4 Sterling Highway

Located at MP 136.4 of the Sterling Highway: 64 power only spaces; 20 pull-throughs; flush toilets; drinking water; hot showers; **propane**; public phone; no time limit.

Creekside Lodge and RV Park is located in a level, graveled, open area. Parking is in clusters of four around central power outlets. A sauna and hot tub are available in the lodge. The closest sewage dump station is one mile at the Ninilchik View SRA overflow area.

DEEP CREEK STATE RECREATION SITE   open all year
Alaska State Park System   MP 137.8 Sterling Highway

Located at MP 137.8 of the Sterling Highway south of Deep Creek bridge: 300 spaces w/o hookups; pit toilets; drinking water; tables; grills; boat launch; fishing; 15 day limit.

Deep Creek SRS is made up of two large campgrounds bordering the creek. Spaces are not designated and RVs are closely parked next to one another. Tables and grills are randomly placed throughout the area. Boat ramps on the creek lead to the inlet. A campground host is on site.

STARISKI STATE RECREATION SITE MP 151.8 Sterling Highway
Alaska State Park System   **open all year**

Located at MP 151.8 Sterling Highway 0.4 mile south of Stariski Creek: 13 spaces w/o hookups; pit toilets; drinking water; covered picnic site; tables; fire rings; fishing; 15 day limit.

Stariski SRS is situated on a bluff directly west of Mount Iliamna. Spaces are gravel-based and level and can accommodate rigs to about 30 feet in length. Individual back-in spaces are separated by stands of spruce trees. A trail leads to the beach.

SHORT STOP STORAGE   **privately operated**
PO Box 596, Anchor Point, AK 99556   **April 15th—Oct 1st**
(907) 235-5327   **MP 153.2 Sterling Highway**

Located at MP 153.2 of the Sterling Highway: 7 spaces with power hookups; **sewage dump station**; flush toilets; drinking water; hot showers; laundry facilities; no time limit.

Short Stop Storage offers laundry facilities and showers, plus a small grocery and bait shop as its main business. RV storage can be arranged.

ANCHOR RIVER STATE RECREATION AREA   **open all year**
Alaska State Park System   **MP 156.9 Sterling Highway**

Turn west at the junction of the old Sterling Highway with the new Sterling Highway at MP 156.9 (by the Anchor River Inn). Follow the road which crosses the Anchor River on a steel bridge. Turn at the first right and follow Beach Access Road to its end (1.7 miles): 40 spaces w/o hookups; pit toilets; no drinking water; picnic sites; tables; fire rings; fishing; dumpsters; 15 day limit.

Anchor River SRA is made up of five separate sites: Silverking, Cohoe, Steelhead, Slide Hole, and Halibut. The first three campgrounds are restricted to day use only. Slide Hole Campground has thirty-three long-term campsites, and Halibut Campground has twenty-three long-term campsites. Spaces are back-ins and level.

Although water is not available at the campgrounds, it has been provided in the past through the courtesy of the "Anchor Angler," which is a tackle shop at the corner of Beach Access Road.

Anchor River SRA is the westernmost public campground on the North American Continent. Looking to the west, three active volcanoes can be seen: Augustine Island, Mount Iliamna, and Mount Redoubt, all part of the "ring of fire" which extends through the Aleutian Islands.

Ma Walli Rock Senior Citizen Handicapped Fishing Area adjoins the state recreation area on Anchor River.

KYLLONEN'S RV PARK
privately operated
PO Box 49, Anchor Point, AK 99556   May 15th—Sept 15th
(907) 235-7451 FAX (907) 235-6435   MP 156.9 Sterling Highway

Turn west at the junction of the "old" Sterling Highway with the new Sterling Highway at MP 156.9 (by the Anchor River Inn). Follow the road which crosses the Anchor River on a steel bridge. Turn right at Beach Access Road 1.3 miles: 23 spaces with full hookups; drinking water; tables; fire rings and grills; fishing; trails; public phone; no time limit.

Kyllonen's RV Park overlooks the Anchor River and Cook Inlet. Trees shield the campground from the road. Spaces are gravel-based, back-ins. The longest RV can be accommodated. Boats can be launched at the beach or at the mouth of the Anchor River. An area has been set aside for fish cleaning and photo taking. A campground host is on site.

ANCHOR RIVER STATE RECREATION SITE
open all year
Alaska State Park System
MP 162 Sterling Highway

Located at MP 162 of the Sterling Highway: 9 spaces w/o hookups; pit toilets; drinking water; fishing; trails; 15 day limit.

Anchor River SRS is located on a gravel-based road on the bank of the Anchor River. There are six side-by-side, back-in spaces and three separated back-ins. No turnaround area is available which may create problems. Boat trailer parking is prohibited at the highway entrance.

RV SERVICES ON THE STERLING HIGHWAY

KASILOF CHEVRON RIVERVIEW LODGE
(907) 262-1573
Located at MP 109.2 of the Sterling Highway: brakes; general repairs; emergency road service; towing; **propane**. Twenty-four hour towing and emergency road service is available.

CHINOOK CHEVRON SERVICE
(907) 567-3473
Located at MP 135.9 of the Sterling Highway: **propane**.

SHORT STOP STORAGE
(907) 235-5327
Located at MP 153.2 of the Sterling Highway: hot showers, laundry facilities; **sewage dump station**.

ANCHOR POINT TESORO
(907) 235-6005
Located at MP 156.3 of the Sterling Highway: **propane**.

HOMER, ALASKA

Homer has something for everyone: scenic viewpoints; hiking; art galleries; restaurants; ocean fishing and more. A pull-out on the outskirts of town overlooks Kachemak Bay, the Homer Spit, Augustine Island and glaciers from the Harding Icefield. What Homer does not have is enough parking space for the estimated 600 recreational vehicles which overflow the Homer Spit on any given summer weekend.

No state campgrounds exist closer than Anchor Point. The dearth of adequate parking space should not deter RVers from visiting Homer especially during the middle of the week when there are fewer campers. Driving to the end of the continuous highway on the North American Continent is, in itself, worth doing. Advance campground reservations are always desirable but, for the most part, parking space can usually be found.

The Kachemak Shorebird Festival is celebrated each year in Homer during the second weekend in May. Events include guided birdwalks and childrens' activities. At least 100,000 migrating birds gather on the Homer Spit at this time of year.

ALASKA MARITIME NATIONAL WILDLIFE REFUGE   (235-6961)
Located at 509 Sterling Highway. In addition to offering wildlife information, displays and printed materials regarding the refuge, the center has video's for on site viewing of the oil spill, birds of the region, and Alaska's role in World War II. They provide a natural history sales outlet as well.

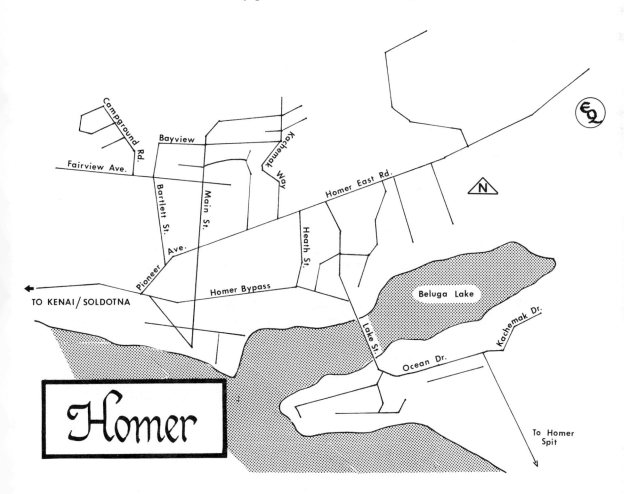

THE VISITOR INFORMATION CENTER   (235-7740)
Located in a log cabin on the Homer Spit past Launch Ramp Road. This Chamber of Commerce center is open from Memorial Day to Labor Day.

THE CENTER FOR ALASKAN COASTAL STUDIES   (235-6667)
Located in an outdoor setting on Kachemak Bay. This is an opportunity to learn about the marine environment under the supervision of volunteer naturalists. A boat trip to Peterson Bay and Gull Island is required in order to reach the site. Call the Center for specific details.

HEALTH AND EMERGENCY SERVICES

South Peninsula Hospital	(907) 235-8101
Homer Fire Department	(907) 235-6100 or 911
Alaska State Troopers	(907) 235-8239
Homer Police Department	(907) 235-3150 or 911

RV CAMPGROUNDS AT HOMER

OCEANVIEW RV PARK   privately operated
455 Sterling Highway, Homer, AK 99603   **April 15th—October 15th**
(907) 235-3951   **MP 172.7 Sterling Highway**

Located at MP 172.7 of the Sterling Highway: 110 spaces; 34 pull-throughs; 80 full hookups; 30 w/o hookups; flush toilets; drinking water; hot showers; picnic sites; tables; grills; cable TV.

Oceanview RV Park offers an excellent view of Kachemak Bay and the Homer Spit. A U-shaped road descends through the campground with tiered, level, back-in, gravel-based spaces. Pull-throughs are located in the center. The largest RV can be accommodated. Cable TV (28 channels) is available. Good Sam discounts are available.

HILLSIDE CAMPGROUND   May 15th—Sept 15th
City of Homer   **Campground Road**

From the Sterling Highway, turn onto Pioneer Avenue, one block, then north on Bartlett Street. Continue up the hill to Fairview, turn west to the entrance on Campground Road: 32 spaces w/o hookups; pit toilets; drinking water; tables; grills.

Hillside Campground has a narrow, dirt road which meanders throughout the area. Spaces, which are not level and are extremely short, are best suited to mini-motorhomes, camper pickups and small trailers. Blocking will be required. Tent campers are the campground's primary users.

CITY OF HOMER CAMPGROUND   May 15th—Sept 15th
City of Homer   **Homer Spit Road**

From the Sterling Highway, follow the Homer Bypass to its junction with Lake Street. Follow Lake Street until it connects with Homer Spit Road: space w/o hookups for 350 campers; chemical toilets; drinking water; boat launch; fishing.

The Homer Spit provides dry camping for RVs and tent campers with the exception of certain, restricted areas. *Disabled parking is available for RVs with attached handicapped (HDP)license plates.* Otherwise, camping is wherever parking can be found. Blocking will be necessary. Restrooms and drinking water are adjacent to the Harbor Master's office.

Camp fees and registrations are handled by camp fee collectors or at the Chamber of Commerce Visitor Center. For reservations: (907) 235-5300.

HOMER SPIT CAMPGROUND   privately operated
PO Box 1196, Homer, AK 99603   May 15th—Sept 15th
(907) 235-8206   Homer Spit Road

From the Sterling Highway, follow the Homer Bypass to its junction with Lake Street. Follow Lake Street until it connects with Homer Spit Road. Located before Land's End Hotel: 114 spaces; 10 pull-throughs; 90 power hookups; 24 w/o hookups; **sewage dump station**; separate tenting area; flush toilets; drinking water; hot showers; laundry facilities; tables.

Homer Spit Campground is located directly on Kachemak Bay near the end of the Homer Spit. Spaces are back-ins, with the exception of a limited number of pull-throughs, in a large, graveled area. The largest RV can be accommodated. Advanced registrations are encouraged.

LAND'S END RV PARK   privately operated
PO Box 273, Homer, SK 99603   May 15th—Sept 15th
(907) 235-2525   FAX (907) 235-6695   end of Homer Spit

From the Sterling Highway, follow the Homer Bypass to its junction with Lake Street. Follow Lake Street until it connects with Homer Spit Road. Drive to the end of the Homer Spit and enter the campground just before the fuel holding tanks to the right: 74 spaces; 58 power only hookups; 16 w/o hookups; **sewage dump station**; porta-potty; flush toilets; drinking water; hot showers; laundry facilities; fire rings; boat launch; fishing; separate tenting area; public phone; no time limit.

Land's End RV Park is a large, level gravel-based area located on Kachemak Bay. There are three parallel sewage dump stations. Small boats can be launched directly from the beach. An area for group meetings is available. It offers an excellent view of Kachemak Bay.

ROCKING J RANCH   privately operated
47895 East End Road, Homer, AK 99603   June 15th—Sept 30th
(907) 235-6239   MP 20.3 East End Road

Located at MP 20.3 East End Road. From the Sterling Highway, turn onto Pioneer Avenue which becomes Homer East Road, also known as East End Road. The campground is located on an **extremely rough road** approximately **eight miles past the end of the blacktop**: 20 spaces; 4 full hookups; 16 w/o hookups; **sewage dump station**; flush toilets; drinking water; hot showers; trails; no time limit.

Rocking J Ranch is located on a former cattle ranch. Full hookups are on level, gravel spaces; dry camping is provided on a large field which is very muddy when wet. A trail leads past Swiftwater Creek to the head of Kachemak Bay. Horses are available for rent. A small grocery store is located in the area. It would be prudent to call before making this drive to ensure a hookup space.

RV SERVICES AT HOMER

PUBLIC SEWAGE DUMP STATION
Turn right just past the post office from the Sterling Highway on Heath Street. The sewage dump station parallels the highway. Potable water is also available at the site.

PIONEER CAR WASH   (907) 235-7675
Turn from the Sterling Highway onto Pioneer Avenue for three blocks: two bays and outside wash areas; self-service or full service available.

ROSI AUTO ELECTRIC   (907) 235-8822
Located on Main Street between Pioneer Avenue and the Homer Bypass: general electrical repairs.

MASTER'S TOUCH RESTORATION   (907) 235-3884
Turn onto Pioneer Avenue from the Sterling Highway. Drive five blocks, turn right on Heath: alignment; body repair; suspension; brakes; mufflers; tank repair; radiators; welding; RV parts in stock; twenty-four hour towing; emergency road repairs.

AIRPORT TEXACO SHOP   (907) 235-5459
From the Sterling Highway, follow the Homer Bypass to its junction with Lake Street. Follow Lake Street until it connects with Homer Spit Road: **sewage dump station**; **propane**; brakes; mufflers; general repairs; tank repairs; welding; emergency road service; diesel repairs. Free sewage dump station use with full fuel fill-up.

HOMER SPIT TESORO   (907) 235-5530
From the Sterling Highway, follow the Homer Bypass to its junction with Lake Street. Follow Lake Street until it connects with Homer Spit Road: petroleum products; **sewage dump station**; **propane**.

THE AUTO CLINIC, INC.   (907) 235-7456
From the Sterling Highway, follow the Homer Bypass to its junction with Lake Street. Follow Lake Street until it connects with Homer Spit Road. Turn onto Kachemak Drive, past the airport: electrical repairs; general repairs; electronic diagnostics; large bays; specialists in transmission and drive train repairs.

THE SHOP   (907) 235-8861
From the Sterling Highway, turn onto Pioneer Avenue which later changes to Homer East Road. Continue until the junction of Kachemak Drive is reached. Turn right: spring replacement; brakes; general repairs; mufflers; towing; full time diesel mechanic; some warranty work.

TERMINAL OIL SALES, INC.   **(907) 235-8818**
From the Sterling Highway, follow the Homer Bypass to its junction with
Lake Street. Follow Lake Street until it connects with Homer Spit Road.
Located at the end of Homer Spit Road: **propane**.

HOMER OPTIONS

THE STERLING HIGHWAY TO THE SEWARD HIGHWAY
The Sterling Highway runs north from Homer to Soldotna and
Kenai. From Soldotna the highway turns east past Sterling, the
cutoff road to Skilak Lake, and Cooper Landing to MP 37 where it
terminates at the Seward Highway.

THE ALASKA MARINE HIGHWAY SYSTEM   (1-800-642-0066)
The Alaska Marine Highway System offers two options on the M/V
Tustumena between mid-June and September from Homer:
Seldovia, Port Lions, Kodiak and Seward, or a six day trip to
Dutch Harbor in the Aleutian Islands. Naturalists from the U.S.
Fish and Wildlife Service are on board the ferry during the summer
months to describe marine and bird life.

The Tustumena is not a "cruise ship" and time in ports such as Sand
Point, Cold Bay and Dutch Harbor is limited and may be at night.
However, the opportunity to see the Alaska Peninsula and the Aleutian
Islands is one which might be considered. Dates of travel to the Aleutians
are approximately three weeks apart.

Contact the Alaska Marine Highway System office on the Homer Spit
(235-8449) for up-to-date information. Space is limited; reservations
should be made as far in advance of travel dates as possible. Refer to the
section on the Alaska Marine Highway System for specific information.

Enjoying the view from the Alaska Marine Highway System

RVing in Alaska:
Campgrounds and Services

Appendices

Appendix A
Interstate Airlines Serving Alaska

The following national air carriers serve Alaska. This information is included for travelers whose schedules may not allow them to drive the highway.

Alaska Airlines   serving Anchorage, Fairbanks, Juneau, Ketchikan and statewide Alaska
1-800-426-0333

American Airlines   (see comment below)
1-800-433-7300

Continental Airlines   serving Anchorage
1-800-525-0280

Delta Air Lines   serving Anchorage, Fairbanks, and Juneau
1-800-221-1212

MarkAir Inc.   serving Anchorage, Fairbanks and statewide Alaska
1-800-478-0800

Morris Air   serving Anchorage only
1-800-466-7747

Northwest Airlines   serving Anchorage
1-800-225-2525

United Airlines   serving Anchorage, and Fairbanks
1-800-241-6522

American Airlines does not fly to Alaska directly, but the airline has a cooperative agreement with Alaska Airlines which gives them access to Anchorage.

Appendix B
Recreational Vehicle Rental Agencies

RV rentals offer an excellent alternative to travelers or others whose time may be restricted. Many rental agencies provide direct pickup and delivery to Anchorage International Airport as a courtesy.

Detailed questions should be asked when price quotes are obtained about insurance coverage, preparation fees, and other charges over and above the daily rate. It would be prudent to review your vehicle coverage with your insurance agent to determine whether or not you may already be covered by your personal vehicle policy before taking additional coverage.

A common problem for RV renters is unfamiliarity with the units they rent. Be certain to ask where switches for dual systems are located, how to connect and clean storage tanks, and how to use other systems before leaving the rental agency.

ABC MOTORHOME RENTAL **(907) 279-2000**
2360 Commercial Drive, Anchorage, AK 99501 **1-800-421-7456**
cars, vans, trailers, and boats available. Also offers bed and breakfast service and free airport pickup

ALASKA ADVENTURES RV RENTALS **(907) 333-7997**
6924 Foothill Drive, Anchorage, AK 99504 **1-800-676-8911**
deluxe 21' and 33' motor homes, fishing packages available, boat rentals, free airport pickup

ALASKA PANORAMA RV RENTALS **(907) 562-1401**
712 West Potter Drive, Anchorage, AK 99518 **FAX (907) 561-8762**
pickup campers, Class A's, housekeeping packages, free airport pickup

ALASKA VACATION MOTOR HOME RENTALS **(907) 274-4222**
PO Box 243903, Anchorage, AK 99524 **FAX (907) 274-2063**
courtesy airport pick-up and return between 8 a.m. and 6 p.m.

CLIPPERSHIP MOTORHOME RENTALS **(907) 562-7051**
5401 Old Seward Highway, Anchorage, AK 99518 **FAX (907) 562-7053**
motorhomes, mini-vans, free airport pickup

COMPACT RV RENTALS **(907) 333-7368**
PO Box 91246, Anchorage, AK 99509 "the affordable Alaska road trip" small pick-up truck and camper combinations includes queen-sized bed, cooking cabinet, table, cooler and water container

FIFTH AVENUE AUTO AND RV CENTER **(907) 272-0544**
1801 East 5th Avenue, Anchorage, AK 99501 **FAX (907) 277-0655**
self contained, late models, Class A & C, free airport pickup

FORGET-ME-NOT MOTORHOME RENTALS   (907) 248-7777
1551 East Tudor Road, Anchorage, AK 99502
housekeeping packages, free airport pickup

GREAT ALASKAN HOLIDAYS   (907) 248-7777
3901 West International Airport Way, Anchorage, AK 99502
fully equipped, located at the airport   out of Alaska **1-800-642-6462**

MURPHY'S RV RENTALS & SALES   **(907) 276-0688**
PO Box 202063, Anchorage, AK 99502-2063   **1-800-582-5123**
fully self-contained, open year round, free airport pickup

NUMBER ONE MOTOR HOME RENTALS . . .   **(907) 277-7575**
322 Concrete, Anchorage, AK 99501   FAX **(907) 277-9182**
open year round, free airport pickup   out of Alaska **1-800-888-4313**

SOURDOUGH CAMPER RENTALS   **(907) 563-3268**
PO Box 9-2440, Anchorage, AK 99509   FAX **(907) 563-8817**

SWEET RETREAT MOTOR HOME RENTALS   **(907) 344-9155**
6820 Arctic Blvd. Anchorage, AK 99518   FAX **(907) 344-8279**
housekeeping and fishing packages, free airport pickup

Agencies Outside of Anchorage

ALASKA AFFORDABLE VACATIONS   **(907) 262-9229**
PO Box 3637, Soldotna 99669   Alaska toll-free **1-800-770-9229**
"one price includes all you need."

ALASKA RECREATIONAL RENTALS   **(907) 262-2700**
PO Box 592, Soldotna, AK 99669   FAX **(907) 262-2700**
located on the Kenai Peninsula, fully self-contained RVs, sleep six

DENALI MOTORHOME RENTALS   **(907) 479-26731331**
PO Box 83970, Fairbanks, AK 99708   Alaska toll-free **1-800-722-6392**
self contained, late models, free airport, hotel, train pickups

FIREWEED RV RENTALS   **(907) 474-3742**
PO Box 61058, Fairbanks, AK 99706   "your home away from home"

TANANA MOTORHOME RENTALS   **(907) 479-7373**
4523 Stanford Drive, Fairbanks, AK 99709

Appendix C
CAMPERS WITH DISABILITIES

In addition to the information already presented in the chapter on Parks and Wildlife, here are other resources available to the disabled camper.

ACCESS ALASKA, 3710 Woodland Drive, Suite 900, Anchorage, Alaska 99517 (907) 248-4777 provides visitor information brochures from businesses in the Anchorage area which suggest that they "provide services" for disabled persons.

ALASKA ASSOCIATION FOR THE DEAF offers help to hearing-impaired and deaf persons regardless of age. Newsletters available upon request. Voice mail (907) 333-4351; teletype (907) 333-7545.

ALASKA KIDNEY CENTER operates dialysis centers in Anchorage and Fairbanks. No other kidney centers exist in Alaska. For travelers who need this service, arrangements should be made as far in advance of the time of travel as possible. Three months is not too much advance notice for the Anchorage center which must request and review medical records before patients can be accepted.

Since more requests for service are made during the summer months, a partial payment is required in advance of the time of service. Phone or write to the following address:

> Head Nurse, Transient Dialysis
> Alaska Kidney Center
> 4201 Tudor Center Road, Suite 220
> Anchorage, Alaska 99508
> (907) 563-3149

ALASKA WELCOMES YOU, PO Box 91333, Anchorage, Alaska 99509 (907) 344-3259 provides guided tours to a variety of destinations in the state such as the Kenai Peninsula, Portage Glacier, Denali Park and so on. They have a twelve-person van that is equipped with a wheelchair lift and which has space for six wheelchairs. The driver is trained to attend to the needs of the disabled. Tours last from one day to several weeks.

CHALLENGE ALASKA, PO Box 110065, Anchorage, Alaska 99511 (907) 563-2658 has a variety of scheduled activities for disabled persons such as fishing, kayaking, sailing and, in the winter months, skiing. For the most part, activities are intended for Alaskans but visitors are welcomed to participate as their schedules allow. They will provide referrals for places to see and visit which are compatible to the disabled.

KING OF THE RIVER, PO Box 107, Soldotna, Alaska 99669 (907) 262-2139 (VOICE/TT) has special equipment for the physically disabled and sign language interpreters for deaf and hard-of-hearing persons. The owners are themselves deaf and making the Kenai River accessible for the disabled angler is one of the company objectives. Their boat can accommodate wheelchairs. They operate from Deep Creek as well as the Kenai River. Half-day and full day trips for king salmon are possible.

RELAYalaska, a telecommunications system for the deaf, hearing-impaired and speech-impaired allows text telephone (TT) users and voice phone users to talk through specially trained operators. To reach RELAYalaska toll-free from a TT, dial 800-770-TYPE. To reach them from a voice phone, dial 800-770-TALK. This service operates 24 hours-a-day, 365 days a year and can be used anywhere in the world.

Sign language interpreter referrals can be arranged by voice line at (907) 277-3323 or TTY line at (907) 276-7232. Long distant operator assist, call 0-700-889-6737.

Appendix D
RVING MEMBERSHIP ORGANIZATIONS

Good Sam Chapters

Glacier Sams
Mildred Zenger, President
(907) 789-7671 – Juneau

Klondike Sams
Doug Thomas, President
(403) 667-1028 – Whitehorse

Midnight Sun
Lowell Skore, President
(907) 248-5845 – Anchorage
Camping second wekend of
summer months

Rovin' Singles
Janet Morrow, President
(907) 337-2260 – Anchorage
Camping fourth weekend of
summer months

Sourdough Sams
Caroline Miller, President
(907) 688-2137 – Anchorage
Camping first weekend of
summer months

Top of the World
Jim McMillan, President
(907) 696-4584 – Eagle River
Camping third weekend of
summer months

Tundra Rollers
Ginger Edmission, President
Post Office Box 1726
Fairbanks, AK 99707

Valdez Wanderers
Paul Kellett, President
(907) 835-2769 – Valdez

Family Motor Coach Association (FMCA)
Arctic Travelers Chapter
Post Office Box 111954
Anchorage, AK 99511-1954

Appendix E
Golf Courses on the Highway System

An estimated 25 million people in the United States claim to be golfers. When *Highways Magazine* ran an article titled "Five Great RV Park Golf Courses," Alaska's golf courses were not listed. Nor was mention made regarding the annual "Farthest North Golf Classic" played each spring on a course laid out on the polar sea-ice which covers the Bering Sea near Nome. These apparent oversights have prompted the inclusion of appendix item E which is intended to encourage duffers throughout the country to pack their clubs when they come north.

Anchorage Area Courses

Anchorage Golf Course
3651 O'Malley Road
(907) 522-3363
Par 72, 18 holes, 6,115 yards

Eagleglen Golf Course
Elmendorf Air Force Base
(907) 552-3821
Par 72, 18 holes, 6,024 yards

Moose Run Golf Course
Arctic Valley Road
(907) 428-0056
Par 71, 18 holes, 6,429 yards

Russian Jack Springs Course
5300 DeBarr Road
(907) 333-8338
Par 31, 9 holes, 1,934 yards

Wasilla/Palmer Area Courses

Palmer Municipal Course
1000 Letak Avenue, Palmer
(907) 745-GOLF
Par 72, 18 holes, 7,125 yards

Settlers Bay Village
Mile 8 Knik Road, Wassila
(907) 376-5466
Par 37, 9 holes, 4,001 yards

The Kenai Peninsula

Birch Ridge Golf Course
Sterling Highway at Bowdry Street
(907) 262-5270
9 holes

Kenai Municipal Golf Course
1420 Lawton Drive
(907) 283-7500
18 holes

Fairbanks

Chena Bend Golf Course
Fort Wainwright
(907) 353-6749
Par 72, 18 holes, 6,646 yards

Fairbanks Golf&Country Club
1820 Yankovich Road
(907) 479-6555
Par 35, 9 holes, 2,888 yards

Southeast

Mendenhall Golf Course
(907) 789-7323 – Juneau
9 holes

Appendix F
Additional Resources

Alaska Ferry RV Reservation Service, PO Box 34098, Juneau, AK 99803. Call toll-free 1-800-643-4898 or FAX (907) 463-4410. Call or write for car deck and cabin space reservations on the Alaska Marine Highway System ferries.

Alaska's Inside Passage, Southeast Alaska Tourism Council, PO Box 20710, Juneau, AK 99802-0710. Write or call toll-free 1-800-423-0568 for a free brochure which describes how to see six of Alaska's top ten attractions in southeast Alaska as well as other activities.

Alaska Marine Highway Schedule, PO Box 25535, Juneau, AK 99802-5535, call toll-free 1-800-642-0066. Request a free catalog and make reservations as early as possible. Summer Schedule May 1st–September 30th; Winter Schedule Oct 1st–April 30th.

Alaska State Vacation Planner, Division of Tourism, Frontier Building, Suite 700, 3601 C Street, Anchorage, AK 99503, call 563-2167.

Alaska–Yukon RV Caravans, 3810 Eastwood Loop, Anchorage, AK 99504-4435. Write or call toll-free 1-800-426-9865 for a 16 page color brochure. Fly-drive-cruise tours, independent RV tours, and 39-day Canada-Alaska "escorted tours" can be arranged.

Anchorage Visitors Guide, Anchorage Convention and Visitors Bureau, 1600 A street, Suite 200, Anchorage, AK 99501-5162.

Arctic Circle Adventure, Northern Alaska Tour Company, PO Box 82991, Fairbanks, AK 99708, call (907) 474-8600 or FAX (907) 474-4767. These one-day tours to the Arctic Circle or two-day tours to Prudhoe Bay offer an excellent alternative to driving your RV on the Dalton Highway.

Gray Line, Brochure Department, 300 Elliott Avenue West, Seattle, WA 98119, call toll-free 1-800-628-2449. FAX (206) 281-0621. Gray Line has an unusual service for southbound RVers. Upon arrival in Anchorage, the RV is checked in at a designated transfer point and shipped to Tacoma, Washington. The traveler(s) then board a ship and sightsee the Columbia Glacier, Sitka, Skagway, Juneau, Ketchikan and the Inside Passage. They complete the voyage and are reunited with the RV nine days later.

The Maps Place, 3545 Arctic Blvd., Anchorage, AK 99503, call (907) 562-6277. Detailed maps of all kinds are available (recreational, topographical, aerial, etc.).

Wild Rose Guidebooks, PO Box 240047, Anchorage, AK 99524-0047, call (907) 274-0471. Write or call for a free catalog listing more than 200 books and publications on Alaska. Book orders are mailed second day air.

INDEX

TRAVEL NOTES

The author and his wife

Dick and Joanne Anderson have made their home in Alaska since 1970. They have lived in Barrow, Bethel and Nome in addition to Anchorage where they now live. An interest in motorhomes led to the first publication of *RVing in Alaska: Campgrounds and Services* .

"We had knocked around the state for years," says Dick, "and I thought we had seen it all until we started writing this book. We found ourselves on roads and in places I didn't even know existed."

Now in an expanded version, *RVing in Alaska: Campgrounds and Services*, offers a number of new campground descriptions, new maps and new photographs for its readers.